AN INTRODUCTION TO THE TEXTUAL CRITICISM OF THE NEW TESTAMENT

A. T. ROBERTSON, M.A., D.D., LL.D., LITT.D.

By PROFESSOR A. T. ROBERTSON

SOME MINOR CHARACTERS IN THE NEW TESTAMENT
PAUL AND THE INTELLECTUALS (Epistle to the Colossians).
STUDIES IN THE TEXT OF THE NEW TESTAMENT.
THE MOTHER OF JESUS.
AN INTRODUCTION TO THE TEXTUAL CRITICISM OF THE NEW TESTAMENT.
THE CHRIST OF THE LOGIA.
THE MINISTER AND HIS GREEK NEW TESTAMENT.
A HARMONY OF THE GOSPELS FOR STUDENTS OF THE LIFE OF CHRIST.
SYLLABUS FOR NEW TESTAMENT STUDY.
TYPES OF PREACHERS IN THE NEW TESTAMENT.
PAUL THE INTERPRETER OF CHRIST.
A SHORT GRAMMAR OF THE GREEK NEW TESTAMENT.
STUDIES IN THE EPISTLE OF JAMES.
STUDIES IN MARK'S GOSPEL.
A GRAMMAR OF THE GREEK NEW TESTAMENT IN THE LIGHT OF HISTORICAL RESEARCH.
A TRANSLATION OF LUKE'S GOSPEL.
JOHN THE LOYAL: A SKETCH OF JOHN THE BAPTIST.
EPOCHS IN THE LIFE OF JESUS.
EPOCHS IN THE LIFE OF PAUL.
THE PHARISEES AND JESUS. The Stone Princeton Lectures for 1916.
LUKE THE HISTORIAN IN THE LIGHT OF RESEARCH.
THE STUDENT'S CHRONOLOGICAL NEW TESTAMENT.
THE GLORY OF THE MINISTRY.
THE DIVINITY OF CHRIST IN THE GOSPEL OF JOHN.
PAUL'S JOY IN CHRIST: STUDIES IN PHILIPPIANS.
MAKING GOOD IN THE MINISTRY: A SKETCH OF JOHN MARK.
THE NEW CITIZENSHIP.
COMMENTARY ON MATTHEW: The Bible for Home and School.
KEYWORDS IN THE TEACHING OF JESUS.
LIFE AND LETTERS OF JOHN A. BROADUS.
THE TEACHING OF JESUS CONCERNING GOD THE FATHER.
STUDIES IN THE NEW TESTAMENT.
NEW TESTAMENT HISTORY (Airplane View).

AN INTRODUCTION TO THE TEXTUAL CRITICISM OF THE NEW TESTAMENT

BY

A. T. ROBERTSON, M.A., D.D., LL.D., LITT.D.

PROFESSOR OF NEW TESTAMENT INTERPRETATION,
SOUTHERN BAPTIST THEOLOGICAL SEMINARY,
LOUISVILLE, KENTUCKY.

Οἱ δὲ λόγοι μου οὐ μὴ παρελεύσονται
—LUKE xxi. 33.

SECOND EDITION, 1928

WIPF & STOCK · Eugene, Oregon

Wipf and Stock Publishers
199 W 8th Ave, Suite 3
Eugene, OR 97401

An Introduction to the Textual Criticism of the New Testament
By Robertson, A. T.
ISBN 13: 978-1-4982-0089-9
Publication date 9/3/2014
Previously published by Doubleday, 1928

To the Memory of
B. B. WARFIELD

PREFACE

My interest in the text of the New Testament was first created by John A. Broadus in 1886 when he taught the subject in the Senior Greek class in the Southern Baptist Theological Seminary. He was master of the theme and won the respect of Caspar René Gregory who called him *"vir doctissimus"* (*Prolegomena* to Tischendorf's N. T., p. 1266). Broadus taught the subject with zest and great skill. For a generation now I have taught the textual criticism of the New Testament to the same class, only now three or four times as large. Until it passed out of print I used Warfield's *Introduction to the Textual Criticism of the New Testament* in connection with Tischendorf's *Novum Testamentum Graece*, ed. viii maj. I have used other books, since the handbook by Warfield could no longer be obtained, but they have not been satisfactory to me. Those by Kenyon, Nestle, and Souter give excellent discussions of the history and material of Textual Criticism, but insufficient presentation of the method. The new edition (Vierte Auflage) of Nestle's *Einführung in das griechische Neue Testament* (1923) by Ernest von Dobschütz brings the work of Nestle up to date with great fulness of details. The fine handbook by Lake is too brief though very much to the point. Many other New Testament teachers have expressed to me similar regrets that

Warfield's book is out of print. I tried to get Dr. Warfield to revise the book, but he declined on the ground that his interest had come to be chiefly in the sphere of dogmatic theology since his removal to Princeton. At the Western Theological Seminary in Pittsburgh he held the chair of New Testament Criticism in 1886 when he wrote the treatise. No one else outside of Hort in his famous *Introduction and Appendix* (Vol. II, *The New Testament in the Original Greek* by Westcott and Hort in 1882) had so clearly and so fully set forth the principles of textual criticism that the student could readily grasp the science and apply it. And Hort's volume has also long been out of print and is too difficult for beginners. But it is hardly a suitable book for classroom use. Dr. Warfield several times urged me to revise his book, but I shrank from the work involved after the long years devoted to my grammatical studies. I once passed the burden on to my gifted colleague, Prof. W. H. Davis, but he was not ready to take hold of it now though he has rendered me valuable service with the book. He has read the manuscript and the proof and he made the beautiful plates for the Facsimiles of important manuscripts. So in sheer desperation I have come back to it that my own class and others also may have the method of Hort with sufficient fulness for the student. The book is in no sense a revision of the work of Warfield, but a new attempt to apply my own long experience in teaching this fascinating subject and to utilize modern knowledge since Warfield wrote.

My task would have been greatly simplified if Gregory had carried out his purpose of preparing a new edition of Tischendorf's *Novum Testamentum Graece* (1869) instead of going to the front and losing his life. That was a fine exhibition of patriotism for his adopted country (Germany) on the part of a man of seventy, but not the least of the tragedies of the world war. New Testament students may have to wait another generation before they can get a book like that of Tischendorf that presents the new evidence combined with the old. Meanwhile we must continue to use the *apparatus criticus* of Tischendorf and supplement it with laborious details. It was in 1911 that Gregory spent a week in my home and he was full of enthusiasm for his great undertaking at which he had labored for a lifetime in Leipzig, but he little knew how soon he would be gone.

It is a pleasure to me to unite thus the names of Broadus, Warfield, and Gregory and to cherish the hope that some one who reads these words may take up the task that Gregory dropped and carry it on to completion.

I have to thank Rev. H. W. Tribble, B.A., Th.M., Fellow in New Testament Greek, for the useful indices.

A. T. ROBERTSON.

LOUISVILLE, KY.

PREFACE TO SECOND EDITION

Errata have been corrected. On page 243 notice has been taken of Streeter's *Four Gospels*, in which he proposes a change in the nomenclature of the Western Class of manuscripts. See also Chapter VI of *Studies in the Text of the New Testament*.

CONTENTS

CHAPTER		PAGE
I	THE TEXTUS RECEPTUS	17
II	THE CRITICAL TEXT	28
III	ANCIENT BOOKS	41
IV	THE USE OF TISCHENDORF	55
V	THE GREEK MANUSCRIPTS	65
VI	THE VERSIONS	102
VII	THE FATHERS	131
VIII	TRANSCRIPTIONAL EVIDENCE OF SINGLE READINGS	148
IX	INTRINSIC EVIDENCE OF SINGLE READINGS	163
X	THE EVIDENCE OF SINGLE DOCUMENTS	171
XI	THE EVIDENCE OF GROUPS OF DOCUMENTS	178
XII	THE EVIDENCE OF CLASSES OR FAMILIES OF DOCUMENTS	184
XIII	THE PRAXIS OF CRITICISM: ILLUSTRATIONS OF THE VARIOUS CLASSES	200
XIV	THE FUTURE OF THE STUDY	221
	FACSIMILES OF EARLY TEXTS	247
	A SELECTED BIBLIOGRAPHY	265
	INDICES	
	NEW TESTAMENT REFERENCES	281
	SUBJECTS AND PERSONS	289

FACSIMILES OF EARLY TEXTS

	PAGE
CODEX AMIATINUS. LUKE V : 1	247
MINUSCULE. IX OR X CENTURY. JOHN XX : 11, 12	247
CODEX VATICANUS. MARK XVI : 8	249
CODEX SINAITICUS. HEB. XIII : 22	251
CURETONIAN SYRIAC. MATT. XV : 20	253
SAHIDIC VERSION. V CENTURY. REV. XI : 6	253
WASHINGTON CODEX. MARK XVI : 20	255
PAPYRUS P[1]. III CENTURY. MATT. I : 1–3	257
CODEX ALEXANDRINUS. ACTS XX : 28	259
CODEX BEZAE. GREEK. LUKE VI : 1	261
CODEX BEZAE. LATIN. LUKE VI : 1	261

AN INTRODUCTION TO THE TEXTUAL CRITICISM OF THE NEW TESTAMENT

AN INTRODUCTION TO THE TEXTUAL CRITICISM OF THE NEW TESTAMENT

CHAPTER I

THE TEXTUS RECEPTUS

It is worth while to explain precisely what the *Textus Receptus* is so that students may know at the very outset why it cannot now be followed. The first printed copy of the Greek New Testament was printed in 1514 though not published till 1522. It was done by CARDINAL XIMENES at Alcala (Latin Complutum) and was the New Testament volume of his Complutensian Polyglot (6 vols.). We do not know what manuscripts were employed except that they were evidently late. But we do know that the few Greek MSS. employed did not contain 1 John v: 7, the words about the Trinity. The words ("three who bear witness in heaven: the Father, the Word, and the Holy Spirit; and these three are one. And") were translated from Latin MSS. into Greek by Ximenes with the help of Stunica, and put into his text. They are found in only two Greek MSS., one of the fourteenth, one of the sixteenth century. It crept into some (not the earliest) MSS. of Jerome's Vulgate by the mistake of Priscillian and other Latin fathers in taking Cyprian's comment as part of the

18 INTRODUCTION TO TEXTUAL CRITICISM

text. The Preface of the Complutensian Greek N. T. claims that the MSS. used were the oldest and most accurate obtainable. The MSS. were lent by Pope Leo from the Vatican Library. But the Complutensian text has had little influence apart from the corrections made from it by Erasmus in his edition of 1527.

ERASMUS actually published his edition of the Greek New Testament in 1516 and so six years before Ximenes in 1522. Erasmus did his work at the suggestion of Froben, the printer at Basel, and it was published in one volume and at a low cost. It was an instant success and made a literary sensation and reached four editions by 1535. He published caustic notes that stirred the ire of the priests, as can be seen in "The Romance of Erasmus's Greek New Testament" in *The Minister and His Greek New Testament*, and in Froude's *Life and Letters of Erasmus*. He based his printed text on 2, a poor minuscule of the twelfth century and corrected it by the cursive (minuscule) Greek manuscript 1 (a tenth century MS. kin in source to 118, 131, 209 and of considerable value). He also used 2 (fifteenth century) for Gospels, 2ap (thirteenth century) for Acts and Paul, and 1r (twelfth century) alone for Apocalypse. It is probable that he had also Latin manuscripts of the Vulgate which he occasionally put into Greek. He confessed doing this for the last six verses of the Apocalypse save verse 20, which had been already translated by Laurentius Valla. The issue of 1522 contained 1 John v: 7 from an entry that had been forged in 61, a sixteenth century manuscript (now in Dublin). Erasmus seemed to feel that he had published the original Greek New Testament

THE TEXTUS RECEPTUS

as it was written, for he used at the end the words *ad Graecam veritatem*. But his first edition in 1516 had little critical value and was inferior to the Complutensian Edition of Ximenes. In 1519 Erasmus issued a revised edition which corrected misprints. The third edition of 1522 introduced the passage in 1 John v: 7 because of a foolish promise made to Stunica (editor of the Complutensian. Ximenes died in 1517) that he would insert it if he found it in any Greek MS. When the MS. 61 of the sixteenth century was produced, Erasmus rightly inferred that it had been translated from the Latin, but he put it in because of his rash promise and thus it got into the *Textus Receptus*. In the edition of 1527 Erasmus added the text of the Vulgate besides the Greek text and his own Latin translation. He also made use of the Complutensian, especially in the Apocalypse. The last edition of 1535 was a reprint of that of 1527. The third edition of Erasmus (1522) became the foundation of the *Textus Receptus* for Britain since it was followed by Stephens. There were 3300 copies of the first two editions of the Greek Testament of Erasmus circulated. His work became the standard for three hundred years in spite of the haste and imperfections connected with it. To this day, Valentine Richards (*N. T. Textual Criticism, Cambridge Biblical Essays*, 1909, p. 512) laments that the text of Erasmus is still reprinted at Cambridge as reproduced by Stephens and Scrivener, while the Mill edition of Stephens is the standard in Oxford. And that at the home of Westcott and Hort (Cambridge) and of Sanday and Turner (Oxford)!

In 1550 ROBERT ESTIENNE (STEPHANUS) published the third edition (*Editio Regia*) of his Greek New Testament (the first in 1546, the second in 1549) which was based directly on the work of Erasmus with marginal readings from fifteen other manuscripts, one of which was the Codex Bezae (D). This text became the *Textus Receptus* of Britain. Stephanus was a Parisian printer. His edition of 1551 was published at Geneva and was the first New Testament to give our verse divisions, a device that on the whole has done more harm than good.

THEODORE BEZA published nine editions of the Greek New Testament (four in folio 1565–82–88–98, five in octavo 1565–67–80–91 and 1604), but they are practically reprints of the work of Stephanus (Stephens). In his first edition (1546) he made some use of the work of Ximenes.

There were seven ELZEVIR editions published at Leyden and Amsterdam between 1624 and 1678. They are based on the work of Beza and of Stephanus and have little critical value as they are very much alike. But the second edition in the year 1633 contains in the preface the words "*Textum ergo habes nunc ab omnibus receptum*," and thus we get the phrase *Textus Receptus*. This Elzevir edition of 1633 became the standard for the continent as the 1550 Stephanus edition had become for Britain.

The mere recital of these facts shows that the *Textus Receptus* rests upon late Greek manuscripts which have undergone many copyings and are subject to many errors through the long years of transmission. The Authorized Version of 1611 into English (King James

Version) is based primarily upon the Stephanus-Beza-Elzevir text. There was some use made of other manuscripts, but no use could be made of documents that were not then discovered.

It should be stated at once that the *Textus Receptus* is not a bad text. It is not a heretical text. It is substantially correct. Hort has put the matter well: "With regard to the great bulk of the words of the New Testament, as of most other ancient writings, there is no variation or other ground of doubt, and therefore no room for textual criticism" (*Introduction*, p. 4). Hort continues: "The proportion of words virtually accepted on all hands as raised above doubt is very great; not less, on a rough computation, than seven-eighths of the whole. The remaining eighth, therefore, formed in great part by changes of order and other comparative trivialities, constitutes the whole area of criticism." It is clear, therefore, that the *Textus Receptus* has preserved for us a substantially accurate text in spite of the long centuries preceding the age of printing when copying by hand was the only method of reproducing the New Testament. But the case is even better than this presentation, for Hort concludes: "Recognizing to the full the duty of abstinence from peremptory decision in cases where the evidence leaves the judgment in suspense between two or more readings, we find that, setting aside differences of orthography, the words in our opinion still subject to doubt only make up about one-sixtieth of the whole New Testament. In the second estimate the proportion of comparatively trivial variations is beyond measure larger than in the former; so that the amount of what can in any sense be called substantial variation is but a small fraction of the whole residuary variation, and can hardly form more than a thoussandth part of the entire text." The real conflict in the textual criticism of the New Testament is concerning this "thousandth part of the entire text." If one wonders whether it is worth while, he must bear in mind that some of the passages in dispute are of great importance, such as the correct reading in 1 Tim. iii: 16 whether υἱός, ὅ, or ὅς and the close of Mark's Gospel (xvi: 9–20). No amount of toil is too great if only we can be sure that we possess the original text of the New Testament.

There are still defenders of the *Textus Receptus* as nearer the original than any other; but the tide has turned definitely against the traditional text. Martin defends the *Textus Receptus* with critical apparatus in his *Critique Textuelle* (1883–86). See also Miller, *The Oxford Debate on the Textual Criticism of the New Testament* (1897), Miller's *Present State of the Textual Controversy* (1899), Burgon and Miller's *The Traditional Text* (1896), Burgon's *The Last Twelve Verses of Mark* (1871), Burgon and Miller's *The Causes of the Corruption of the Traditional Text of the Holy Gospels* (1896). Burgon did valuable work in collecting references to New Testament quotations in the Fathers. Scrivener's *Plain Introduction to the Criticism of the New Testament* (2 ed., 1874) is a valuable contribution to the study of minuscule or cursive manuscripts. He in the main defended the *Textus Receptus*. Scrivener in his Greek New Testament (1887) really gives the text of Stephanus with the variations of Beza, Elzevir,

Lachmann, Tischendorf, Tregelles, Westcott and Hort, and the Greek Text of the Revisers. The Scrivener edition of 1881 had given the *Textus Receptus* with the variations of the Revisers. The best modern edition of the *Textus Receptus* is by Nestle (1901) with some critical apparatus.

Souter (*Text and Canon of the New Testament*, p. 96) observes that there "already seems to have arisen a fictitious worship for the letter of Erasmus's last edition" (1535) by the time that Stephanus issued his third edition in 1550 which was the first to give any critical apparatus with variations in readings.

The unlimited reign of the *Textus Receptus* is usually given as 1516 to 1750, the period of struggle from 1750 to 1830. But already during this period of the stereotyped text derived from late Greek manuscripts scholars were struggling towards a better text. BEZA in 1582 made some use of D for the Gospels and Acts and D_2 for Paul's Epistles. In 1606 LUCAS of Bruges (*Notae ad Varias Lectiones Editionis Graecae Evangeliorum*) was the first scholar to make use of the three sources for the text of the New Testament (Greek manuscripts, versions, quotations). In 1657 the *London Polyglot* was edited by BRIAN WALTON and others. It gives the text of Stephanus (1550) with many various readings from A and sixteen manuscripts besides the Latin Vulgate, Peshitta Syriac, Aethiopic, and Arabic. And then RICHARD SIMON produced his *Histoire critique du texte du Nouveau Testament* (1689) which was translated into English the same year, and also *Histoire critique des versions du Nouveau Testament* (1690. English translation, 1692), *Histoire critique des principaux commentateurs du Nouveau Testament* (1693. Not translated), and *Nouvelles Observations sur la texte et les versions du Nouveau Testament* (1695). Souter adds (*Text and Canon of the New Testament*, p. 98): "It would be impossible to exaggerate the value and suggestiveness of Simon's works."

Thus we see the two tendencies already at work against each other. There was the adherence to the stereotyped *Textus Receptus* which had won the field. The Stephanus text was supreme in England and the Elzevir text on the continent, but they were practically the same. "The text, which was to enslave the Greek Testament for two hundred years and more, was based really on Erasmus's last edition, the Complutensian Polyglot, and a handful of manuscripts — in fact, on something like a hundredth part of the Greek evidence now at our disposal, not to speak of versions and citations" (Souter, *Text and Canon of the New Testament*, pp. 96–97). The other tendency already at work was the effort to improve the traditional text. This was the work of a few scholars already mentioned and it was to bear rich fruit in the future in spite of the indifference and the hostility of the majority. So the struggle went on.

In 1707 JOHN MILL gives in the main the text of Stephanus of 1550, but he presents a wealth of textual material with an able introduction. He used many new Greek manuscripts (78 in all) and did good work on the versions, particularly the Old Latin and the Vulgate, and patristic quotations. He used the uncials A B D D_2 E E_2, E_3, K and the cursives 28, 33, 59, 69, 71, the Peshitta Syriac, the Old Latin and the Vulgate. He was the first to make proper use of the quotations and "with the possible exception of Tischendorf, probably no one person has added so much material for the work of criticism" (Lake, *The Text of the New Testament*, p. 61).

RICHARD BENTLEY (1662-1742) planned a Greek New Testament that would correspond to the text of the fourth century. He had colossal learning and made great preparations with the help of John Walker to reproduce a pure text with the agreement of both Greek and Latin manuscripts. But the great Master of Trinity College, Cambridge, died without publishing his edition of the Greek New Testament. "Bentley's work must not be overlooked. The impulse he gave to these studies was such, that but for him there would have been no Lachmann and no Hort" (Souter, *Text and Canon*, p. 99). Bentley's efforts were opposed by the obscurantist Conyers Middleton and others.

J. A. BENGEL in 1734 published, indeed, the *Textus Receptus* "because he could not then publish a text of his own. Neither the publisher nor the public would have stood for it" (Gregory, *The Canon and Text of the New Testament*, p. 447). So Bengel only dared to put the good readings into the text when they had already appeared in some previous printed edition. But he made marginal notes of five classes of readings (the genuine readings, those better than the text, those just as good, those not so good, and those to be rejected). This was a clear scheme, but even so he angered so many that he published a "Defence of the Greek New Testament" in German and then in Latin

(1737). He divided the manuscripts into Asiatic and African somewhat like the Syrian and Alexandrian of Westcott and Hort. "In some ways he is the father of modern criticism" (Lake, *The Text of the New Testament*, p. 61), though he felt bound to print the *Textus Receptus*. He advanced the view that manuscripts should be weighed and not counted. His *"Gnomon"* is one of the great commentaries on the New Testament for scholarly and spiritual insight.

J. J. WETTSTEIN (1751-52) published a Greek New Testament in two folio volumes. His text was in the main the Elzevir text. He was the first to distinguish the uncial manuscripts by capital letters and the cursives by Arabic numbers, and he gave the largest and best critical apparatus then in existence. Below the Elzevir text he gave the readings which he considered genuine. His nomenclature for the manuscripts still survives and has been supplemented and improved by Gregory in his *Die griechischen Handschriften des Neuen Testaments* (1908). His commentary is so rich in illustrative material "that those who know the commentary best would not hesitate to place it first among all that ever one man has produced" (Souter, *Text and Canon of the New Testament*, p. 99).

The *Textus Receptus* thus held on through the time of Mill, Bentley, Bengel, Wettstein. But its days were numbered. GRIESBACH published his Greek New Testament in 1774-77 with a rich apparatus and with a theory of textual criticism that compelled attention. He found three families of manuscripts (Western, Alexandrian, Byzantine or Constantinopolitan). The Alexandrian he found chiefly in A B C L, the Egyptian versions, and Origen's quotations. The Western he found in D, the Latin versions and fathers. The Byzantine was the text of the Byzantine Empire and the least valuable. But the Byzantine text is practically the *Textus Receptus*. So Griesbach counted heavily against the *Textus Receptus*. Hug and Scholz worked at the same time, but did nothing equal to Griesbach. The *Textus Receptus* was now challenged by the foremost scholars of the world.

The student will now do well to turn to Tischendorf's *Novum Testamentum Graece* and read the data given there concerning the addition in 1 John v: 7.

CHAPTER II

THE CRITICAL TEXT

In the preceding chapter it was shown that it required courage as well as great toil to make use of the new discoveries concerning the text of the New Testament. The foundations of historical textual (or lower) criticism were really laid by Mill, Bentley, and Bengel (Hort, *Introduction*, Vol. II of *The New Testament in the Original Greek*, p. 179), as we have already seen. Mill examined individual documents to see the worth of each. Bentley deliberately set out to restore the text of the fourth century. Bengel began to weigh documents and his Asiatic and African classes corresponded roughly with Hort's Syrian and Pre-Syrian classes. Griesbach like Bentley called Bengel's Asiatic text Byzantine or Constantinopolitan and his African he divided into Western and Alexandrian. Hort (*Introduction*, p. 183) points out that Griesbach "failed to apprehend in its true magnitude the part played by mixture in the history of the text during the fourth and following centuries," and he "was driven to give a dangerously disproportionate weight to internal evidence, and especially to transcriptional probability" (*ibid.*, p. 184). But Hort adds about Griesbach that he venerates his name "above that of every other textual critic of the New Testament" (*ibid.*, p. 185). Schaff holds that Griesbach's editions of the Greek

New Testament "mark the beginning of a really critical text, based upon fixed rules" (*Companion to the Greek New Testament and English Versions*, p. 250). Hort observes that the successors of Griesbach abandoned his effort "to obtain for the text of the New Testament a secure historical foundation in the genealogical relations of the whole documentary evidence" (*Introduction*, p. 186). Hence Hort felt that he was in reality taking up the work of Griesbach afresh.

The third period of the history of the textual criticism of the New Testament (from 1830 onward) has thus its roots in the second (1750 to 1830), "a period of strife between those who followed the so-called *Textus Receptus* blindly, and those who were determined to secure the most ancient witnesses they could and to trust them" (Souter, *Text and Canon*, p. 100). In the third period the bondage of the *Textus Receptus* is broken and the triumph of the critical text is won. From the very first the printed Greek New Testament was bitterly assailed by the ignorant monks as a great calamity. Erasmus was attacked in Britain and on the continent. "Stephanus had to flee from the wrath of the doctors of the Sorbonne to Protestant Geneva" (Schaff, *Companion to the Greek Testament*, p. 288). Owen attacked Walton, Whitney assailed Mill, Middleton condemned Bentley, Wettstein opposed Bengel, Frey attacked Wettstein, Matthaei abused Griesbach. It was a pitiable story, but truth was to win in the end.

The battle went on. The fight for the true text of the New Testament was carried on by Lachmann, by Tregelles, by Tischendorf, by Alford, by Westcott and Hort, even by Scrivener at last, by Gregory, by

Nestle, by Von Soden. But even in this list of heroes of scholarship there has been suffering. Fritzsche called Lachmann "the ape of Bentley." England allowed Tregelles almost to starve and he went blind in deciphering manuscripts. Simonides slandered Tischendorf and actually claimed that he wrote the Codex Sinaiticus himself.

LACHMANN in 1842-50 gave a new turn to the whole subject. Souter calls him "the protagonist" of this third period as he considers Bentley "the great hero of the second period" (*Text and Canon*, p. 101). But as we have seen, Hort holds Griesbach to be the great man in textual criticism before his own day. Lachmann was Professor of Classical Philology in Berlin and had worked at the textual problems of Lucretius, Catullus, Tibullus, Propertius, Gaius. Like Bentley of Cambridge he was one of the greatest philologians of the world. So he had the principles and experience of a classical philologian rather than those of a professional theologian. He did not so reverence the *Textus Receptus* that he was afraid to publish his own text. In 1831 he published a small edition of such a text with the variations of the *Textus Receptus* (Elzevir, 1624) at the end. This was a bold proceeding and was distinctly giving second place to the *Textus Receptus*. Tregelles (*An Account of the Printed Text of the Greek New Testament*, 1854, p. 99) says of Lachmann: "Lachmann led the way in casting aside the so-called *textus receptus*, and boldly placing the New Testament wholly and entirely on the basis of actual authority." Hort (*Introduction*, p. 13) is equally explicit in giving the honor for beginning the new era to Lachmann:

"A new period began in 1831, when for the first time a text was constructed directly from the ancient documents without the intervention of any printed edition, and when the first systematic attempt was made to substitute scientific method for arbitrary choice in the discrimination of various readings." But even De Wette thought that Lachmann was wasting his time and strength! The method of Lachmann consisted in boldly dropping Bentley's and Griesbach's Byzantine or Constantinopolitan text (Bengel's Asiatic) which depended on late documents. His idea was to restore the text of the oldest manuscripts, that is the text of the fourth century, rather than the original text, but to make a definite start and to get away from the tyranny of the *Textus Receptus*. He tried to reproduce the text in general use in the time of Jerome and printed his text in both Greek and Latin in two volumes, *Novum Testamentum Graece et Latine* (1842–50). So he used only two types of text, the Oriental (Griesbach's Alexandrian) and Occidental (Griesbach's Western). The Oriental text he found in A B C, parts of H, P, and Origen. But Origen does not belong to the fourth century and B and C were imperfectly known in Lachmann's time. Sometimes he had A alone. When his Oriental or Eastern documents disagreed, he would fall back on the Occidental or Western (D E G a b c d e ff g Vulgate, Irenaeus, Cyprian, Hilary, Lucifer, Primasius for the Apocalypse). When they all failed him, he made use of the mass of late documents. He had imperfect data, for Aleph (the Sinaitic Manuscript) had not yet been discovered and B (Vatican Codex) had not been photographed and edited. "Lachmann would certainly have done at least what Westcott and Hort did, if he had had the materials they had at his disposal" (Souter, *Text and Canon*, p. 101).

TREGELLES carried the work of Lachmann a step further. He was of Quaker origin and was associated for a time with the Plymouth Brethren. He was very poor and his work was published by subscription: *The Greek New Testament, edited from Ancient Authorities, with the Latin Version of Jerome from the Codex Amiatinus* (in seven parts from 1857 to 1879). The Gospels were printed in 1857 and 1860 before the publication of Aleph, and the Pauline Epistles had been begun in 1865 before the appearance of Vercellone's edition of B (in 1868). Tregelles followed in the main the principles and text of Lachmann, but gives a fuller critical apparatus. It is easier to understand than that of Tischendorf, though nothing like so complete. His aim was not to produce the text of the oldest Greek manuscripts, those of the fourth century as Lachmann did, but to reproduce the oldest text obtainable. In other words he was weighing documents, not by their own age, but by the age of the text which they contained. "To Tregelles must be ascribed the honour of introducing this method of procedure, which he appropriately called 'Comparative Criticism.' It is a truly scientific method, and leads us for the first time to safe results" (Warfield, *Textual Criticism of the N. T.*, p. 112). By means of the dated manuscripts it is possible to divide documents that agree with them into two great classes, those that give an early text and those that give a late text. Sometimes late documents preserve an early type of text. This is a great advance that Tregelles made. He was stricken with paralysis while working on the last chapters of the Apocalypse in 1870 and died in 1875. "Tregelles's great service was to draw English-speaking scholars away from the *textus receptus*" (Souter, *Text and Canon*, p. 107), as Lachmann had done on the continent. And it is worth a great deal to get a text that is older than the fourth century, even one of the third or the second century. But that is not the original text that we so much desire to have.

TISCHENDORF published at intervals from 1864 to 1872 in eleven parts his great and monumental work: *Novum Testamentum Graece. Editio octava critica maior*. 2 vols. A one volume edition (*editio critica minor*) gives the same text with a much smaller critical apparatus. It may be said at once that the eighth edition is the one absolutely essential work for the student of textual criticism of the New Testament. Nowhere else can one obtain the same wealth of material. Gregory had planned a ninth edition that would bring the work up to date by the addition of the new discoveries, but his untimely death during the Great War prevented the consummation of his plans. Tischendorf was stricken by apoplexy on May 5, 1873 and died of paralysis December 7, 1874. The *Prolegomena* to Tischendorf was completed by Gregory (1884 to 1894) and is now in one volume. No one has ever toiled so much on the documents that relate to New Testament textual criticism as Tischendorf. His working power was amazing. He travelled far and wide and was supported by the Saxon government and later by the Russian. He was professor in Leipzig. The mere catalogue of his publications covers pp. 7–22 in Gregory's *Prolegomena*. His editions of the texts of Biblical manuscripts (some of the Septuagint) fill seventeen large quarto and five folio volumes. They include such as ℵ, B, B₂, C, D₂, E₂, L. There were twenty-four editions of his Greek New Testament. The best handy edition of Tischendorf's New Testament is that by Gebhardt (1881) which gives also the readings of Tregelles and of Westcott and Hort. "He regarded himself as an instrument in the hands of Providence for the discovery and publication of documentary proofs for the vindication of the original text of the New Testament and to God he ascribed the glory" (Schaff, *Companion to the Greek Testament* p. 261). His greatest discovery was that of ℵ (Aleph), the Codex Sinaiticus. He tells the story in his volume, *Die Sinaibibel (Ihre Entdeckung Herausgabe und Erwerbung.* 1871). It reads like a romance. Schaff (*Companion,* pp. 108–111) tells the story for those who wish to read it, how Tischendorf made three journeys to Mount Sinai (1844, 1853, 1859), how he first rescued forty-three leaves of the Septuagint from a wastebasket in the library of the Convent of St. Catherine, how on the first discovery of the whole manuscript he secured a temporary loan of the codex and had it carried on a camel to Cairo, how he copied the 110,000 lines of the codex with the help of two countrymen and was allowed to take it as a conditional present to the Czar of Russia. Tischendorf had an exaggerated idea of the worth of ℵ which he called "*omnium codicum uncialium solus integer omniumque antiquis-*

simus." In his seventh edition of the Greek New Testament he had leaned more to the *Textus Receptus*, but the discovery of ℵ turned him back to the critical text. He did not possess critical judgment of much value. Hence his text is of small importance, but his *critical apparatus* is of the highest importance. Both Tregelles and Tischendorf failed in their efforts to deal consistently or successfully with the variations between the most ancient texts (Hort, *Introduction*, p. 13). So important is it for the student to know how to use Tischendorf's 8th Edition that a special chapter (IV) will be devoted to the subject.

ALFORD deserves mention because of his gradual conversion to the text of the old documents. At first in his *Greek Testament* (1849) he gave too much attention to the *Textus Receptus*, but in his sixth edition (1868) he followed Tregelles and Tischendorf and made good use of ℵ. He upheld Lachmann and Tregelles for "the bold and uncompromising demolition of that unworthy and pedantic reverence for the received text which stood in the way of all chance of discovering the genuine word of God" (*Greek Testament*, Vol. I, p. 76). Already in 1873 Lightfoot, Trench, and Ellicott were urging *The Revision of the English Version of the New Testament* largely on the ground of the new light on the text. Philip Schaff wrote an *Introduction* to the American edition.

WESTCOTT AND HORT produced "the greatest edition ever published" (Souter, *Text and Canon*, p. 103) in 1881 almost at the same time as the Revised Version of the English New Testament. It had been in the hands of the revisers in the form of proof and naturally had a great influence on them. It first appeared in two volumes. Vol. I contains the text, Vol. II the Introduction (324 pages) and Appendix (Notes on Select Readings, 140 pages, Notes on Orthography and Quotations, pp. 141-188). Vol. II is the work of Hort and it is far and away the ablest discussion of the science of the textual criticism of the Greek New Testament in existence. It is a great pity that it is now out of print. The text of Westcott and Hort has had numerous editions in different sizes of type and binding. The small flexible leather binding makes a volume suitable for the pocket. It is today the text that is used by scholars all over the world. These two Cambridge scholars have produced a text that is not final, but that is infinitely superior to all others that preceded it since the first printed Greek New Testament in 1514. They spent twenty-eight years in preparing their text and have laid down their theory on lines that have stood the test of time. This is not to say that one today agrees with every conclusion of Westcott and Hort. They were undoubtedly too much under the influence of B even when standing alone (*Introduction*, p. 230). But they lifted the whole matter out of the realm of empiricism to the level of historical science. "Their introduction, in which textual principles are enunciated with convincing power, and a brilliant classification and characterization of authorities are given, is an achievement never surpassed in the scholarship of any country" (Souter, *Text and Canon*, p. 103).

They saw clearly that we need to know not merely the text of the old documents of the fourth century as Lachmann did or the old text as Tregelles did, but also the best and the purest text possible. We want to know not simply the age of the parchment or the age of the text, but the excellence of the text (Warfield, *Textual Criticism*, p. 114). This is the purpose of Westcott and Hort, to restore the original text, as far as it is possible to do so. The theory of Westcott and Hort which will be taught in this volume, with such modifications in details as new discoveries demand, rests upon the classification of the evidence of documents (external evidence) into families (genealogy). There are four of these families (or classes), one Syrian and three Pre-Syrian. The Syrian (Antiochian, Byzantine, or Constantinopolitan) is more recent than the Pre-Syrian Classes. Hence when the Syrian is opposed by the Pre-Syrian it is bound to be wrong. The three Pre-Syrian Classes are the Neutral, the Western, and the Alexandrian. The Syrian Class is broadly represented by the late documents. The Neutral is found chiefly in ℵ B, Egyptian versions, Origen. The Western is seen mainly in D, Old Latin, Old Syriac, Irenaeus, Tertullian, Cyprian. The Alexandrian, when found alone, is seen mainly in C L Origen. But the Alexandrian seldom stands alone. It usually appears either with the Neutral or with the Western (by mixture, to be discussed later). Hence at bottom the differences between the Pre-Syrian Classes whittles down to that between the Neutral and the Western. When the Alexandrian class stands alone, it is wrong just as the Syrian is when alone. As between the Neutral and the Western, Westcott and Hort much prefer the Neutral save in some Western non-interpolations. Modern discovery has tended to give rather more weight to the Western readings than Westcott and Hort did. But in its broad outline their theory stands intact today. One cardinal point with Westcott and Hort is to learn the value of each document by applying transcriptional and intrinsic evidence to the document as a whole by the examination of separate readings. This matter will be worked out later. The same process is applied to groups and to families. Thus Westcott and Hort showed how to apply the principles of internal evidence (transcriptional and intrinsic) to the external evidence of documents. By means of this powerful agent they have been able to attack the most difficult problems that had baffled Lachmann and Tregelles. The aim of the present volume is to put the modern student in possession of their principles of textual criticism so that he can apply them himself to each problem in detail and so be able to make his own text of the New Testament.

GREGORY's main contribution was to be the thorough revision of Tischendorf's *Novum Testamentum Graece*. His sudden death cut off that ambition, though he was about ready to write out the results of a lifetime of research. He had already prepared his *Vorschläge für eine Kritische Ausgabe des griechischen Neuen Testaments* (1911). In broad outline Gregory was a disciple of Westcott and Hort and his aim was to reproduce as far as possible the original text of the first century. His books reveal his system and ideals. *Prolegomena* (1884-94) is Vol. III of Tischendorf's *magnum opus*. He was Professor of Textual Criticism of the New Testament in the University of Leipzig.

He wrote also *Canon and Text of the New Testament* (1907), *Textkritik des Neuen Testaments* (1900–09), *Die griechischen Handschriften des Neuen Testaments* (1908), *Einleitung in das Neue Testament* (1909). No one was so well equipped with knowledge of the new discoveries as he. Jacquier has a sympathetic portrayal of his work (*Le Nouveau Testament dans l'Église Chrétienne,* Tome 2, 1913, pp. 495–99).

WEYMOUTH in 1905 issued *The Resultant Greek Testament*. He aimed to give the readings in which the majority of modern editors are agreed. He gives the readings of Stephanus (1550), Lachmann, Tregelles, Tischendorf, Lightfoot, Alford, B. Weiss, Westcott and Hort, and the Revision Committee of 1881.

NESTLE in 1908 published his *Novum Testamentum Graece cum apparatu critico ex editionibus et libris manuscriptis collecto* (*Stuttgart*). It can be had in pocket form also with flexible back. His text is almost exactly that of Westcott and Hort.

B. WEISS (1894 to 1905) differs little in his text from that of Westcott and Hort which has come to deserve the name of the critical text.

PALMER in 1881 published the Greek text behind the Revised English Version. He gave both the Stephanus text and the text of the Revisers.

SOUTER in 1910 reissued this text with new and up-to-date critical apparatus with the advice of Sanday. It is an exceedingly useful volume.

BALJON'S *Novum Testamentum Graece* (1898) has a brief critical apparatus and makes use of the Syriac Sinaitic MS. for the Gospels and gives Blass's so-called *Roman Text* for the Acts, but it is much too brief to take the place of Tischendorf. The views of Blass, Hoskier, Kenyon, and other modern scholars on special points will come up for discussion later.

VON SODEN made a most ambitious attempt to present the oldest attainable text with new nomenclature and new principles. From 1902 to 1910 (pp. 2203) he published Teil I of *Die Schriften des Neuen Testaments in ihrer ältesten erreichbaren Textgestalt, hergestellt auf Grund ihrer Textgeschichte: Untersuchungen*. Then Teil II: *Text mit Apparat* in 1913. In 1913 he published also *Griechisches Neues Testament* (*Text mit Kurzem Apparat*). Lake (*Text of the New Testament*, p. 99) says that the time has not yet come to estimate rightly the value of the work of Von Soden, whose untimely death cut short his work. His theories are not likely to be adopted, but his views will be presented in Chapter XIV (close) as a matter of historical interest. His text does not differ greatly from that of Westcott and Hort and once again bears witness to the worth of their work.

The student will do well just here to read in Tischendorf the evidence concerning Ἐν Ἐφέσῳ in Eph. i: 1.

CHAPTER III

ANCIENT BOOKS

1. *Meaning of Book*

The English word book is supposed to come from the Anglo-Saxon bōc, bēce, beech, on the bark of which books were written. So the word Bible (βίβλος, βιβλίον) is βύβλος, the outer coat of the pith or inner bark of the πάπυρος, on which ancient books were so often written. But book refers not merely to the material on which something is written, but in particular to the record on the material. Today that is the usual meaning. The material has varied greatly during the centuries preceding printing. Back of paper was parchment; back of parchment and along with it was the papyrus; and before that and along with it was the wax tablet, the clay tablet (the Assyrian and Babylonian books), ostraca (pieces of pottery), stone (commonest at first), metal, bark, anything, everything. The making of books is very ancient and much study was early a weariness to the flesh. We may well invoke blessings on the man who invented books, for thus we get *the* Book as Sir Walter Scott called the Bible as he lay dying. See Birt, *Das antike Buchwesen* (1882); *Die Buchrolle in der Kunst* (1907); Schubart, *Das Buch bei den Griechen und Römern* (1907).

2. *Paper before Printing*

It was the bringing of paper to Western Europe (Italy and Spain) by the Arabs that furnished the means for numerous copies of the Greek New Testament before the invention of printing (about the middle of the fifteenth century with the use of movable type in the Gutenberg Bible, 1440-45). Paper, like printing, came from China, probably as a result of the capture of Samarcand by the Arabs in A.D. 704. Factories in Bagdad produced it and specimens of the new paper made from linen cloth or linen rags survive from the twelfth century. In the fourteenth century the manuscript book trade began to use it freely in the West and in the fifteenth it was superseding the use of parchment. Sometimes it is not easy to tell whether a book is a late paper manuscript or an early printed book. But the combination of paper and printing rapidly put an end to manuscript books, though before printing paper won its way slowly. The paper manuscripts of the Greek New Testament are all late and of no distinctive value (Souter, *Text and Canon*, p. 9).

3. *Parchment*

Parchment preceded paper as papyrus preceded parchment. But parchment and papyrus were long used side by side. Kenyon (art. *Writing* in Hastings D B) says that leather rolls in Egypt are extant from B.C. 2000. But there is a papyrus account sheet belonging to the reign of Assa in Egypt possibly 3360 B.C., certainly 2600 B.C. (Deissmann, *Light from the Ancient East*, 1910, p. 22, note 8). So both parchment and papyrus are very ancient. The Assyrian monuments show scribes holding rolls of parchment. The Persians used parchment for the royal records. Herodotus states that the Ionians of Asia Minor once used the skin of sheep and goats. Varro (*apud* Pliny H. N. xiii: 11) says that Eumenes II of Pergamum (B.C. 197–158) restored the use of parchment for writing when the king of Egypt forbade the export of papyrus from Egypt. It is probable that parchment was the common material for copies of the Old Testament books. At Pergamum the skin was dressed in a special way to make it smooth and more suitable for writing. It was hence termed περγαμηνή, our parchment. Strictly speaking *vellum* refers to material derived from calves and antelopes and parchment to that made from sheep, etc. But practically no distinction was later made and parchment was applied to all such material. Vellum is a fine quality of leather prepared for writing on both sides. It is probable that the Jews used either parchment or papyrus as they wished. The use of vellum for note-books in the place of wax tablets may have led also to the change from roll to codex, the leaf book like our modern book form. Originally the roll was employed for either skin or papyrus. The codex seems to have arisen in the third century A.D., "the final victory of vellum and the codex form being achieved in the early part of the fourth century" (Kenyon, *Writing*, Hastings' D B). Parchment may be of different thicknesses just like paper. It depends on the thickness of the skin in each case. Scrapers could only go so far without spoiling the skin. A fine thin skin would be from a young animal. Reuss thinks that parchment was too expensive for early use (*Geschichte der heiligen Schriften*, 1860), but Jordan (*Writing*, Hastings' *Dictionary of the Apostolic Church*) holds the very opposite, that papyrus finally became so expensive that it gave way to the new vellum that was at once cheaper and far more durable. "Among the Greeks, this transition from papyrus to parchment was checked by two material considerations, viz., the lightness and delicacy of the papyrus fabric, and the relief which, in contrast to the glossy and often dazzling parchment, that fabric afforded to the eye of both writer and reader — though the larger characters generally used for writing on the parchment sheet were relatively more legible to the eyes." Jordan quotes Martial as saying about A.D. 84 that books on papyrus were dearer and more valuable than those on parchment. The manufacture of papyrus was confined to the Nile Delta while parchment could be made anywhere. According to Quintilian (*Inst. Orat.* x. iii: 31) it was not possible to write with ease on parchment which was still not so polished as it was later and hence he had to write in large letters. But it is more than doubtful if this is the meaning of Paul when he spoke of the "large letters" used by him in the Epistle to the Galatians (Gal. vi: 11). Some of the parchment was purple and highly ornamented. The great Greek Bibles that have come down to us (א, A, B, C, etc.) are written on parchment. Probably to that fact is due their preservation through the centuries. Palimpsests, like C, are parchments that had the writing rubbed out, or nearly so, and written over again.

4. *Papyrus*

We have seen that parchment supplanted papyrus (πάπυρος, Egyptian pa-p-yos or *papu*) definitely in the fourth century A.D. The process began earlier, but from the fifth century B.C. to the fourth century A.D. the Greeks mainly employed papyrus for their books. Papyrus has the longest record of use as writing material of anything except stone. The papyrus plant flourished chiefly in Egypt, but it existed also in Sicily and Syria. The papyrus reed grows mainly in marshes and stagnant pools. The ark of bulrushes in which the child Moses was placed (Ex. iii: 3) was probably made of the papyrus reed. The inner bark or pith of the papyrus was split in pieces of any desired length and laid side by side, then moistened with sticky water or glue, and other pieces put crosswise over them. Then the pieces were pressed and dried and smoothed into excellent paper (our word paper is from papyrus). Egyptian papyrus rolls are in existence at least from the twenty-seventh century B.C. The writing was along the horizontal lines if only on one side. The manufacture of papyrus sheets was carried to the point of efficiency so that toughness and durability were combined with great thinness. The sheets of papyrus were glued together to make a roll of any length. The modern discovery of papyri begins in 1752 in Herculaneum where a whole library of papyrus rolls was found quite charred by the heat. The first discovery of Greek papyri in Egypt was made in 1778 when some Arabs found forty rolls in an earthen pot in the Fayûm. More papyri rolls were found in 1820 on the site of the Serapeum above Memphis. In 1877 a great mass of Greek and other papyri was found in the Fayûm. Another great find was made in 1892 in the Fayûm. These finds were divided among the great

European museums and libraries. The natives had discovered most of them. In 1889-90 Professor W. M. Flinders-Petrie found many mummies or mummy-casings adorned with breast-pieces and sandals made of papyri. These Petrie papyri came mainly from the third century B.C. Grenfell and Hunt in 1896-97 dug up an enormous mass of papyri at Oxyrhynchus which they are still editing and publishing. At Hibeh, at Tebtunis, and again at Oxyrhynchus they continued their discoveries. Some of the papyri contain classical books, some of lost writings. Many small portions of the Septuagint and the New Testament have been found (to be noted later). But the great mass of them are mere fragments and odds and ends (non-literary papyri) that tell the life of the people (love letters, business letters, receipts, tax-lists). These Greek papyri give the κοινή language of the time with great variety and freshness and show how the people wrote and thought. See Thompson, *An Introduction to Greek and Latin Palaeography* (1912); Kenyon, *The Palaeography of Greek Papyri* (1912); Wilcken, *Grundzüge und Chrestomathie der Papyruskunde* (1912); Deissmann, *Licht vom Osten* (4 Aufl., 1923), *Light from the Ancient East* (tr. 1910); Mayser, *Grammatik der Griechischen Papyri* (1906); the cyclopedia articles, Milligan's *Greek Papyri* (1910), and the many volumes of papyri.

5. *Ostraca and Wax Tablets*

There were also ostraca (pieces of pottery) and wax tablets that were used. The poor people used the ostraca (see Crum, *Coptic Ostraca*, etc., 1902). Wax tablets were employed in schools in taking notes, and in letters. They were like our slates. Zacharias made use of a writing tablet, πινακίδιον (Luke i: 63). The wax tablet would be like our post card. Often one would use the same tablet for his reply. The pointed stilus was used to write on the wax tablet. Two could be fastened together, a folding tablet, and probably formed a link in the transition from roll to codex. One of these folding tablets could carry as much as Second or Third John or Philemon.

6. *The Roll*

Both parchment and papyrus were first used in rolls. Separate sheets would be pasted together for any desired length. Each leaf was usually square and could hold more than one narrow column, the number depending on the width of the leaf or sheet of papyrus or parchment. The number of columns never exceeded four and two became common. One would in Greek write first on the left column and go on to the right. The roll would then be folded so that the outside sheet would be the beginning. As one reads, he would unroll with his right hand and roll up what was read with his left. The title of a book would be given at the end of the roll or on a separate slip fastened at the top (or at both places). The roll was wound on a stick of some kind to keep it smooth. The book (βιβλίον) of Isaiah (Luke 4: 17, 19) handed to Jesus in Nazareth was a roll. This is the meaning of βίβλος (book-roll) in Matt. i: 1; Mk. xii: 26; Luke iii: 4; xx: 42; Acts i: 20; vii: 42; xix: 19 and of βιβλίον (diminutive of βίβλος) in John xx: 30; xxi: 25. Βιβλαρίδιον (Rev. x: 2, 8 ff.) is a double diminutive. Each of the larger New Testament books (Matthew, Luke, John, Acts, Apocalypse) would make one roll of large size. Usually the rolls were written only on one side, but occasionally on both. The roll (βιβλίον) in Rev. v: 1 written ἔσωθεν καὶ ὄπισθεν was written on both sides. When not in use the roll would often be kept in a leather cover which could be sealed as in Rev. v: 1. In Rev. v: 2; x: 2 it is probably the unsealed roll that is in mind, not the unrolled book. Probably the four rolls containing the Four Gospels would be kept in one cylinder in the early days.

7. *The Codex*

Sometimes the papyrus sheets were made into codices (a leaf book) instead of the ordinary roll (Jerome, *Ep*. lxxi). It seems that papyrus codices appeared in Asia Minor as early as the first century B.C. But parchment was usually used for the codex book form. *Membrane* is simply Latin *Membrana*, Greek μεμβράνα (skin), and originally loose parchment sheets. Wood and metal tablets could not be folded, but were hinged, usually like a chain or accordion, not like our book. But some tablets were diptychs, polyptychs and these may have suggested the codex. But it was common to fold a single sheet of parchment for a letter. In folding the sheet of vellum into quires, hair-side would face hair-side and flesh-side flesh-side all through the book. The sheets folded together varied in number in the Greek world (four, five, six sheets). Thus there would be eight, ten, twelve, leaves or sixteen, twenty, twenty-four pages. The Latin world generally folded together four sheets of vellum and that would make eight leaves or sixteen pages (quaternio, or quire). The sheets were numbered, as a rule, but the leaves were left unnumbered till the fifteenth century and the pages till the sixteenth. The rolls gradually gave way to the codices. Gregory thinks that the change from book roll to codex or leaf-book came about 300 A.D. (*Canon and Text of the New Testament*, p. 322). He thinks also that Christian scribes introduced the leaf-book or codex because the Christians needed to be able to find a passage in the New Testament quickly. Hence parchment codex and Christian literature go together (Jordan, *Writing*, Hastings' *Dictionary of the Apostolic Church*). The pages in the codex were generally square and could hold as many as four narrow columns, though two was the common number. The lines in the columns were of uniform length and usually kept straight with the same number of letters (approximately) in each line. The codices were not always bound, but wooden boards would be employed when done at all. "In earlier days a complete vellum Bible in one volume is an excessive rarity, but in the thirteenth century thousands of them were produced in single volumes of comparatively small bulk" (Souter, *Text and Canon*, p. 8). Our modern printed books follow the codex or leaf-book form.

8. *Pen and Ink*

An iron pen or stilus was used to write on the wax tablets. For the papyrus roll and the parchment codex a reed-pen (*calamus*) was employed as in III John 13 διὰ μέλανος καὶ καλάμου. The ink here was black. For writing on papyrus a soot-ink was used. It was a mixture of pine-soot and glue dissolved in water. For parchment or vellum by the fifth century gall-apple ink was employed as the soot-ink did not suit parchment so well. But still the soot-ink was probably used in New Testament times as in II Cor. iii: 3 ἐνγεγραμμένη οὐ μέλανι. Inkstands were also in use. The reed-pen was shaped much like the quill of later times and a pen-knife was necessary for splitting it. Before the pen a small brush was probably employed. The ink used varied in permanency as with us. In the case of palimpsests chemical reagents can sometimes restore the original writing.

9. *Styles of Writing*

Every scribe had his own handwriting as now. But there were two forms in current use, the literary style like our print, and the cursive hand like our writing. These varied with different centuries. The large uncial letters, often with exquisite curves, made a beautiful page. The non-literary hand would use smaller uncials. But with the rise of the codex and the disappearance of papyrus a more running smaller hand came into general use. It appears first in the seventh century A.D. By the ninth century this small cursive hand (minuscule) was employed even for literary purposes and the uncial soon vanished. But in the fourth century A.D. the great manuscripts, like ℵ and B, are written in uncial letters. The letters all run close together to save space (continuous writing) and one has to pick out each word quickly, a difficult task for a modern reader. The early manuscripts have hardly any accents or breathings until the ninth century when the minuscule style is driving out the uncial. There was practically no punctuation. Sometimes dots, double dots, spaces, were used to indicate a break. In the best manuscripts a new paragraph would sometimes be indicated by a short horizontal line on the margin. Hence our *paragraph* (παρά, γράφω), written by the side. Some of the later books have pictures drawn at the start or at the main divisions. The purple manuscripts on purple vellum were in silver or gold letters (*editions de luxe*). Sometimes ornamented letters stand out from the column to attract attention. The στίχος was an average line of poetry and so was used as a line of measurement. Books were said to contain so many στίχοι. Κῶλα and κόμματα were divisions according to the sense. It was easy to misread continuous writing and to make mistakes in copying.

10. *Scribes*

There were professional copyists who would take down a book at the dictation of the author. This was Paul's habit, to use an amanuensis, one of whom, Tertius, gives his own name (Rom. xvi: 22). Paul would always sign his own name at the end (II Thess. iii: 17). Sometimes he would write a whole section (Gal. vi: 11) and all of it if a short one (Philemon 19). Silvanus was probably the amanuensis for Peter in his First Epistle (v: 12). Scribes (γραμματεῖς, *librarii, antiquarii*) were regularly employed in publishing books. A reader would read aloud slowly and each scribe would copy by the sound. This habit explains many variations in spelling, itacism, for instance (ι, υ, υι, ει, οι, η, ῃ all pronounced alike). In case of copying the eye would also mislead as well as the ear in dictation. The memory would also play tricks and the pen go astray. Then each scribe had his own degree of culture. Copyists would usually sit on the floor with the writing materials around them. But in some instances small hand tables by the stool would be used. It is possible that ℵ and B belong to the fifty-five copies of the Bible that the Emperor Constantine told Eusebius to have made and to send to Constantinople. Eusebius was bishop at Caesarea in Palestine (cf. Gregory, *Canon and Text*, pp. 326–28).

11. *Libraries*

The ancients had many books and had their own way of keeping them. Libraries of clay tablets have been handed down to us from Assyria. Rameses I in Egypt had two libraries. The two most famous libraries of ancient times were those of Pergamum and Alexandria. Mark Antony transferred that of Pergamum to Alexandria. After that public libraries became common in the Graeco-Roman world. The ruins of Herculaneum have shown us the ruins of a small library of papyrus rolls. Few libraries, ancient or modern, contain all the books on any one subject. Books were common in the time of Hammurabi. Assyrian and Babylonian libraries of clay tablets have been brought to light.

12. *Autographs*

If we only had the autographs of the New Testament writers, this book would not have been written. The whole great library on the textual criticism of the

New Testament would be needless. The papyri of Egypt have preserved for us many thousands of autograph letters, as one can see for himself, or pictures of them in a book like Deissmann's *Light from the Ancient East*. Gregory expressed the hope that the autograph of Mark's Gospel may yet turn up from the sand heaps of Egypt and settle the dispute about the close of the book (*Canon and Text*, p. 512). Perhaps so, but only in Egypt is there any hope for such a discovery. The brittle papyrus books have not survived elsewhere to any extent. It is fairly certain that the New Testament writers did not use parchment, though Paul speaks of "the parchments" (τὰς μεμβράνας in II Tim. iv: 13) in distinction from "the books" (τὰ βιβλία), the papyrus rolls. Certainly it cannot be proved that Paul meant parchment codex or even parchment roll in contrast to papyrus roll. He may mean merely sheets of parchment. But even if he does not refer to leather rolls of the Old Testament (Hebrew or Septuagint), he may still mean parchment sheets of the Old Testament (portions of it) or even of the Gospels. He prized "the parchments" "especially" (μάλιστα). Probably the New Testament autograph copies were in the running uncial hand, not the literary uncial and not in the cursive of the seventh century A.D. The material was probably papyrus for John (II John 12) expressly speaks of it by the use of διὰ χάρτου, though, of course, this instance, proves nothing positive about the others. There was nothing to prevent the use of parchment if one had it and could afford it. Wax tablets would only suit the briefest letters. One may believe what he will about the alleged autograph of Mark in Venice and the supposed autograph of Peter in Hebrew. Both are obviously legendary inventions. We shall probably never see an autograph copy of any New Testament book. Jesus himself wrote nothing save on the ground. But it is possible by the science of textual criticism to restore almost completely the *ipsissima verba* of the autograph New Testament books. And that is much, for the Greek New Testament pictures Jesus himself to men. Erasmus so felt when he wrote the Preface to his Greek New Testament: "These holy pages will summon up the living image of His mind. They will give you Christ Himself, talking, healing, dying, rising, the whole Christ in a word; they will give Him to you in an intimacy so close that He would be less visible to you if He stood before your eyes." On this whole subject of New Testament Autographs, see Kenyon's *Textual Criticism of the New Testament* (pp. 19-44). On the circulation and collection of the New Testament writings see Milligan's *The New Testament Documents*" (pp. 171-229).

The student can now read in Tischendorf the evidence for Acts viii: 37.

CHAPTER IV

THE USE OF TISCHENDORF

We now turn from the history of criticism to the matter of criticism. Until a new work on a grand scale and one that is thoroughly up to date has been produced, the student is compelled to make constant use of Tischendorf's Eighth Edition (*octava critica maior*). It is necessary, therefore, for the student to know how to use these two volumes. Volume I is devoted to the Gospels and Volume II to the rest of the New Testament in this order (Acts, Catholic Epistles, Pauline Epistles with Hebrews, Apocalypse). Westcott and Hort follow this order as does Von Soden, though Nestle does not. It would be well for all editions of the Greek New Testament to conform to the order of Tischendorf, simply for convenience of reference.

The work of Tischendorf is in Latin, once the language of all scholars and so the common medium of communication between scholars of all lands and tongues. But, now, alas, Latin is no longer required for the A. B. degree, but, like Greek, has been made optional in many colleges and universities. The result is that there is no language which a modern scholar can be assumed to know, not even always his own. Many ministers today study neither Greek nor Latin in college, but take up Greek at the theological seminary. These come to the use of Tischendorf with the door shut in the face. There is no recourse save a hurried effort to learn a little Latin in order to go on with the study of the textual criticism of the New Testament.

But Tischendorf abbreviates his Latin very often as *c.* for *cum*, *al.* for *aliis*, *et.* for *etiam*, *om.* for *omittunt*, etc. It is almost short-hand Latin in places. He does this to save space. It behooves the student, therefore, not simply to know Latin, but to know how to fill out the abbreviations of Tischendorf and, when necessary, to fill in *lacunae* in his sentences.

Besides all this, there are very many symbols and abbreviations of all sorts that can only be understood by actual use of the two volumes. In Vol. I, pp. ix to xx Tischendorf gives brief explanations of some of these. Gregory's *Prolegomena* (pp. 1317-1323, Compendia et Sigla) is devoted wholly to the elucidation of the methods of notation employed by Tischendorf. He has done it in a masterly fashion with much detail and with great clearness. The volume contains 1428 pages. This book again is in Latin. Lake gives a couple of pages (*The Text of the New Testament*, pp. 92-93) to the explanation of Tischendorf's system of notation.

The best way to learn Tischendorf's system is by taking several examples, for no one example brings out all the points in it. But several examples will show most of them at any rate. Take the evidence given at the beginning of Matt. xiii: 1.

εν c. ℵ B Z 16. 33. 61. a b c e ff$^{1.2.}$ g$^{1.}$ k vg arm aeth Or^{3,2et3} ...ς Ti add δε c. C D E F G K L M S U V X Γ Δ Π al pler f h q syr^{utr} cop |

Note the absence of accents and breathings on the two Greek words quoted. The perpendicular line | at the end means that the evidence presented on the readings in question ends here. Beyond that line a new subject is discussed. The dotted line .... near the middle of the evidence marks the division between the evidence for the two readings, εν without δε on the one hand, and εν with δε added on the other. In both instances c. stands for *cum* and means *on the authority of* the documents that follow. The word *add* is for *addunt*.

Nothing that comes before c. (or *cum*) is really evidence. All the evidence follows c. What comes before c. is the opinion of editors in their printed editions of the Greek New Testament. Ti before *add*, for instance, is a reference to the seventh edition (1859) of Tischendorf's *Novum Testamentum Graece* which was published before Tischendorf discovered ℵ. In the seventh edition Tischendorf printed δε, but, since ℵ does not have it, he follows ℵ B and their supporters in not giving it. The arbitrary sign ς (*sti*) means the text of Stephanus (1550), Elzevir (1624), Griesbach (1827), and Scholz (1830, 1836) who usually agree. By using a bracket after ς Tischendorf indicates difference between these four editions. Usually the three later editors agree with Stephanus. $\varsigma.^e$ = Elzevir, S^z = Scholz, Gb = Griesbach. The use of ' means "probable" (Gb', Griesbach thinks it probable), " means "very probable" (Gb", Griesbach thinks it very probable); but ⁰ means dissents, ⁰⁰ very much dissents. So that ς (Gb⁰⁰) means the reading Stephanus, Elzevir, Scholz, Griesbach (text), but Griesbach very much prefers himself the other reading. Gb + means that Griesbach puts it into his text, but with doubt.

The evidence on both sides is always given in the same order (first the Greek manuscripts, then the versions, then the Fathers).

In giving the Greek manuscripts the uncials (majuscules) always come first and then the cursives (minuscules) second. W (Washington codex) gives δε here (not in Tischendorf). The uncials are represented by capital letters. The uncials are always given or counted. It is important to bear this fact in mind. The cursives are usually represented by Arabic figures. The cursives are much more numerous than the uncials and are not so important as a rule. Hence they are not all given every time. In this instance only three uncials, ℵ B Z, support εν without δε and three cursives, 16. 33. 61. But the reading εν with δε is supported by fifteen uncials (besides W) all of which are mentioned by their symbols. But the cursives that give δε are so numerous that Tischendorf merely gives *al pler* (*aliis plerisque*), "very many others," or "most others," that is, "very many other Greek MSS." But after the named or numbered uncials, this necessarily means "very many other (cursives)," minuscules not uncials. It is quite important for the student to bear this point in mind. The uncials are never so grouped. They are always named or counted. The minuscules are usually lumped together as *al pler*, *al omn* (*aliis omnibus*), etc.

After the Greek manuscripts (uncials and cursives) Tischendorf gives the versions (manuscripts also). He always places the Latin versions before the other versions. He uses *it* for Old Latin which we now know has to be divided into African Latin and European Latin. When both of these versions agree, the symbol is *it*. If the manuscripts of the Old Latin disagree as here, they are represented by separate documents on each side. Here we have a b c e ff$^{1.2.}$ g$^{1.}$ k for εν alone, and f h q for the addition of δε. The Latin Vulgate (= vg) follows for εν alone with no variation in the manuscripts. The Old Latin manuscripts are represented by small letters (a b c etc.), the Vulgate manuscripts by syllables like am, gat, tol.

The other versions follow in order of importance. Versions of first-class importance are the Latin, Syriac, and Egyptian. Those of secondary importance are the Armenian, Aethiopic, Gothic, Georgian, Arabic, Slavonic, etc. These are all represented by simple abbreviations like arm., aeth., go., except where there are several versions in one language as in the Syriac and Egyptian.

Tischendorf at first knew of only two Syriac versions (the Peshitta and the Harclean). When these agree he represents them by syr^{utr}, i. e., both (utrisque) Peshitta and Harclean. When they disagree, he gives them as syr^{sch} (the Peshitta edition of Schaaf) and syr^p (Syriac posterior, i. e., later than the Peshitta, in other words, White's edition of the Harclean Syriac). In the eighth edition Tischendorf makes use of the Curetonian Syriac (syr^{cu}) and of the Jerusalem (or Palestinian) Syriac (syr^{hr}), but he retained syr^{utr} for both Peshitta and Harclean Syriac. He did not, of course, know of the Sinaitic Syriac (syr^{sin}) discovered in 1892 by Mrs. Lewis and Mrs. Gibson. In the reading above in Matt. xiii: 1 Tischendorf quotes syr^utr for δε.

The symbol cop for δε stands for Coptic (Αἰγύπτιος, Egyptian). It is also termed Memphitic (mem) or Bohairic (boh) as it is now usually called. There are two other Egyptian versions, the Sahidic (sah) or Thebaic (theb) and the Bashmuric (bash). Tischendorf quotes only cop for this reading of δε. The Armenian (arm) and Aethiopic (aeth) support εν without δε.

The Fathers follow the versions. Their names are given in abbreviated form. It happens that on Matt. xiii: 1 no father is quoted by Tischendorf except Origen who does not give δε. He is referred to by Or^{3, 2 et 3} (Vol. III, pp. 2 and 3). The abbreviations for the Fathers are very numerous and can be picked up by use. Gregory in his *Prolegomena*, pp. 1153–1230, gives a useful list of all the abbreviations employed by Tischendorf in quotations from early writers. Most of them are self-explanatory as Act Barn (Acta Barnabae), Amb (Ambrose). But in the case of Ambrose there are two pages of abbreviations for the various writings of Ambrose. So Ambrst is for Ambrosiaster (Pseudo-Ambrose), Amm or Ammon is for Ammonius, Ath for Athanasius, Aug for Augustine, Chr or Chrys for Chrysostom, Cyp for Cyprian, Cyr for Cyril of Alexandria and Cyr^hr or Cyr^hier for Cyril of Jerusalem, Did for Didymus of Alexandria, Ephr or Ephraem for Ephraem Syrus, Epiph or Epph or Epphan for Epiphanius, Eus for Eusebius (Bishop of Caesarea), Evv apocr for evangelia apocrypha, Fulg for Fulgentius, Greg for Gregory Magnus, Gregory^naz or Naz for

Gregory of Nazianzus, Greg^{nyss} or Nyss for Gregory of Nyssa, Greg^{thaum} or Thaum for Gregory Thaumaturgus, Hier for Sophronius Eusebius Hieronymus (Jerome), Hipp for Hippolytus Romanus, Jac^{nis} or Jac^{nisib} for James Nisibenus, Ign for Ignatius, Ir or Iren for Irenaeus, Just or Justin for Justin Martyr, Lact or Lactant for Lactantius of Africa, Marc or Mcion for Marcion, Nov or Novat for Novatian, Or for Origen, Pamp or Pamphil for Pamphilus (presbyter of Caesarea and teacher of Eusebius), Pel or Pelag for Pelagius, Phot for Photinus, Polyc for Polycarp, Prim or Primas for Primasius, Ps-Ath for Pseudo-Athanasius, Ruf or Rufin for Rufinus, Sev or Sever or Sev^{ant} or Sev^{antio} for Severus of Antioch, Tat for Tatian, Tert for Tertullian, Thdor^{ant} or Thdor^{mops} for Theodore of Antioch (or Mopsuestia), Thdor^{heracl} for Theodore of Heraclia, Thdrt for Theodoret of Syria, Thphyl for Theophylact of Constantinople, Vig for Vigilius.

There are many more of these Fathers and various devices are employed by Tischendorf in referring to the numerous writings of some of them which are all explained by Gregory in his *Prolegomena*, pp. 1153–1230 (Compendia et Sigla).

But it will be best to take another example from Tischendorf and go rapidly over it so as to clinch what we have learned about his use of symbols. We shall take Matt. vi: 1 all four readings.

δε c. ℵ L Z 1. 22. 33. 209 al plus^{10} g^1 cop syr^{utr} aeth pers^p Op . . . ς Ln om. c. B D E K M S U Δ Π al pl it^{pler} vg go syr^{cu} al Chr Hil al |

We miss, as always, any reference to the readings of

the Greek manuscripts unknown to Tischendorf like Σ (Codex Rossanensis), Σ^b (Codex Sinopensis), Φ (Codex Beratinus), Ψ" (Codex Laurensis), Ω (Codex Dionysiacus), כ (Codex Andreensis), and in particular W (Washington Manuscript of the Four Gospels). The papyri fragments of the New Testament recently found in Egypt are also wanting as is any reference to the Sinaitic Syriac Palimpsest of Mrs. Lewis. But we can only use Tischendorf's work as it is.

The new points raised here are al plus[10] = aliis codicibus minusculis plus quam decem = with other minuscules more than ten besides the four named. The single old Latin ms. g^1 in favor of δε explains the use of it$^{pler(plerisque)}$ on the other side, most of the old Latin, but not quite all. The symbol pers^p means the Persian text of the Polyglott in distinction from that of Whitlock (pers^w). Op means Opus Imperfectum in Matthaeum of unknown authorship. Ln stands for Lachmann. After syr^{cu} we have al (aliis) for other versions not named just as al after Hil means other fathers not named. Chr is for Chrysostom and Hil for Hilary. The other symbols were explained in connection with Matt. xiii: 1.

| δικαιοσυνην (Gb) c. א* et ^{b} B D 1. 209. al it^{pler} vg Or$^{int\ 4,\ 512}$ Hil Aug Hier (*iustitiam hoc est eleemosynam*) al. . . . ς̄ ελεημοσυνην c. E K L M S U Z Δ Π al pler f k syr^p (et.$^{mg\ gr}$) go arm al Chry . . . א^a δοσιν (scriptum est -σειν,), item ut^{vid} syr ^{cu}|. (Gb) means that Griesbach prefers δικαιοσυνην in opposition to Stephanus, Elzevir, Scholz. The use of asterisk * and ^{b} with א calls for explanation. א was worked over by several scribes. The asterisk is only used when one of

these scribes has made a notation. Here both the original manuscript (ℵ*) and the scribe[b] (ℵ[b]) read δικαιοσυνην in opposition to ℵ[a] who reads δοσιν. The appearance of the asterisk indicates the real reading of the manuscript. The corrector usually lines up on the other side as ℵ[a] and not as here, on the same side with the original ms. But here we have two correctors at work on ℵ, one opposing, one confirming. Students must clearly understand that the correction is not the original manuscript, but merely the opinion of a late scribe written on the original in a different hand. Or[int 4, 512] means Origen in a Latin translation (*interpretatio Latina* quoted by Jerome, Rufinus, or some unknown commentator). Aug is for Augustine, Hier for Jerome (Hieronymus). The Latin phrase in parenthesis is quoted from Jerome as being his interpretation of *iustitiam*. The addition of (et.[mg gr]) to syr[p] means "also" (etiam) the Greek margin to the Harclean Syriac (syr[p]) or syriac posterior. Here we have a third reading δοσιν (-σειν = -σιν, itacism) supported by ℵ[a] one of the correctors at work on ℵ. But this is not the reading of the real ℵ (ℵ*) above. Ut [vid] = ut videtur, meaning that the reading of the Syriac of Cureton is not clear, but apparently agrees with ℵ[a]. |Δ προσ το μη| The uncial Δ stands alone in adding μη before θεαθηναι. |ουρανοισ c. ℵ* D 1. 33. Chr (et. [mo 2]) . . . ς̄ Ln Ti praem τοισ c. ℵ[c] B E K L M S U Δ Π al pler :: cf ad 5, 45| Most of these symbols have already been explained. Note ℵ* again, the real ℵ in contrast with the corrector ℵ[c] who places τοις before ουρανοις. The (et. [mo 2]) after Chrysostom means "etiam duo codices Moscuenses" which are praised by Matthaeius (see

Gregory, *Prolegomena*, p. 249). And praem = praemittunt, place τοις before ουρανοις. The use of :: marks a note by Tischendorf. He refers (cf.) the reader to Matt. v: 45 where some of these same authorities read τοις ουρανοις.

It is not necessary to give more examples from Tischendorf at this point. Constant use of his work with the help of Gregory's *Prolegomena* and the guide of the teacher will enable the student to handle with ease the condensed and more or less complicated, but indispensable apparatus criticus of Tischendorf which sadly needs revising and bringing up to date.

The student at this point may do well to read again in Tischendorf I John v:7; Eph. I:1; Acts viii:37.

CHAPTER V

THE GREEK MANUSCRIPTS

1. *The Apparatus Criticus*

We have seen that the textual critic has three sources for his study (Greek manuscripts, translations or versions made from Greek manuscripts, quotations of early writers from Greek manuscripts or from manuscript translations). Printed Greek New Testaments are not used at all as witnesses since they, valuable as they are, are merely the opinions of modern scholars, since the age of printing, as to what they think the Greek New Testament is or was. Hence the printed Greek New Testaments merely reduplicate what is in known manuscripts or give the conjectures of modern scholars where emendations may be made. This is simply collusive testimony. In some cases we do have a printed text of a single Greek manuscript, as in the case of the Alexandrian Manuscript (A) by Woide in 1786, or a photographic copy as that of the Alexandrian Manuscript by Thompson in 1881–3. A photographic copy of the Vatican Manuscript (B) was made in 1889–90. Such photographic copies, if well done, give the text of the single manuscript accurately. Hence only Greek manuscripts of various kinds are employed as primary witnesses for the Greek text.

Secondary witnesses are translations into various languages during the early centuries. These are also preserved in manuscripts. A student may use a standard printed version of one of these languages, like the Latin Vulgate, when the manuscripts are in substantial agreement. When manuscripts disagree on important points, appeal must be made to the separate manuscripts. This is the plan pursued by Tischendorf.

Citations from the early Christian writers (called Fathers) may be in any of the early languages. They also exist in manuscript form. Printed editions can be used with safety only when the manuscripts that give the quotations are in substantial agreement. This is likewise the plan of Tischendorf.

Hence, at bottom, all the testimony for the original Greek New Testament is manuscript evidence.

The evidence derived from different parts of this vast critical apparatus varies greatly in value and in importance. No one man has the time to make original research into all of it. Certainly the student who is learning the science cannot do it. But he can get a working knowledge of the chief points in it and he must learn how to use it intelligently in order to reach just conclusions concerning the text of the Greek New Testament. It is worth all the time and trouble that it takes for the modern minister to be able to form an intelligent judgment on the disputed passages without having to rely on the *ipse dixit* of this or that theological doctor. One does not wish to be the slave of modern scholars any more than of medieval scholars. It is mere traditionalism to have to take the critical text without understanding why, as it is mere obscurantism to accept the traditional *Textus Receptus* simply because it lies behind the King James Version.

2. Four Types of Text.

Formal discussion of the four types of text found in the manuscript evidence will be made in Chapters XII and XIII. But it is necessary to give an advanced sketch of this crucial point in order to make an intelligent and helpful discussion of the Greek manuscripts, the versions, the quotations. The character of the leading Greek manuscripts, versions, and fathers will be largely determined by these class affiliations or genealogy.

The four types are the Syrian Class (the α-text), the Neutral Class (the β-text), the Alexandrian Class (the γ-text), the Western Class (the δ-text). This is the nomenclature as to names adopted by all modern scholars except Von Soden (see Kenyon, Textual Criticism of the N. T., p. 59). Lake (*The Text of the New Testament*, p. 66) applies α to the Neutral, β to the Western and δ to the Syrian. But that is a small detail. The names of the Classes are the Same.

The Syrian Class (the α-text) is represented by the late uncials like E F G H K, and A in the Gospels, the mass of the minuscules, the later versions and later fathers.

The Neutral Class (the β-text) is represented by ℵ B Boh., Origen.

The Western Class (the δ-text) is represented by D, Old Lat., Old Syr., Cypr., Iren., Tert.

The Alexandrian Class (the γ-text) is comparatively infrequent and is represented by C L Orig., and a few other documents. But no document has an exclusively Alexandrian text. Some documents, like W, appear now in one class, now in another.

The relations of these four types of text to each other will be shown in Chapters XII and XIII. Only it may be said here pointedly that a purely Syrian reading is always wrong as the addition of καὶ ἐν τῷ σώματι ὑμῶν ἅτινά ἐστι τοῦ θεοῦ to I Cor. vi: 20 on the authority of C³ D² ᵉᵗ³ K L P 37. al pler syr^utr arm^usc(et zoh) Chr¹⁸⁰ Thdrt^(1,1074)

Likewise a reading supported only by the Alexandrian Class is always wrong. The Neutral is usually right as against the Western, but by no means always so.

3. *The Kinds of Greek Manuscripts*

There are four of these (papyrus fragments, uncial codices, minuscule codices, lectionaries), but only two of them amount to much, as we shall see. The papyrus fragments are few and the lectionaries are numerous but of late date and unimportant. The uncials and the minuscules are the Greek manuscripts that are relied upon for the original text. The uncials are earlier and more reliable, as a rule, than the minuscules or cursives, though there are exceptions. This point will be examined in detail.

4. *The Number of the Greek Manuscripts*

It is not possible to give an accurate number because new discoveries are constantly adding more. When Warfield wrote his *Introduction to the Textual Criticism of the New Testament* in 1886 he was astonished at the number (p. 28): "The most astonishing thing about the manuscripts of the New Testament is their great number: as has already been intimated, quite two thousand of them have been catalogued upon the lists,

—a number altogether out of proportion to what antiquity has preserved for other ancient books." But Kenyon (*Textual Criticism of the N. T.*, p. 129) in 1912 gives 4065 as those known and catalogued:

Papyri	14
Uncials	168
Minuscules	2318
Lectionaries	1565
	4065

He adds: "Also there are, no doubt, many mss. in existence which have not yet found a place in the recognized lists." But Gregory (*Textkritik des N. T.*, pp. 1083, 1210, 1929) gave 4084 as the total number known in 1909, and in 1912 he adds 5 papyri, 3 uncials, 9 minuscules, 4 lectionaries, 4,105 in all (*Theologische Literaturzeitung*, 1912, col. 477). Dobschütz in Nestle's *Einführung in das Griechische Neue Testament* (vierte Aufl., 1923, p. 85) gives the list thus:

Papyri	32
Uncials	170
Minuscules	2320
Lectionaries	1561
	4083

Obviously it is not possible for any one to claim intimate knowledge of this vast collection of manuscripts.

But the wealth of manuscript evidence is a great blessing and helps us to restore the original text. There is but a single manuscript that preserves the most of the Annals of Tacitus. Only one manuscript gives the Greek Anthology. The poems of Catullus come to us in three manuscripts later than the fourteenth century A.D. The best attested texts like those of Sophocles, Euripides, Vergil, and Cicero can only count the mss. that give them by the hundreds. And these are from 500 to 1600 years after the autographs were written. The manuscripts of Aeschylus, Aristophanes, Sophocles, and Thucydides are 1400 years after the death of the authors. Those of Catullus and Euripides are 1600. Those for Plato are 1300 and those for Demosthenes are 1200. Only Vergil has one manuscript in the fourth century and two in the fifth (cf. Kenyon, *op. cit.*, p. 5).

But this is not all. There are some 8,000 manuscripts of the Latin Vulgate and at least 1,000 for the other early versions. Add over 4,000 Greek manucripts and we have 13,000 manuscript copies of portions of the New Testament. Besides all this, much of the New Testament can be reproduced from the quotations of early Christian writers. It was obviously impossible for the New Testament to perish from the earth unless the world itself were to be destroyed. Even then much of it will go to heaven in the minds and hearts of the saints.

5. *The Notation of the Greek Manuscripts*

As already noted, Greek manuscripts of the New Testament fall into four kinds (papyrus fragments, uncials, minuscules, lectionaries or lessons). There is a separate notation for each of these groups. Unfortunately modern scholars are not entirely agreed in the way in which they are numbered. Von Soden has developed an elaborate system of his own which is not likely to be adopted because of its complexities. But a brief discussion of his plan will be given in Chapter XIV. The method here adopted is that of Tischendorf and Scrivener as modified by Gregory after consultation with many New Testament scholars all over the world. It goes back to Wettstein, in fact.

In brief, it is as follows. Capital letters are employed for the uncial manuscripts. First the Roman letters were employed, A to Z, till they were exhausted. Then the Greek letters that differ from the Latin came into use, Γ to Ω. A start was then made with the Hebrew letters which have not yet been used up.

For the minuscules Arabic numbers are used. Arabic numerals are also employed for the lectionaries whether in uncial or minuscule handwriting.

This is the notation for the Greek manuscripts found in Scrivener's *Introduction to the Criticism of the N. T.* (4th ed. 1894), Gregory's *Prolegomena* to the eighth edition of Tischendorf's *Novum Testamentum Graece* (1894), Gregory's *Textkritik* (1909), and Tischendorf's *Novum Testamentum Graece* (8th ed. 1869).

Very few of the New Testament manuscripts include all the parts of it. א (the Sinaitic Manuscript) is the only uncial that contains all the New Testament and not many of the minuscules have all of it. Four other uncials (A B C Ψ) originally contained all the New Testament. Only forty-six minuscule copies of the Greek New Testament are known according to Kenyon that contain all the books. These complete minuscules, according to Kenyon (*Textual Criticism of the N. T.*,

p. 132) are as follows: 18, 35, 61, 69, 141, 149, 175, 180, 201, 205, 209, 218, 241, 242, 296, 339, 367, 386, 498, 506, 517, 522, 582, 664, 680, 699, 824, 886, 922, 935, 986, 1072, 1075, 1094, 1352, 1384, 1503, 1597, 1617, 1626, 1652, 1668, 1678, 1704, 1785, 2136.

But Gregory adds three more, 757, 1424, 2191. And Von Soden counts 167 Greek manuscripts which contain the N. T. "tout entier" (Jacquier, *Le Texte du N. T.*, p. 64). So it goes.

The reason for this was probably the difficulty in putting all the New Testament books on a single roll. It would be of impossible length on the papyrus roll. "Such a copy, even when written in a small hand and with narrow margins, would occupy a roll more than two hundred feet in length, which is far in excess of even the largest Egyptian papyri (which, being intended less for reading than for show are often of great length), and is seven or eight times the length of an average Greek papyrus" (Kenyon, *op. cit.*, p. 35). It was the combination of the codex form of book with the minuscule style of writing that made it easy to put all the New Testament in one volume. Each book at first existed and circulated separately. It was only after the codex supplanted the roll in the fourth century that we begin to have a complete New Testament like א or nearly complete like B. But already there were manuscripts that had the Gospels or the Acts and the Catholic Epistles or the Pauline Epistles or the Apocalypse.

Hence Tischendorf and Scrivener gave a separate notation to each of these four groups. This plan made the letters hold out better for the uncials. Thus the

Vatican Manuscript B which stops in the middle of Hebrews is a different manuscript from B_2 as it is called with the figure 2 at the bottom, Codex Vaticanus 2066 (Gregory's 046) for the Apocalypse. So Codex Bezae (D) has the Gospels and Acts while Codex Claramontanus (D_2) has the Pauline Epistles. Once more E is Codex Basiliensis which contains most of the Four Gospels while E_2 (Codex Laudianus) has the Acts and E_3 (Codex Sangermanensis) has the Pauline Epistles. But this method is at best confusing and disconcerting. Sometimes B^{apoc} or D^{paul} is employed for greater clearness.

But a more serious difficulty is due to the fact that the number of known uncials is at least 168 and possibly 171 (Kenyon, *op. cit.*, p. 57). Seventy-two of these uncials had been designated by Latin, Greek, and Hebrew letters. Gregory has developed a method which scholars generally have accepted that relieves this difficulty. (1) Papyri fragments are designated by an antique P ($\mathfrak{p}$) with a number like $\mathfrak{p}^{16}$. (2) Uncials are designated by Latin and Greek letters, but only one Hebrew letter, א, is retained. Each letter is confined to one uncial manuscript except in the case of eight (D E F G H K L P). The series that had been grouped under O, T, W, θ are abandoned. By these Latin and Greek letters and one Hebrew letter forty-five uncials are numbered. The other uncials are designated by Arabic numbers in thick or Clarendon type with o prefixed in the same type. The numbers 01 to 045 are used as alternative designations for the first forty-five already designated by letters. (3) Minuscule manuscripts are designated by Arabic numbers in ordinary type. Only the four groups are abolished. Each minuscule which has the Gospels keeps its number as far as it goes. Those without the Gospels follow on in regular order. It is not an ideal plan, but something had to be done and this has been accepted. Souter has adopted Gregory's system in his *Revisers' Greek New Testament*. The difficulty cannot be wholly overcome till a new edition of Tischendorf's *Novum Testamentum Graece* can be produced.

Nine uncials give us the Four Gospels complete (ℵ B K M S U W Ω 0141). D has frequent lacunae. Only seven give all the Acts (ℵ A B P_2 049, 056, 0142), for D gives out at Acts xxii: 29. Nine give the Catholic Epistles (ℵ A B K_2 L_2 P_2 049, 056, 0142). Seven give the Pauline Epistles (ℵ A D_2 G_3 P_2 056, 0142). Only four uncials give the Apocalypse (ℵ A P_2 046).

Lectionaries are designated by *Evl.* when they contain the Gospels, and *Apost.* when they give the Acts or the Epistles. Gregory suggests 1 before the Arabic number for Gospel lectionaries and 1^2 for Epistle and $1+^2$ for Gospel and Epistle.

6. *Papyrus Fragments*

The papyri discoveries have not added much to our knowledge of the text of the New Testament. But it is far from impossible that Egypt may give us a Gospel or an Epistle of the third century or even of the second (Kenyon, *op. cit.*, p. 40). Gregory is not without hope about the close of Mark: "I regard it nevertheless as one of the possibilities of future finds that we receive this Gospel with its own authentic finish" (*Canon and Text of the N. T.*, p. 512).

But the papyri of the first century A.D. do give us a quite definite conception of the kind of books that the New Testament writings looked like as to material, shape, and style of writing. They were almost certainly on sheets of papyrus like the "pen and paper" of II John 12 and like the thousands of letters from Egypt. The longer ones would be on rolls like the book roll in Nazareth offered to Jesus (Luke iv: 20) and again like the rolls in Egypt. The New Testament writers knew parchment also as Paul did and he valued them much, μάλιστα τὰς μεμβράνας (II Tim. iv: 13). The Epistle to the Romans would make a roll of less than twelve feet.

But this would depend somewhat on the width of the columns and the size of the letters. There were two styles of writing during the papyrus period in the first century A.D. One was the literary hand which itself varied greatly in size and elegance. Each letter stood to itself and there was no division between words. We have examples of this literary hand for the first century A.D. in a papyrus that contains three orations of Hyperides. The other style was the non-literary hand or cursive style where the letters are smaller and run together as in the first century papyrus copy of Aristotle's Ἀθηναίων Πολιτεία. We have no way of knowing which style was used by New Testament writers. It is probable that the Gospels and Acts were written on papyrus rolls (or even parchment rolls) in the literary hand. But the Epistles, certainly the smaller Epistles, were probably written in the cursive or running hand. It is quite possible that Paul is calling attention to his own use of a large literary script in Gal. vi: 11.

76 INTRODUCTION TO TEXTUAL CRITICISM

But it is worth while to give the list of the papyrus fragments of the New Testament so far as known. The symbol is an antique P (𝔭).

𝔭¹. Matt. i: 1–9, 12, 13, 14–20. Third century and the oldest known manuscript of a portion of the N. T. At the University of Pennsylvania. Supports the text of B or the Codex Vaticanus (β-text, Neutral Class). Found at Oxyrhynchus.

𝔭². John xii: 12–15. Fifth or sixth century. In Florence. Greek on the *verso* and Luke vii: 18ff in Sahidic on the *recto*. In the book or codex form.

𝔭³. Luke vii: 36–43; x: 38–42. Sixth century. In Vienna. In book form. Same type of text as the Vatican and Sinaitic Codices.

𝔭⁴. Luke i: 74–80; v: 3–8; v: 30–vi: 4. Fourth century. In Paris. In book form. Like the Vatican Codex save three new readings.

𝔭⁵. John i: 23–31, 33–41; xx: 11–17, 19–25. Third century. In British Museum. With 𝔭¹ oldest specimen of the Greek N. T. Same type of text as Codex Sinaiticus and Codex Vaticanus. "Nearly the outermost sheet of a single quire of some twenty-five sheets, containing the whole Gospel of St. John; a quite unparalleled form of book" (Kenyon, *op. cit.*, p. 42).

𝔭⁶. John xi: 45. Date unknown. In Strassbourg. Agrees with the Syrian Class (α-text).

𝔭⁷. Luke iv: 1, 11. Date unknown. At Kieff. Agrees with the Vatican Codex (β-text, Neutral Class).

𝔭⁸. Acts iv: 31–7; v: 2–9; vi: 1–6, 8–15. Fourth century. In Berlin. Mixed text, chiefly Neutral (β-text) or Western (δ-text).

THE GREEK MANUSCRIPTS

$\mathfrak{p}^9$. 1 John iv: 11–13, 15–17. Fourth or fifth century. At Harvard. In book form. Neutral type of text.

$\mathfrak{p}^{10}$. Rom. i: 1–7. Early fourth century. At Harvard. Rough uncial hand and not clear what type of text. Badly copied.

$\mathfrak{p}^{11}$. 1 Cor. i : 17–20; vi: 13–18; vii: 3, 4, 10–14. Fifth century. At St. Petersburg (Petrograd). First papyrus fragment of the N. T. discovered. Not very legible and type of text uncertain, apparently Neutral.

$\mathfrak{p}^{12}$. Hebrews i: 1 and 2. Third or fourth century. In Amherst Library. Written on the margin of a letter from a Christian at Rome.

$\mathfrak{p}^{13}$. Heb. ii: 14–v: 5; x: 8–xi: 13; xi: 28–xii: 27. Late third or fourth century. In British Museum. Written on back (*verso*) of a roll, with epitome of Livy on the *recto*. Longest specimen of N. T. papyrus known. Neutral type of text. Gives much of Hebrews wanting in B. Can be used to supplement B.

$\mathfrak{p}^{14}$. 1 Cor. i: 25–27; ii:6–8; iii: 8–10, 20. Fifth century. In Monastery of St. Catherine on Mt. Sinai. In book form. Type of text uncertain.

$\mathfrak{p}^{15}$. 1 Cor. vii: 18–viii: 4. Fourth century. Oxyrhynchus Papyri 1008.

$\mathfrak{p}^{16}$. Phil. iii: 9–iv: 1. Fourth century. Oxyrhynchus Papyri 1009.

$\mathfrak{p}^{17}$. Heb. ix: 12–19. Fourth century. Part of leaf. Oxyrhynchus Papyri, no. 1078.

$\mathfrak{p}^{18}$. Rev. i: 4–7. Late third or fourth century. Oxyrhynchus Papyri, no. 1079.

𝔭¹⁹. Matt. x: 32–xi: 4. Fifth century. Oxford. Oxyrhynchus Papyri 1170.

𝔭²⁰. James ii:19–iii: 9. Third Century? Oxford. Oxyrhynchus Papyri 1171.

𝔭²¹. Matt. xii: 24–33. Fifth century. Oxford. Oxyrhynchus Papyri 1227.

𝔭²². John xv: 25–31. Third or fourth century. Oxford. Oxyrhynchus Papyri 1228.

𝔭²³. James i: 10–18. Fourth century. Oxford. Oxyrhynchus Papyri 1229.

𝔭²⁴. Rev. v: 5–8, vi: 5–8. Fourth century. Oxford. Oxyrhynchus Papyri 1230.

𝔭²⁵. I Pet. v: 5–13, Fourth century. Oxford. Oxyrhynchus Papyri 1353.

𝔭²⁶. Rom. i: 1–16. Sixth or seventh century. Oxford. Oxyrhynchus Papyri 1354.

𝔭²⁷. Rom. viii: 12–ix: 9. Third century. Oxford. Oxyrhynchus Papyri 1355.

𝔭²⁸. John vi: 8–12, 17–22. Fourth century. Oxford. Oxyrhynchus Papyri 1596.

𝔭²⁹. Acts xxvi: 7, 8, 20. Third or fourth century. Oxford. Oxyrhynchus Papyri 1597.

𝔭³⁰. I Thess. iv: 13–II Thess. i: 1. Third or fourth century. Oxford. Oxyrhynchus Papyri 1598.

𝔭³¹. Titus i: 11–15, ii: 3–8. Third century. Manchester. Rylands Papyri No. 5.

𝔭³². Rom. xii: 3–8. Sixth or seventh century. Manchester. Rylands Papyri No. 4.

𝔭³³. John viii: 14–22. Fourth century. Oxford. Oxyrhynchus Papyri 1780. Leaf of codex.

𝔭³⁴. John xvi: 14–30. Third century. Oxford. Oxyrhynchus Papyri 1781. Leaf of codex.

It is held by Grenfell and Hunt that No. 1781 is a leaf from the same Manuscript as Brit. Mus. No. 782 (𝔓⁵). It is the earliest known portion of the Gospel of John. I am indebted to my colleague, Dr. W. H. Davis, for calling my attention to these last two fragments.

Dobschütz (op. cit., p. 86) observes that the most of these fragments are leaves of books, certainly numbers 15, 16, 17, 20, 21, 23, 24, 29, 33, 34. Rolls were clearly 18, 22. The oldest are numbers 1, 5, 18, 20, 22, 27, 31, 34.

Dobschütz also notes (ib.) two fragments used as talismans, but uncertain whether papyrus or parchment. He notes them:

T[1] Matt. vi: 9–13. Fourth century. Athens. Wilcken, A. f. Pap. I, 1901, pp. 429 ff.

T[2] Matt. iv: 23–24. Sixth century. Oxford. Oxyrhynchus Papyri 1077.

In the main the papyri fragments corroborate the Neutral text, that of B and ℵ. See further Wessely, *Griechische und Koptische Texte Theologischen Inhalts II* (1911); Pistelli, *Papiri Evangelici* (Papiri della Societa Italiana, Vol. I); Savary, *Les papyrus grecs et la critique textuelle du Nouveau Testament* (Revue de l'Orient Chrétien, 1911, p. 414).

7. *Uncial Codices.*

The fourth century A.D. marks a turning point in the history of the Greek N. T., as Kenyon (*op. cit.*, pp. 45ff) shows. The conversion of Constantine caused persecutions to cease and led to the multiplication of copies of the Scriptures. They could now be produced with all the resources of literary scribes and on a large scale. Constantine himself ordered fifty Greek Bibles from Eusebius, Bishop of Caesarea, for the churches in Constantinople. It is quite possible that ℵ and B are two of these fifty, though the actual copying was probably done in Egypt or by Egyptian scribes.

In the fourth century also the papyrus roll gave way to the parchment codex for literary use. The use of papyrus for literary purposes now rapidly declined, though non-literary papyri continued in great numbers up to the eighth century. Jerome states that Pamphilus in Caesarea replaced the papyrus rolls in the library there by vellum books. The codex or book-leaf form made it possible to put the whole Greek Bible in one vellum volume as was done in the case of B and ℵ. The inconvenient roll made it impossible to have all the Bible, not even all the New Testament, on one roll. But now a complete Bible for the first time could be bound together containing both the Old Testament and the New Testament. And it was a Greek Bible. The canon for the New Testament was not yet fixed and these old Greek Bibles do not always agree in the books contained in them. Thus B has the Old Testament Apocrypha save the Maccabean books and ℵ has the Epistle of Barnabas and a portion of the Shepherd of Hermas.

And the New Testament is now copied in the literary uncial hand, not in the private cursive hand. Vellum allows heavier strokes in writing than papyrus. Hence the vellum codices show at the start a larger and more handsome style. The cursive hand continued for ordinary affairs, but the formal book-hand rules now

THE GREEK MANUSCRIPTS

in copies of the Greek New Testament. Uncial means inch-long letters and is derived from Jerome's phrase in his Preface to his Latin translation of the Book of Job, *uncialibus, ut vulgo aiunt, litteris.* These letters are formed singly and without connection with other letters, while the cursive style binds the letters together. Initial letters at the beginning of paragraphs were made quite large, real inch letters. The size and shape of the letters varied from age to age and with different scribes. Some scribes would slant the letters to the right, others would make them upright. The uncial period lasted for six centuries, fourth to tenth century. As a specimen of the uncial style take Mark i: 1 in the Codex Vaticanus (B):

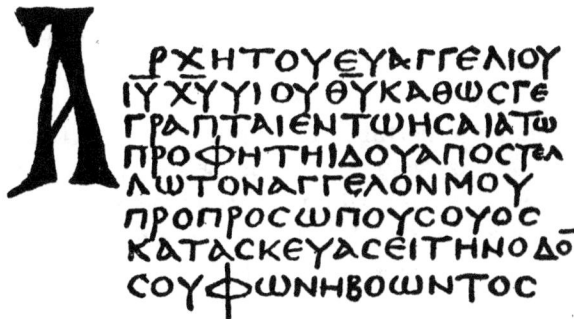

This is really what children call printing letters, one at a time. But one can gain skill in it and do it with great ease and rapidity. In fact, this was the only way the ancients knew how to print books. Publishing houses employed numerous scribes who took down the books from dictation (from the reader) or who copied from another manuscript. One can see by trying it how easy it is to skip a letter or a word or to repeat a word or a line. The marvel of it is that one could catch up such writing at a glance and pronounce it with no separation of words, with no breathings and with no accents. The lines above some letters indicate abbreviation of words, a kind of shorthand for common words. A few letters at the end of lines are made smaller to keep the column regular.

It is not always easy to tell the date of the uncials as very few of them have dates on them. But the style of writing and of parchment indicate the date as a rule. For the rules of palaeography see Thompson's *Handbook of Greek and Latin Palaeography* (1893), Kenyon's *Palaeography of Greek Papyri* (1899).

The uncials are not all of equal importance. There are six for the Gospels that may be called primary uncials because they outreach the others in age and in value. These six are B, ℵ, A, C, D, W. The others are of secondary importance in comparison with these six. The one of least value in the Gospels is A because here it has many Syrian readings. The one of most worth is B. But it is worth while to have some description of each of these six primary uncials.

B (*Codex Vaticanus*) or 03 (Gregory). In Vatican Library in Rome. Fourth century (probably middle of the century). Probably the oldest and certainly the best of the uncials. It originally contained all the Greek Bible, but it has lost Gen. i: 1–xlvi: 28 and Psalms cv: 27 to cxxxvii: 6 in the Old Testament. In the New Testament it stops at Heb. ix: 13 and so has lost Heb. ix: 14 to the end, the Pastoral Epistles, Philemon and the Apocalypse. It has three columns to the page with forty-two lines to the column. The page is square and the vellum is fine. The New Testament is in the same hand, the Old Testament in two other hands. There have been two correctors, one (B²) nearly contemporary, with the manuscript, the other (B³) of the tenth or the eleventh century. In the tenth century some one inked over the writing. A good photographic copy is now accessible to scholars. The original manuscript has no accents, breathings, or stops. It is disputed whether it was written in Egypt or Caesarea, but Egypt seems more likely. B in the Gospels and Acts is the best representative of the Neutral Class (β-text), though in the Pauline Epistles it has also Western readings (δ-text).

א (*Codex Sinaiticus*) or 01 (Gregory). In St. Petersburg (Petrograd). Fourth century also, but almost certainly toward the close of the century, since it has the Ammonian sections and the Eusebian canons while B has not. It probably belongs around the date 375 A.D. Tischendorf numbered it by the first letter of the Hebrew alphabet because he was not willing for it to come at the end of the Roman alphabet. It is next to B in date and in value. It has a mixed text, now Neutral with B, now Western with D, and occasionally the Alexandrian text (γ-text) with C L. It has been corrected by several scribes. One in the sixth century is known as אª, another in the sixth century אᵇ, one in the seventh אᶜ or אᶜᵃ who made many corrections, three others of minor importance in the same century (אᶜᵇ, אᶜᶜ, אᶜᵈ), and אᵉ of the twelfth century. א alone of all uncials contains the whole of the New Testament. An excellent photograph of the manuscript was made by Kirsopp Lake in 1911. At the beginning of paragraphs a letter sticks out a little. Tischendorf discovered it in 1844 at the Monastery of St. Catherine on Mt. Sinai, but it was 1859 before he got it all. He tells the romantic story in his *Die Sinaibibel* (1871) and in several other books. See also Scrivener's *Introduction to the Criticism of the N. T.*, (ed. iv, vol. 1, pp. 90ff.). It is written on thin and fine vellum. Each page has four narrow columns with 48 lines each. Tischendorf issued the seventh ed. of his *Novum Testamentum Graece* in 1859 before he got possession of ℵ and before he had used B. Hence that edition is like the α-text (Syrian or Textus Receptus) while his eighth edition made use of ℵ and B and represents the β-text (Neutral) and differs from the seventh in 3000 places. Kenyon (*Textual Crit.*, pp. 71f.) gives an interesting list of the more striking readings where ℵ differs from the Textus Receptus.

A (*Codex Alexandrinus*) or 02 (Gregory). Fifth century (probably first half). In the British Museum. It contains the whole New Testament except Matt. i: 1–xxv: 6; John vi: 50–viii: 52; II Cor. iv: 13–xii: 7. It was probably written in Alexandria. It is the first of the primary uncials used to any extent by modern scholars, by Walton's Polyglot in 1657, except the slight use made of D by Stephanus in 1550 and Beza in 1581. A photographic facsimile was made by E. Maunde Thompson in 1879 and a smaller one by Kenyon in 1909. It is on thin vellum, worn through in places. It is written in a large square hand, two columns to the page. Enlarged capital letters mark the beginning of a new paragraph. Four hands are discovered in the New Testament, but an Arabic note at the beginning says it was written by Thecla the Martyr. The only important corrector, A^a, is nearly contemporary with the manuscript. It has a mixed text. In the Gospels there is a decided Syrian type (α-text), in the Acts, Epistles, and Apocalypse it has the Neutral type (β-text), occasionally Alexandrian. It is the best manuscript for the Apocalypse.

C (*Codex Ephraemi Rescriptus*) or 04 (Gregory). Fifth century. In Paris. It was apparently written in Egypt. It contains fragments of all the books except II Thessalonians and II John. It is a *palimpsest*. That is to say, the original manuscript, which contained the Greek N. T., has been scraped or rubbed again so that a Greek translation of the sermons or treatises of Ephraem of Syrus in the twelfth century was written over the vellum that once contained the whole Greek Bible. It is not the only time that sermons have covered up the Bible, alas. By the use of chemicals the scripture can be restored in most places, but it is always hard to restore a palimpsest text. There are frequent lacunae and much of the manuscript was thrown away when the treatises of Ephraem were written on the rest. The original was in one column while the superimposed writing is in two columns. Enlarged initials mark new paragraphs and the Eusebian or Ammonian sections are in the margin. Tischendorf notes two correctors, one in the sixth, the other in the ninth century (this one put in accents and breathings). It has a mixed text, now Neutral (β-text), now Alexandrian (γ-text), now Syrian (α-text). Like A it marks the transition from the Neutral to the Syrian text (the later Textus Receptus).

D (*Codex Bezae*) or 05 (Gregory). Sixth century, but Souter assigns it to the fifth. At Cambridge, England. It contains only the Gospels and Acts, but with some small lacunae. It was apparently used by Stephanus to some extent in 1550 and by Beza cautiously in 1581. It is the most peculiar of all the uncials, but has great importance because it is earliest Greek form of the Western text (δ-text). It is a bilingual manuscript, the left page in Greek, the right in Latin, one column on each page. A good photographic copy is now accessible to scholars (1899). The relation between the Greek and the Latin is still in dispute, whether one has been assimilated to the other. Dr. Rendel Harris, *A Study of Codex Bezae* (1891), argues that the Greek has been assimilated to the Latin. The forms of the Greek and Latin letters are curiously alike. There may be truth in both views. Dr. Chase, *The Old Syriac Element in the Text of Codex Bezae* (1893) and *The Syro-Latin Text of the Gospels* (1895), argues that there are Syriac forms and idioms in D and it is generally admitted that there are some. The Syriac influence was probably in the East before the Greek manuscript was brought West that was used by the scribe who wrote D. But Latin dominated the West and the Greek of D seems to be accommodated in places to the Latin order. The Gospels are in the Western order (Matthew, John, Luke, Mark). It was apparently written in the West. It is curious also that D is so much like the Old Latin and the Old Syriac versions. It is purely Western in the type of text, but has some remarkable readings of its own like that after Luke vi: 4 (about working on the Sabbath) which the student can read in

THE GREEK MANUSCRIPTS

Tischendorf's *Novum Testamentum Graece*. See also the long passage at the end of Matt. xx: 28 like that in Luke xiv: 8–11. There are missing places in the Greek manuscript such as Matt. i: 1–20; vi: 20–ix: 2; xxvii: 2–12; John i: 16–iii: 26; Acts viii: 29–x: 14; xxi: 2–10,15–18; xxii:10–20; xxii: 29–xxviii: 31. The Latin is also defective. There are many omissions at the end of the Gospel of Luke as is seen in Luke xxiv: 12, 20, 36, 40, 51. In the Acts there are so many additions in D that Blass has suggested two editions of the text by Luke himself, a matter that will receive discussion later. The scribe has also made numerous slips in matters of detail, blunders due perhaps partly to the manuscript and partly to the copyist himself who may have known Latin better than he did Greek like τήν for τῇ (Acts xiii: 14; xiv: 20 A dozen scribes in later times made corrections.

W (*the Washington Codex*) or 032 (Gregory). Date uncertain, not earlier than the fourth century and not later than the sixth. In Washington. It was brought from Egypt in 1906 by Mr. C. L. Freer of Detroit. A photographic facsimile was made by Prof. H. A. Sanders of the University of Michigan and published in 1912 with a discussion of the chief readings of interest. In 1914 E. J. Goodspeed published a discussion of the manuscript, *The Freer Gospels*, comparing the text with that of Westcott and Hort. It is a parchment of 187 leaves in 26 quires of eight leaves each. Goodspeed assigns it to the fifth century, but Sanders to the fourth. The hand is a clear, sloping uncial. The first quire of John is in another hand. The Gospels are in the Western order (Matthew, John, Luke, Mark). The binding in boards with paintings of the evangelists may be as late as the eighth century. There are no chapter or section titles in the margin. At the beginning and end of each Gospel there are brief titles. Paragraphs are noted with some punctuation, and a little abbreviation. There is only one corrector who has added a word in the margin in seven instances. It has a mixed text, Neutral, Western, Alexandrian, or even Syrian. The most remarkable thing in this manuscript is a peculiar addition that it gives to the longer ending to Mark's Gospel after xvi: 14 (14a), an apocryphal addition hitherto known only vaguely from a reference by Jerome (*Contra Pelag.*, ii. 15).

The other uncials are secondary and call for very few remarks.

D_2 or D^p (*Codex Claromontanus*), Gregory's 06, sixth century, at Paris, Graeco-Latin, Western text.

E (*Codex Basiliensis*), Gregory's 07, eighth century, at Basle. Four Gospels with lacunae. Chiefly Syrian type.

E_2 (*Codex Laudianus*), Gregory's 08, sixth century, Oxford, bilingual copy of Acts with Latin on left and Greek on right. Western text. Earliest ms. that contains Acts viii: 37. See E. S. Buchanan, *The Epistles of Paul from the Codex Laudianus* (1914).

F (*Codex Boreeli*), Gregory's 09, ninth century, Utrecht, mutilated copy of the Gospels. Syrian text.

F_2 (*Codex Augiensis*), Gregory's 010, ninth century, Graeco-Latin copy of Pauline Epistles, with lacunae, Hebrews in Latin only. Two columns. Western text.

G (*Codex Seidelianus or Wolfii A*), Gregory's 011, ninth century, British Museum, Gospels with lacunae, Syrian text.

THE GREEK MANUSCRIPTS 89

G$_3$ (*Codex Boernerianus*), Gregory's 012, ninth century, Dresden, Graeco-Latin copy of Paul's Epistles without Hebrews. Western text. Really part of the, same ms. as Δ of the Gospels at St. Gall.

H (*Codex Seidelianus II*), Gregory's 013, ninth century, one leaf at Cambridge and rest at Hamburg, mutilated copy of the Gospels. Syrian text.

H$_2$ (*Codex Mutinensis*), Gregory's 014, ninth century, at Modena, defective copy of the Acts, but with Catholic and Pauline Epistles added in a minuscule hand.

H$_3$ (*Codex Coislinianus*), Gregory's 015, sixth century, at Paris, Moscow, etc., portions of some of Paul's Epistles, representative of text of Euthalius in fourth century. Neutral Text.

I (*Codex Freer*), Gregory's 016, sixth century, much damaged ms. of the Pauline Epistles.

K (*Codex Cyprius*), Gregory's 017, eleventh century, Paris, one of the nine complete uncial manuscripts of the Gospels. Syrian type of text.

K$_2$ (*Codex Mosquensis*), Gregory's 018, ninth century, Moscow, Catholic and Pauline Epistles. Syrian text.

L (*Codex Regius*), Gregory's 019, eighth century, Paris, Gospels with some lacunae, contains both the short and the long ending for Mark after Mark xvi: 8. It is badly written. Neutral type, sometimes the Alexandrian.

L$_2$ (*Codex Bibliothecae Angelicae*), Gregory's 020, ninth century, at Rome, has from Acts viii: 10 to Heb. xiii: 10 with Catholic and Pauline Epistles. Syrian text.

M (*Codex Campianus*), Gregory's 021, ninth century, Paris, complete copy of the Gospels. Syrian text.

N (*Codex Purpureus Petropolitanus*), Gregory's 022, sixth century, 228 leaves scattered at St. Petersburg, Patmos, etc., of the Gospels, on purple parchment like O, Σ, Φ. Mixed text, mainly Syrian. See Cronin's *Codex Purpureus Petropolitanus* (1899).

O (*Codex Sinopensis*), Gregory's 023, sixth century, Paris, portions of Matthew, on purple vellum in letters of gold. Mixed text, mainly Syrian.

P (*Codex Guelpherbytanus A*), Gregory's 024, sixth century, at Wolfenbüttel, a palimpsest manuscript of parts of the Gospels. Mixed text, more frequently Syrian than Neutral.

P_2 (*Codex Porphyrianus*), Gregory's 025, ninth century, St. Petersburg, Acts to Apocalypse with lacunae, one of the seven uncials for the Apocalypse, a palimpsest with cursive upper writing (Euthalian edition of the Acts and Pauline Epistles). Mixed text, Western, Neutral, Syrian.

Q (*Codex Guelpherbytanus B*), Gregory's 026, fifth century, Wolfenbüttel, portions of Luke and John, palimpsest. Mixed text, with more of the Neutral than P.

R (*Codex Nitrensis*), Gregory's 027. sixth century, British Museum, palimpsest copy of Luke's Gospel, Syriac treatise over the Greek. Mainly Neutral text.

S (*Codex Vaticanus 354*), Gregory's 028, first ms. with exact date A.D. 949 by Michael, Rome, complete copy of the Gospels. Syrian text.

T (*Codex Borgianus*), Gregory's 029, fifth century, Rome, bilingual with Greek on the left and Sahidic on the right, seventeen leaves of Luke and John. Neutral text, ranked next to B and ℵ by Hort.

U (*Codex Nanianus*), Gregory's 030, tenth century, Venice, complete copy of the Gospels. Syrian text.

V (*Codex Mosquensis*), Gregory's 031, ninth century, Moscow, complete copy of the Gospels. Syrian text.

X (*Codex Munacensis*), Gregory's 033, tenth century, Munich, mutilated copy of the Gospels, thin uncial like the minuscule type. Syrian text, occasionally Neutral.

Y (*Codex Macedonianus*), Gregory's 034, ninth century, London, Gospels with lacunae. Syrian text with pre-Syrian readings now and then.

Z (*Codex Dublinensis*), Gregory's 035, sixth century, Dublin, palimpsest fragment of portions of Matthew. Neutral text.

Γ (*Codex Tischendorfianus IV*), Gregory's 036, tenth century, Oxford and St. Petersburg, fragments of the Gospels, (all of Luke). Syrian text.

Δ (*Codex Sangallensis*), Gregory's 037, ninth century, St. Gall, part of same ms. as G_3, Graeco-Latin (the Latin interlined between the Greek lines), the four Gospels nearly complete. In Mark the text is Neutral, while in the other Gospels it is Syrian, evidently copied from a different manuscript.

Θ Gregory's 038, ninth or tenth century, St. Petersburg, Gospels with lacunae. Syrian.

Λ (*Codex Tischendorfianus III*), Gregory's 039, ninth century, Oxford, Luke and John complete, probably same ms. as the minuscule 566 in St. Petersburg which has Matthew and Mark. Neutral text in the main like the minuscules 20, 157, 164, 215, 262, 300, 376, 428, 565, 686, 718, 1071, all of which minuscules state that they were copied "from the ancient copies at Jerusalem."

Ξ (*Codex Zacynthius*), Gregory's 040, eighth century, London, palimpsest, most of Luke i: 1–xi: 33 with marginal commentary, and chapter division like Codex B. Neutral text.

Π (*Codex Petropolitanus*), Gregory's 041, ninth century, St. Petersburg, almost complete copy of the Gospels. Syrian text.

Σ (*Codex Rossanensis*), Gregory's 042, sixth century, at Rossano, in letters of silver on purple vellum, with O earliest illustrated ms. (save Egyptian papyri), fragments of the Gospels, Syrian text.

Φ (*Codex Beràtinus*), Gregory's 043, sixth century, at Berat, letters of silver on sumptuous purple vellum, mutilated copy of Matthew and Mark. Mixed text, mainly Syrian.

Ψ, Gregory's 044, sixth century, Mt. Athos, from Mark ix: 5 to end of Pauline Epistles except a leaf in Hebrews, agrees with L in giving the short ending before the long one after Mark xvi: 8. Text in Mark is Neutral or Western rather than Syrian as mainly elsewhere.

Ω, Gregory's 045, eighth century, Mt. Athos, Four Gospels save Luke i: 15–28. Neutral type.

B_2 (*Codex Vaticanus 2066*), Gregory's 046, eighth century, Rome, one of the seven uncials for the Apocalypse. Neutral text.

For the rest of the uncials one may turn to Gregory's *Die griechischen Handschriften des Neuen Testaments* (1908), his *Textkritik des Neuen Testaments* (1909), and to his *Prolegomena* (1894) to Tischendorf, or to Jacquier's

Le Text du Noveau Testament (1913, pp. 100–106), or to Nestle-Dobschütz, *Einf.* (vierte Aufl., 1923, pp. 86–98), and for a popular picture to Gregory's *Canon and Text of the N. T.* (1907). Some of these vellum leaves are published with the Oxyrhynchus Papyri as Nos. 847, 848, 1080, 1169. In the case of 1080 it is of miniature size evidently designed to be carried in the pocket.

8. *Minuscule Codices*

The uncial codex gives way finally in the tenth century to the minuscule codex. But the minuscule codex had been gaining on the uncial for two centuries. As we have seen, the cursive style of writing in private documents had been in existence all the while. The new thing that came about was the use of the cursive or minuscule hand for literary purposes or book form. The specimens of non-literary papyri now in existence go as far as the early part of the eighth century and show the easy transition to the running hand used in the ninth century for books. The minuscule literary hand is much smaller than the uncial and it also has a different form for some of the letters as is seen in A α, Γγ, Δδ, Ζζ, Μμ, Νν, Ξξ, ΣCσς, Υυ. These smaller minuscule letters were written in a running hand with ligatures just like English script. Not every example of the minuscule hand is thus linked together just as one occasionally sees English script that is practically like printed letters (separately). The distinction is more generally true of vellum than of papyrus writing. It was not until the thirteenth century, as we have seen, that paper came into common use in the West by the side of vellum. It was only the invention of printing in the sixteenth century that secured the final victory of paper over vellum (Kenyon, *Text. Crit.*, p. 126). Only vellum was fit for the first kind of writing.

The number of the minuscules is not really known since no one has really collated and studied them all. Lake (*The Text of the N. T.*, p. 19) says that the number now known is "about three thousand" instead of the 2318 of Kenyon or 2352 of Gregory. Exact figures are not possible and new manuscripts are constantly coming to light. The books to consult for lists of the known minuscules are Scrivener's *Plain Introduction* (4th ed. by Miller, 1894), Abbot's *Notes on Scrivener's Plain Introduction* (1885), Gregory's *Prolegomena* (1894), Gregory's *Die griechischen Handschriften des N. T.* (1908), Gregory's *Textkritik des N. T.* (1909), Gregory's *Vorschläge für eine Kritische Ausgabe des griechischen N. T.* (1911), Von Soden's *Die Schriften des N. T.* (1910), Nestle's *Introduction to the Greek N. T.* (Tr. of 2nd ed., 1901), Nestle's *Einführung in das Griechische N. T.* (4te umgearbeitete Auflage, by Dobschütz, 1923), and Gregory's *Canon and Text of the N. T.* (1907).

The minuscules are denoted by Arabic figures, but according to no fixed system. The notations in Tischendorf, Scrivener, Westcott and Hort have separate numbers for the four principal divisions of the N. T. (Gospels, Acts and Catholic Epistles, Pauline Epistles, Apocalypse). Kenyon (*op. cit.*, p. 126), notes that the same minuscule is known as Evan. 582 for the Gospels, Acts 227, Paul. 279. So another appears as Gospels 584, Acts 228, Paul 269, Apoc. 97. This is very inconvenient. New minuscules call for notation, also. So Gregory kept Scrivener's (really that of Scholz) list names as far as Gospels 449, Acts 181, Paul 229, Apoc. 101. But after that Gregory's numbering is different as far as Gospels 774, Acts 264, Paul 341, Apoc. 122 (the end of Scrivener's lists). Gregory got the consent of most New Testament scholars in Europe and America that his notation for the minuscule Gospels should stand. Manuscripts that do not include the Gospels follow at the end of the lists or fill in accidental gaps. Gregory gives tables of cross-references to Scrivener's notation in his *Die griechischen Handschriften des N. T.*

Some of the minuscules show a sort of kinship and can be traced back to the same uncial. This is true of 1 (tenth century), 118 (thirteenth century), 131 (eleventh century), 209 (twelfth century). This group frequently agrees with ℵ B L (cf. Lake, *Texts and Studies*, 1902).

The so-called Ferrar Group is a name originally applied to four manuscripts of the Gospels (13, 69, 124, 346), all of the twelfth century except 69 (fourteenth or fifteenth). Dr. Ferrar of Dublin proved that they come from a common original. Abbé Martin proved that they all except 69 came from Calabria or Sicily. Dr. Rendel Harris (*On the Origin of the Ferrar Group*, 1893; *Further Researches into the History of the Ferrar Group*, 1900) has shown that the group has affinities with the Old Syriac and with Tatian's *Diatessaron*. The Ferrar Group now includes also 230, 543, 788, 826, 828, 983, 1689, 1709 (a dozen in all). This group all give the pericope about the adulterous woman (John vii: 53–viii: 11) after Luke xxi: 38.

Minuscule 33 in Gospels (Acts 13, Paul 17) is in

bad condition and hard to read (Paris, tenth century). But it has a mixed text (Neutral, Alexandrian, Syrian).

Paul 67 (Acts 66, Apoc. 34), twelfth century, likewise has some Neutral and Alexandrian readings, while 58 and 137 for Acts preserve Western readings and 61 has Neutral and Alexandrian readings.

Erasmus in 1516 relied mainly on 2, a late fifteenth century minuscule. In his *editio princeps* Erasmus used also 1 and 1^r (for the Apocalypse). Since 1^r stopped at xxii: 15 Erasmus retranslated the Latin into Greek for Rev. xxii: 16–21, for which he had no Greek manuscript whatever.

9. *Lectionaries*

These lessons do not give a continuous text, but only selected portions for detached reading. Frequently arbitrary changes are made in the text, for this purpose, particularly at the beginning or close of the lesson. The earliest date is in the sixth century. The majority of them are in the uncial hand, which holds on a century longer (eleventh) than in the continuous text. The number is given as 1565 by Gregory. Those that give Gospel lessons are called *Evangeliaria* or *Evangelistaria* (Evl.), those that give the Acts or Epistles *Apostoli* or *Praxapostoli* (Apost.). These lectionaries often add a parallel phrase from another Gospel (sort of harmony). These ecclesiastical lessons probably go back to a great antiquity. They are valueless in matters of detail. They give some support to the Western text, besides the Syrian. Lake (*Text of N. T.*, p. 52) argues that they prove that, before the Syrian text became supreme, the Western text had a similar vogue. He finds the Western type of text in the Luxeuil lections and in the Liber Comicus of the Acts. For a popular account of the lectionaries see Gregory's *Canon and Text of the N. T.* (1907) and for a formal list his *Prolegomena* (1894). Dobschütz (*op. cit.*, p. 102) gives a list of twenty of the oldest.

The words were not separated, as we have already seen. We have seen also that some of the manuscripts indicate the beginning of a new paragraph. No ms. comes to us wholly without editorial care. The oldest uncial, B, "occasionally marks a break in the sense by a point at the height of the top of the letter or by a little blank space, and begins a new paragraph now and then by allowing the first letter of the line to project a little beyond the edge of the column. But it has no capital letters, no divisions between words, no further punctuation, no breathings, no accents" (Warfield, *Textual Crit.*, p. 39). In ℵ the letter that begins the new paragraph stands out a little further than the rest of the column. In A capital letters occur in the margin with beginning of paragraphs. Breathings and accents apparently do not occur till the eighth century. The minuscules have them and also other helps like modern printing.

But chapter divisions were very early, how early no one knows. Clement of Alexandria (*Strom.* vii. 14, 84) speaks of 1 Cor. vii: 1 ff. as μεγίστην περικοπήν. Tertullian (*ad Uxorem*, II, 2) refers to 1 Cor. vii: 12–14 as *de illo capitulo*. Eusebius (*Hist. Eccl.* vii, 25) refers to some (Dionysius of Alexandria and others) who reject the Apocalypse καθ' ἕκαστον κεφάλαιον. B gives the oldest system known to us, the Vatican sections in the fourth century. For the Gospels, there are 170 for Matthew, 62 for Mark, 152 for Luke, 50 for John. Paul's Epistles are treated as one book including Hebrews. They are obviously made according to sense. Codex Zacynthius of Luke, Ξ, has the same system.

Next in point of age come the τίτλοι or κεφάλαια *majora*. τίτλος is the heading and κεφάλαιον the contents of the chapter. The early scribe called the first section προοίμιον and began κεφ.ᾱ after that, as in Mark i: 23. They occur in the fifth century in A, but not in B ℵ. There are 68 in Matthew, 48 in Mark, 83 in Luke, 18 in John. This was the commonly accepted chapter divisions in the Gospels as is seen in A, C, N, R, Z, etc. The τίτλοι were gathered into tables at the beginning of each Gospel or written at the top or foot of each page.

The *Eusebian Canons* are the indices or tables (κανόνες) for sections in the Gospels that give common events. It was once supposed that Ammonius in the third century prepared these sections (hence called *Ammonian sections*), but it is not really known that he did. There were 355 (*Ammonian*) sections in Matthew, 233 in Mark, 342 in Luke, 232 in John. There were ten tables or lists ("canons"). The first contained all the sections common to all four Gospels. The second, third and fourth were those common to any given three. The fifth to the ninth were those common to any given two. The tenth included those in only one Gospel. In the margin of each Gospel the number of each section was given. Opposite John xv: 20 was written $\frac{PΛΘ}{Γ} = \frac{139}{3}$. This means that this is section 139 in John and belongs to canon 3. This canon includes passages common to John, Matthew, and Luke. In this canon opposite John 139 we find Matthew 90 and Luke 58. Thus we have a sort of harmony. C, D, and many other mss. have the sections, but not the canons.

Euthalian chapters raise doubtful questions. Von Soden argues that Euthalius lived in the seventh century instead of the fifth. If this is true, the Euthalian apparatus was started by some one else before his day. Evagrius's name occurs in some Euthalian mss. The usual idea is that Euthalius, a deacon of Alexandria, published in 458 an edition of Paul's Epistles with a system of prologues, prefaces, lists of quotations, catalogues of chapters and ecclesiastical lections. The text was also arranged "colometrically," short clauses, according to the sense. J. Armitage Robinson (*Euthaliana* in *Texts and Studies*, 1895) argues that he lived in the fourth century. At any rate the second hand of B has put a variation of the Euthalian chapters in Acts. The Euthalian system is certainly not all due to Euthalius, whether he lived early or late. It was added to and grew. It seems plain that the Euthalian apparatus was early known in the library at Caesarea. But, besides the chapter divisions, there was a kind of stichometry in the text.

Stichometry calls for a word in itself. Every fiftieth line (or στίχος) was indicated by its appropriate numeral. The actual length of the standard Greek στίχος seems to have been the average sixteen syllable hexameter line. It was just like the modern printer's "em" a fixed unit of measurement for paying the scribe. The usual system gives 2600 measuring lines for Matt., 1600 for Mark, 2800 for Luke, 2300 for John. Lake thinks that these mss. are right which give 2560 for Matt., 1610 for Mark, 2750 for Luke, 2024 for John, including Mark xvi: 9–20, but not John vii: 53–viii: 12.

The *colon* or *comma* writing is different, for this applies to the sense. It was first applied to the orators and other books used in public reading to help the reader or speaker. It was applied to the poetical books of the Old Testament and Jerome proposed it for the prophets. It is not known whether Euthalius cared for these sense clauses or not. These clause lines would vary much in length. The great examples of the sense clauses (colon and comma) are D, D_2, H_3. In K there is only a point to mark the sense divisions. Dr. Rendel Harris (*Stichometry*) argues that there was a Syrian sense system for the Gospels, and possibly connected with the Euthalian system in the Gospels.

Our modern chapter divisions were apparently invented in 1228 by Stephen Langton. He applied them first to the Latin Vulgate and they gradually made their way into the printed Greek New Testament. They often cut the sense right in two as Heb. xii: 1–3, for instance, clearly is the climax of chapter 11. The modern verses are meant to be sense clauses, but they often mar the sense far more than they mark it. They were made by Robert Stephanus in 1551 on a journey from Paris to Lyons as he went *inter equitandum*. I have often felt that the horse sometimes bumped his pen into the wrong place. Certainly the paragraph according to sense liberates the text from the bondage of verses and even of chapters, still useful mainly for

THE GREEK MANUSCRIPTS 101

preachers to find their texts by. The first step in interpretation is to ignore the modern chapters and verses.

It would be a good exercise for the student to turn now to Luke ii: 14 in Tischendorf and note the presence of ℵ A B D W for ευδοκιας and of ℵc B³ L P ΓΔΛΞ unc⁸ al om ᵛⁱᵈ for ευδοκια and see the bearing of this evidence on the two readings.

A new minuscule of the Gospels was found by Dr. Adolf Deissmann in the autumn of 1926 while in Asia Minor. It has been secured for the Library of the Southern Baptist Theological Seminary, Louisville, Ky. It has been given the number 2358 by Von Dobschütz in accord with Gregory's notation. It will be edited by Prof. J. W. Bowman of Saharanpur, India. It apparently has affinities with θ and 565, as it comes from the Tiflis region. See brief article in the January, 1928, *Review and Expositor*, "A Newly Discovered Tetra-Evangelion."

CHAPTER VI

THE VERSIONS

1. *Preliminary Remarks*

Since we have over 4000 manuscripts of the Greek N. T. at hand, it would seem to be unnecessary to bother about translations. For most other ancient books no such problem is raised. But the New Testament is so important that we want help from every source. We have seen that H. J. White estimates over 8000 manuscripts of the Latin Vulgate, while de Bruyne suggests over 30,000 (Jacquier, *Le Texte du N. T.*, p. 3). At any rate the number is very great. If all the Greek mss. of the N. T. were suddenly destroyed, we should not lose the New Testament, for the versions would be left. But we should lose the flavor of the original Greek, the delicate nuances of tense, voice, preposition, particle, impossible of translation, as have been pointed out in *The Minister and His Greek New Testament* (1923), and in *A Translation of Luke's Gospel with Grammatical Notes* (1923). The body of the N. T., the substance of the teaching, would be preserved.

For the most part Jesus spoke in Aramaic, but he certainly spoke in Greek on various occasions to the mixed multitudes from Phoenicia, Philistia, and Decapolis. It seems certain that there was an early document prepared by Matthew, as Papias said, called

The Logia of Jesus, that was in Aramaic. The critics call this document Q. This document was used in Matthew's Gospel and in Luke's Gospel either in the Aramaic or in the Greek translation. And Luke pretty certainly used Aramaic sources, oral or written, for chapters 1 and 2 (after the Introduction i: 1-4) and apparently also for the early part of Acts. It is now argued by Burney that the Fourth Gospel was written in Aramaic. At any rate translation played an early and very important part in the propagation of the gospel. Christianity took root first among the Jews of Palestine. But Palestine was a bilingual country, especially in the towns and cities. Decapolis was a Greek region and Greek was the language of commerce in Galilee. In Jerusalem the crowd understood Paul when he spoke in Greek, but better when he spoke in Aramaic. But in most lands the people understood Greek in addition to their own national language. Greek was the *lingua franca* of the Mediterranean world. Hence Paul could speak in Greek in Antioch or Ephesus, Philippi or Troas. He would write in Greek to Galatia or to Rome. The κοινή was current all round the Mediterranean world.

It was current almost everywhere, but not quite. In the back districts the people would cling to their vernacular. At Lystra the people heard Paul speak in Greek, but spoke in their own Lycaonian lingo (Acts xiv: 11). As the Gospel went into the smaller towns and into the remoter hill country there grew up a need for translation. The preachers alone would be able to read the Greek manuscripts of the portions of the New Testament that they had. The free or offhand translation of the preacher would be unsatisfactory unless he was a real scholar. And then in some parts of the Roman Empire the Greek language had not really reached the masses. This was especially true of Western Europe, west of the city of Rome, which was a seat of Greek culture, northern Italy, Spain, Gaul, Germany, Britain. And North Africa knew little Greek. The same thing was true of Eastern Syria in the East and Armenia. In Egypt when one went up the Nile from Alexandria he would find Coptic used, a language that used most of the Greek letters and some Greek constructions, a modification of the Greek and the old Egyptian.

It was precisely on this inner circle that the pressure was first felt for the New Testament in the vernacular. It was in Syria, it was in Egypt, it was in North Africa. Christianity had become strong and the people wanted the New Testament in their own tongue. It was this demand from the Jews in Alexandria that led to the Septuagint translation. The Bible has created love for it by the people and the people have always wanted it and still want it and rejoice when they can get it in book, in sermon, or in address. The story of the Bible in Anglo-Saxon and then in English is one of the romances of heroism of all time. The English Bible has made Britain and America as Luther's Bible made Germany.

There is some difficulty in the use of translations for the purposes of textual criticism. Many of the finer points of the Greek cannot be preserved in translation. For instance, the Latin has no article, the Syriac tenses like all Semitic languages are wholly inadequate to render the Greek tenses, the Coptic has no voice. And then the translation will vary with different persons. One man will be more true to the Greek original and even transliterate the Greek, especially in the Coptic and often in the Latin. Another will make a free paraphrase which is of little value for the words of the text. But even then a translation will bear witness to the presence or absence of a passage in the version.

There are three *primary versions* (the Syriac, the Egyptian or Coptic, the Latin). The rest are *secondary* and of much less value (the Aethiopic, the Gothic, the Armenian, the Slavonic, the Persian, the Georgian, the Arabic, the Francica, the Theotish, the Bohemian, the Anglo-Saxon). Some of the secondary versions are of practically no value.

We must bear in mind that we are dealing with manuscripts of a given version that often differ widely among themselves. It is not always easy to say what is the true text of a given version. This text has to be decided by the same principles of criticism that are employed for the study of the Greek manuscripts themselves. These manuscripts vary greatly in date and some of them are later than the age of printing.

The precise date of each version is not certain. It is not possible to say positively which of the three primary versions is the earliest. Hence these will be discussed in their geographical order. Instead of one version in one language we shall find sometimes a series of versions, one after the other, precisely as we have had in English.

2. *The Syriac Versions*

The Aramaic of Palestine was not identical with the Syriac of Syria (or Assyria), but it was kin to it. Christianity early and naturally spread north to Antioch, almost the second capital of the Roman Empire, rivalling Alexandria and Ephesus. As the Gospel got further away from Antioch, where Greek was dominant, to Damascus, Aleppo, Edessa, and Nisibis, the call would come for a Syriac version of the New Testament. On these Semitic dialects see Neubauer, *The Dialects of Palestine in the Time of Christ* (*Studia Biblica*, i. 39ff.) and James, *The Languages of Palestine*. Gregory points out two difficulties in our use of the Syriac manuscripts for the text of the New Testament. One is the fact that Syriac is so far removed from our own idiom and hard for us to understand. The other is that the translator into the Syriac was probably more familiar with his native Syriac than with the Greek New Testament itself (*Canon and Text of the N. T.*, pp. 395f.). It is by no means certain when the earliest translation into Syriac was made. There is no conclusive evidence one way or the other. Gregory (*op. cit.*, p. 397) suggests 150 A.D. as the date by which the Syrian Christians were pretty certain to have a translation of their own. There was a succession of such efforts.

(a) *The Diatessaron of Tatian*

There is much dispute concerning the origin and date of this famous harmony, the first of the long series since. Tatian was an Assyrian Christian by birth, but a Greek in culture. About A.D 170 he produced in Rome, where he was then resident, a Syriac harmony of the Gospels in continuous text interwoven out of our Four Gospels. In 1836 an Armenian version of a commentary on the *Diatessaron of Tatian* by Ephraem of Syria was published by the monks of the Mechitarist monastery in Venice. In 1876 a Latin translation of this was made by Dr. G. Moesinger which showed that the commentary was a compilation of our Four Gospels. In 1888 Ciasca edited several Arabic manuscripts of the *Diatessaron* itself so that now the famous book is accessible to all. See Hogg's *The Diatessaron of Tatian* (1896) and Hill's *The Earliest Life of Christ: The Diatessaron of Tatian* (2 ed., 1911). It is not clear whether Tatian first made his harmony in Greek or Syriac. Gregory and Souter think that he first made it in Greek at Rome about A.D. 170 by pasting together pieces of the Greek Gospels and then either he or some one under his guidance translated the harmony into Syriac probably on his return to his native land. Burkitt holds that this Syriac harmony (διὰ τεσσάρων, by means of four) was the earliest Syriac text of the Gospels in use in Assyria. Vogels (*Die Harmonistik im Evangelientext des Codex Cantabrigiensis* (1910) holds that there was a Latin harmony also. Certainly Victor of Capua in the sixth century got hold of a copy of Tatian's *Diatessaron* and followed his plan of a continuous text, only using for the Gospels the text of the Vulgate instead of the Old Latin (Codex Fuldensis of the Vulgate). Barton and Spoer (*The Four Gospels in Syriac*, 1894) believe that they have found in a lectionary of the Harklean Syriac four pericopes with striking resemblances to the text of

Tatian's *Diatessaron* (Arabic translation). At any rate there is no doubt that the Syriac *Diatessaron* of Tatian was in current use in Edessa and other parts of Assyria till the end of the fourth century, since Ephraem (died 373) and other Syriac writers expounded the *Diatessaron*. Burkitt (*Evangelion da-Mepharreshe*, 2 vols., 1904) holds that the Assyrian Christians first knew the Syriac Gospels in the interwoven *Diatessaron* of Tatian, because the later title of the Four Gospels in Syriac, *Evangelion da-Mepharreshe*, means "*The Gospel of the Separated Ones.*" "No one would be likely to speak of our four Gospels in that way who had not been earlier accustomed to use them in the combined form" (Souter, *Text and Canon of the N. T.*, p. 55).

The type of text in Tatian's *Diatessaron* is the δ or Western text. Souter (*op. cit,.* p. 56) notes that it is more like D and the Old Latin than it is like the Old Syriac text, though the *Diatessaron* and the Old Syriac do have some common renderings and probably have had some influence on each other. See Chapman, *The Diatessaron and the Western Text of the Gospels* (Revue Bénédictine, 1910). The *Diatessaron* has some affinities also with the β text of B and א.

The relation between the *Diatessaron* and the Old Syriac is not clear. It is discussed by Vogels (*Die altsyrischen Evangelien in ihrem Verhältnis zu Tatian's Diatessaron*, 1911). Burkitt holds that in some places the text of the *Diatessaron* has been conformed to that of the Peshitta Syriac. Von Soden considers the *Diatessaron* of Tatian the chief disturbing factor in the text of the New Testament, but that is probably exaggerating its influence. If we had a copy of the Syriac

Diatessaron or of the Greek original, we could speak with more positiveness about the worth of the two Arabic manuscripts that give us our present text. Sometimes the *Diatessaron* stands alone in its readings.

(b) *The Old Syriac*

A century ago Griesbach and Hug saw that the Peshitta Syriac was a revision of an earlier version which they called Old Syriac. But proof was lacking for long, but now we have two interesting documents of this early version. The Old Syriac version was apparently made about A.D. 200. According to the suggestion of Burkitt, Serapion, Bishop of Edessa, had it done and probably got Palut, third Bishop of Edessa, to do it. This translation would thus be somewhat later than the *Diatessaron* of Tatian and at first would be of interest to scholars who would be glad to have the separated Gospels in Syriac.

The *Sinaitic Syriac* (syr^{sin}) is the older of these two documents, though the one more recently discovered. It seems to belong to the fourth century and is a palimpsest, the upper writing dating 778. It was discovered in the Monastery of St. Catherine on Mount Sinai in 1892 by twin sisters, Mrs. Lewis and Mrs. Gibson, of Cambridge. It is sometimes called the Lewis Syriac (syr^l). The manuscript has been carefully photographed and also copied, though it is hard to decipher in places. The ms. is still at Sinai. It is defective and contains only Matt. i: 1–vi: 10; viii: 3–xvi: 15; xvii: 11–xx: 24; xxi: 20–xxviii: 7; Mark i: 12–44; ii: 21–iv: 17; iv: 41–v: 26; vi: 5–xvi: 8; Luke i: 1–16; i: 38–v: 28; vi: 12–xxiv: 53; John i: 25–47; ii: 16–iv: 37; v: 6–25; v: 46–xviii:

31; xix: 40–xxi: 25. The most remarkable reading in the syr^sin is in Matt. i: 16 where the translation of the text is: "Joseph, to whom was bethrothed Mary the Virgin, begat Jesus, who is called the Christ." Some of the Old Latin mss. have a similar reading and the archetype of the Ferrar Group of minuscules (13, 69, 124, 346) apparently had it as codex 346 still has it. Von Soden has it in his text (1913) bluntly: ἐγέννησεν ᾽Ιησοῦν. Moffatt has translated the Von Soden text in his *New Translation of the N. T.* The effort has been made to make this the original text in our Greek Matthew and the origin of all the later mss. and to antedate the theory of the Virgin Birth of Jesus. But the answer lies in the Sinaitic Syriac itself which not only has "Virgin Mary" (παρθένος Μαριάμ, Von Soden), but which also gives the conception of Mary by the Holy Spirit (Matt. i: 18) and the purpose of Joseph to put her away secretly before the angel spoke to him (i: 19-25). It is not clear why the reading "begat" exists in the ms. The theory of insertion by Ebionitic influence still leaves the contradiction in i: 18ff. It is suggested also that "begat" here is only employed in the sense of ancestry, that Joseph was the putative father of Jesus. The text of the ms. is Western, though not geographically in the West. Some of the other important readings of the Sinaitic Syriac may be given since Tischendorf did not have it:

It agrees with ℵ B in omitting "first-born" in Matt. i: 25.

It omits Matt. xii: 47 with ℵ B L syr^cu.

It omits Matt. xvi: 2–3 and xvii: 21 with ℵ B Syr^cu.

It omits Matt. xviii: 11 with ℵ B L.

In Matt. xix: 17 it reads "Why askest thou me concerning the good" with ℵ B D L syr^{cu}.

In Matt. xx: 22–3 it omits "and to be baptized with the baptism that I am to be baptized with" with ℵ B D L syr^{cu}.

In Matt. xxiv: 36 it omits "neither the Son" against ℵ B D.

In Matt. xxvii: 16–17 it has "Jesus Barabbas" with a few minuscules.

It omits Mark ix: 44–46 with B C L and the latter half of 49 with ℵ B L.

It omits Mark xv: 28 with ℵ A B C D.

It omits Mark xvi: 9–20 with ℵ B.

In Lu. ii: 14 syr^{sin} has εὐδοκία, not εὐδοκίας as in ℵ A B D it vg.

In Lu. iv: 18 it omits "to heal the broken hearted" with ℵ B D L.

In Luke ix:55 it omits "ye know not what manner of spirit ye are of" with ℵ A B C L.

In Luke x: 41 it omits "thou art anxious and troubled about many things" with some Old Latin mss.

In Lu. xi: 2–4, it omits "which art in heaven", "thy will be done, as in heaven, so on earth", "but deliver us from evil" with BL and with ℵ save for the second.

It omits xxii: 43–4 with ℵ^a A B R T boh sah.

It omits in xxiii: 34 "Father, forgive them" with ℵ^a B D boh sah.

In xxiv: 42 it omits "and of a honeycomb" with ℵ A B D L.

It is very defective in John's Gospel.

In John iii:13 it has "which is in heaven" against ℵ B L.

In iv: 9 it has "for the Jews have no dealings with the Samaritans" against ℵ D.

In vi: 69 it has "thou art the Christ, the Son of God."

It omits John vii: 53–viii: 11.

It omits the last words of viii: 59 with ℵ B D it vg.

In xi: 39 it adds "Why are they lifting away the stone?"

In xviii: 24 Caiaphas, not Annas, is the questioner.

The chief books on the Sinaitic Syriac are: Mrs. Lewis, *The Four Gospels Translated from the Syriac Palimpsest* (1894): Bensley, Harris and Burkitt, *The Four Gospels Transcribed from the Sinaitic Palimpsest* (1894); Mrs. Lewis, *Some Pages of the Four Gospels Retranscribed* (1896); Mrs. Lewis, *Light on the Four Gospels from the Sinai Palimpsest* (1913); Burkitt, *Evangelion da-Mepharreshe: the Curetonian Syriac Gospels, re-edited, together with the readings of the Sinaitic palimpsest and the early Syriac patristic evidence; with a translation into English* (1904); Bonus, *Collatio Cod. Lewisiani evangeliorum Syriacorum cum cod. Curetoniano* (1896); Holzey, *Der neuentdeckte Codex Syrus Sinaiticus untersucht* (1896); Hjelt, *Die altsyrische Evangelienübersetzung und Tatian's Diatessaron* (1901).

The *Curetonian Syriac* (syr^{cu}) is the other document that gives the Old Syriac version. Tattam brought a bunch of Syriac mss. to the British Museum. They came from the convent of St. Mary in the Natron Valley, west of Cairo, Egypt. Dr. Cureton, of the British Museum, printed one of these in 1848 and circulated it privately. It was formally published in 1858 with the title, *Remains of a very antient recension of the Four*

Gospels *in Syriac, hitherto unknown in Europe*. It is a Syriac copy of the Gospels and belongs to the fifth century. It was at first thought to be a manuscript of the Peshitta version. But it was held by Cureton to be an older version and has been named from him the Curetonian Syriac (syr^{cu}). Tischendorf made use of it. It has the Gospels in the order Matthew, Mark, John, Luke. At the beginning of Matthew it has the title "*Evangelion da-Mepharreshe*" which is usually understood to be "The Gospel of the Separated Ones" in contrast to the continuous and combined text of Tatian's *Diatessaron* (so Payne Smith, *Thesaurus Syriacus*). The ms. contains portions of each of the Gospels as follows: Matthew i: 1–viii: 22; x: 32–xxiii: 25; Mark xvi: 17–20; John i: 1–42; iii: 5–viii: 19; xiv: 10–12, 15–19, 21–24, 26–29; Luke ii: 48–iii: 16; vii: 33–xvi: 12; xvii: 1–xxiv: 44. It is all in the British Museum save three leaves in Berlin edited by Roediger in 1872 and also by Wright, *Fragments of the Curetonian Gospels* (1873). It is a pity that so much of the ms. is lost. Like syr^{sin} the syr^{cu} has the Western (δ) text like D and the Old Latin. These two Syriac mss. do not always agree, but it seems plain that they both come from a common original. The syr^{cu} has in Matt. i: 16 "Joseph, to whom was betrothed Mary the Virgin, who bare Jesus Christ". It has also Mark xvi: 17–20 which is absent in syr^{sin}. It has also the doxology in Matt. vi: 13 except the words "and the power". It has Matt. xviii: 11, not in syr^{sin}. It adds with D a long passage to Matt. xx: 28. With D also it has the addition in Luke ix: 55. It has all of Luke x: 41. It has with ℵ D all of Luke xxii: 17, 18 as also xxiii: 34. It has "and of a honeycomb" in xxiii: 42. It seems clear that the syr^sin is older than the syr^cu, though both are mss. of the Old Syriac version. Neither ms. is an accurate copy of the original Syriac translation. Besides the books already mentioned one may consult Merx, *Die vier Kanonischen Evangelien nach ihrem ältesten bekannten Texte* (3 vols., 1897–1911); Le Hir, *l'Etude sur une ancienne version syriaque des l'Evangiles* (1859); Bäthgen, *Evangelienfragmente der griechischen Text des Curetonischen Syrers wiederhergestellt* (1885).

(c) *The Peshitta Syriac* (syr^sch).

The sign ^sch refers to Schaaf, one of the early editors of the Peshitta version. Once this version was supposed to be the oldest Syriac translation, but that is not true. The word *Peshitta* (formerly written *Peshitto*) means "simple". It came to be the common or current version like our Authorized Version, like the Latin Vulgate. It may have been first applied to the Old Testament to distinguish it from Origen's Hexapla Version which had been put into Syriac. The name Peshitta is not found earlier than the ninth century. Burkitt holds that the name distinguishes the translation from both the Syriac Hexapla of the Old Testament and the later Harklean Syriac of the New Testament which had notes. But it is certainly later than the Old Syriac and a revision of it just as Jerome in the Latin Vulgate revised previous Latin versions. The Peshitta contains all the New Testament books save Second and Third John, Second Peter, Jude and the Apocalypse. The date of the Peshitta is now seen to be the fifth century. Gregory (*Textkritik*, pp. 508–521) gives a list of 178 Peshitta mss. for the Gospels, 74 for the Acts and Catholic Epistles (James, 1 John, 1 Peter), 81 for the Pauline Epistles, 243 copies (allowing for duplicates), but Jacquier (*op. cit.*) counts 286. Some argue for a date in the third century because of the absence of the disputed books, but it is not certain that at first the Peshitta version went further than the Gospels like the Old Syriac. Chase (*Syro-Latin Text*) thinks it included the Acts also. It seems that Rabbula, Bishop of Edessa from 411 to 435, ordered a revision of the Old Syriac in accord with up-to-date Greek mss. The Peshitta version is probably the outcome of that order. At any rate the type of text is usually the Syrian ($\varkappa$-text) like that seen in the writings of Chrysostom cf Constantinople (died 407). This means that the Old Syriac of the early third century was revised to suit Greek mss. of the early fifth century. The text was changed from Western to Syrian, but the Peshitta sometimes has Pre-Syrian readings (Neutral or Western) as Hort shows (*Introduction*, p. 137). The Peshitta, for instance, does not have John vii: 53–viii: 11. Gwilliam (*The Materials for the Criticism of the Peshitto N. T.*, 1891) finds some Peshitta mss. of the fifth century as does Martin (*Introduction a la critique textuelle du N. T.*, 1883, pp. 132f.), but Gregory (*Textkritik*, pp. 508–521, 1298–1301) does not so list them.

Gwilliam's view that the Peshitta belongs to the second century is supported by Burgon and Miller (*The Traditional Text of the Holy Gospels Vindicated and Established*, 1896; *The Causes of the Corruption of the Traditional Text of the Holy Gospels*, 1896). Dr.

Sanday (Souter, *Text and Canon of the N. T.*, p. 61) called the early date of the Peshitta "the sheet-anchor" of the older hypothesis against the critical text of Westcott and Hort. But the sheet-anchor did not hold. H. L. Hastings has *A Historical Introduction to the Peshitto Syriac New Testament* (7 ed., 1896).

(d) *The Philoxenian and Harklean Syriac*

In the year 508 Philoxenus (Xenaias) had his Rural Bishop (χωρεπίσκοπος) Polycarp make a new revision of the Syriac for himself, the Philoxenian Version (syr^phil). The mss. that are known preserve for us only the books not in the Peshitta version (Second and Third John, Second Peter, Jude, the Apocalypse). The Philoxenian text of the Apocalypse has been published by Gwynn (*The Apocalypse of St. John in a Syriac Version*, 1897). The type of text is Syrian for the most part. Souter (*op. cit.*, p. 61) thinks that this text in Jude 22–3 is correct, καὶ οὓς μὲν ἐκ πυρὸς ἁρπάζετε, διακρινομένους δὲ ἐλεᾶτε, preserved only here and in Clement of Alexandria (about 220) and Jerome (about 400). Westcott and Hort consider "some primitive error probable" in this passage.

But in 616 Thomas of Harkel made a revision of the Philoxenian. This is called the *Harklean Version* (syr^p). Gregory gives 51 distinct mss. for the Harklean version (36 for Gospels, 10 for Acts and Cath. Eps., 5 for Paul, 13 for Apoc.). The reviser says that he did his work in Alexandria by the use of "two or three accurate Greek manuscripts". He did his work in the most literal fashion, doing violence to the Syriac in order to preserve the Greek idiom. But this literalness adds

THE VERSIONS 117

greatly to its value as a witness to the original Greek. The translator added marginal notes giving the readings of some of the mss. used, Greek and Syriac. These marginal readings often differ from the text used and are of considerable value. Tischendorf often notes the reading of the Greek margin thus syr^{pmg}. When Tischendorf made his seventh edition, he knew only two Syriac versions (the Peshitta and the Harclean). He refers to them when they agree as syr^{utr} (utrisque). The Harclean he called posterior (later) and so syr^p. The text of the Harclean is largely pre-Syrian either Western or Neutral. It is interesting, as Souter notes (*op. cit.*, p. 62), that in Alexandria at the beginning of the seventh century there were mss. that differed from the current Syrian type. In the Acts the syr^p agrees often with D and three late Greek minuscules (383, 614, 1518). Hort calls the Harclean "one of the most confused texts preserved" (*Introduction*, p. 156). It needs re-editing.

(e) *The Jerusalem or Palestinian Syriac* (syr^{hr})

This peculiar version belongs to the sixth century and is entirely independent of the other Syriac versions. It was probably made in Antioch (Burkitt, *Journal of Theol. Studies*, 1901, pp. 174–183). It is really more like the Aramaic (Chaldee) of Northern Palestine rather than the usual Syriac. From its resemblance to the Palestinian Targum it has been called Palestinian or Jerusalem Syriac. A number of fragments of mss. give this version. They date from the sixth to the twelfth century. They are chiefly lectionaries. They do not always agree, but they give a text that is mainly pre-Syrian (Neutral or Western). It may be due to the efforts of Justinian and Heraclius to abolish Judaism from Judaea and Samaria. Fragments have been known since 1758, but in 1892 Mrs. Lewis discovered a complete Gospel lectionary (dated 1104) and another complete Gospel lectionary was found by Rendel Harris in 1893 (dated 1118). They were both published in 1899 by Mrs. Lewis and Mrs. Gibson, *The Palestinian Syriac Lectionary of the Gospels*. See also Gwilliam, *The Palestinian Version of the Holy Scriptures* (1893); Mrs. Lewis, *Studia Sinaitica*, No. I (1894); Mrs. Lewis, *Codex Climaci Rescriptus* (1909). The so-called *Karkaphensian Version* is only a collection of texts, not a continuous version.

3. *Egyptian Versions*

These versions are often called Coptic, which is an abbreviation of Αἰγύπτιος. Tischendorf sometimes calls one of the versions Coptic (cop), which is unfortunate. There were many Jews in Egypt, especially in Alexandria, and Christianity soon gained a foothold there. But Greek was much used, especially in lower Egypt around Alexandria, Fayûm, Oxyrhynchus, as the papyri abundantly show. As the Gospel spread farther up the Nile, there would be increasing call for the New Testament in the native tongue. This Coptic language was a debased type of the ancient Egyptian written in letters mostly borrowed from the Greek, with six other letters from the demotic alphabet. This came about in the second century and it formed "a sort of bridge between the Greek and Egyptian" (Kenyon, *Textual Crit. of the N. T.*, p. 177). The dates of the Egyptian versions are uncertain, certainly not earlier than the close of the second century and later than the end of the third. A good guess is between 200 and 250. There are three of these Egyptian versions of which we possess remains, but only two are important. Sir W. M. Flinders-Petrie has reported the discovery at Qau-el-Kebir of a papyrus codex of 43 leaves (86 pages) of the Gospel of John in a dialect somewhat different from either of the three well-known Egyptian dialects. That can be determined only after the publication of the manuscript by Sir Herbert Thompson. The manuscript is thought to belong to the fourth century. It is certainly the oldest ms. of John's Gospel in any Egyptian dialect.

(a) *The Sahidic (sah) or Thebaic (theb)*

It was called Thebaic on the idea that it was made at Thebes. But it belongs to upper Egypt as one would naturally expect a version there first, away from the Greek influence in Alexandria. Sahidic is from the Arabic *Es-sa'id*, Upper Egypt. There are numerous fragments (751 in all) and complete mss. of Matthew, Mark, John, Epistles of Paul (including Hebrews), First and Second Peter, the Epistles of John (all in possession of J. Pierpont Morgan; *Journal of Biblical Literature*, 1912), and a fourth century ms. of Acts in the British Museum (Budge, *Coptic Biblical Texts in the Dialect of Upper Egypt*, British Museum, 1911). The translation is rough and uses many Greek words and often leaves out conjunctions. The type of text is now Neutral, now Western. It is more Neutral in Matthew and John, more Western in Luke and Mark.

This is also the order of the Gospels. It is probably the earliest of the Egyptian versions and as early as 200 A.D. Souter (*op. cit.*, p. 67) notes that the Sahidic does not agree with D or with the Old Latin in making a single addition against all other documents. In Luke xxiii: 53 it has a peculiar reading that the stone at the sepulchre was such that twenty men could not move it. See Horner, *The Coptic Version of the N. T. in the Southern Dialect, otherwise called Sahidic* (3 vols., 1911).

(b) *The Bashmuric or Middle Egyptian* (*basm*)

Very little is known about this version save that it is from a different Greek text. In fact the manuscripts indicate three dialects (Bashmuric, Akhmimic, Fayumic). They cover very little of the New Testament and have not been properly edited. It is more like the Sahidic than the Bohairic. See Crum, *Coptic Manuscripts Brought from the Fayyum* (1893).

(c) *The Bohairic* (*boh*). *Called also Coptic* (*cop*) *and Memphitic* (*mem*).

This version contains the whole New Testament and is the official version of the Coptic Christians. It is probably later than the Sahidic and Bashmuric versions, perhaps about 250 A.D. It is well edited by Horner, *The Coptic Version of the N. T. in the Northern Dialect, otherwise called Memphitic and Bohairic* (4 vols., 1898–1905). It presents the Greek fairly well though no distinction is made between participle and finite verb. There is no passive voice. Mr. Horner gives 36 copies of the Gospels, 18 of the Acts and Epistles, 10 of the Apocalypse, all late, from the ninth century on. But new mss. are occasionally found. The text is Neutral and Alexandrian rather than Western. The general agreement with ℵ B is quite marked and it sometimes supports B against ℵ. All Bohairic mss., however, give the last twelve verses of Mark, but two copies (Huntington 17 and Brit. Mus. Or. 1315) give in the margin an alternative ending like that in L. The Bohairic mss. do not always agree. All the better ones omit John vii: 53–viii: 11 and Luke xxiii: 43–4, and all the best but one omit John v: 4. At first the Apocalypse was not in this version, but was added later.

4. *The Latin Versions*

Tischendorf thought of only two Latin versions, the Old Latin (*it*) and the Vulgate (*vg*). The Old Latin mss. are represented by letters like *a*, *b*, while the Vulgate mss. are signified by syllables like *am*. It is now clear that there were two Old Latin versions (the African and the European) and possibly a third (the Italian). It may be that the so-called Italian version is only a variation of the European. Bentley doubted the Italian version and Burkitt (*The Old Latin and the Itala*, 1896) has made it seem probable that when Augustine speaks of "*Itala interpretatio*" as being "*verborum tenacior cum perspicuitate sententiae*" he really refers to the Vulgate of Jerome which he certainly quotes in the Gospels. As to *f*, one of the two so-called Italian mss., Burkitt calls it a post-Vulgate ms. corrupted by the Gothic.

And *q*, the other Italian ms., would merely be a ms. of the European Latin version. So it seems safest to see only two Old Latin Versions, three Latin Versions altogether. Gregory holds that we should talk about the Old Latin, the Middle Latin, and the New Latin Bible (*Canon and Text*, p. 407).

(a) *The African Latin*

Augustine applied "Itala" to the Vulgate of Jerome, according to Burkitt. But he has been misunderstood and the term "Itala" has been given to the Old Latin in distinction from the Vulgate. In Tischendorf *it* is for Old Latin and *vg* for Latin Vulgate. But even so, what is called Old Latin really represents two versions, one in Africa, one in Europe. And the call for a Latin version came first in North Africa, because Greek had not penetrated here to any great extent, whereas Rome itself was bilingual. In Rome Greek and Latin were referred to usually as "both languages" (ἐκατέρα γλῶσσα, *utraque lingua*) as Souter has shown (*Text and Canon*, p. 33; *Did St. Paul Speak Latin?* The Expositor, April, 1911). Augustine spoke of "*codices Afros*" (*Retr.* i–21,3). Jerome spoke of "*Latinorum interpretum infinita varietas* (*De Doctrina Christina*) as a justification for his own work. Tertullian wrote in Carthage A.D. 195 to 218 and Monceaux (*Histoire Littéraire de l'Afrique Chrétienne*, 1901, pp. 105f.) shows that he used Latin translations of Luke, John, Galatians, First Corinthians, Romans, and Ephesians. There is little reason to doubt, in spite of Zahn, that Tertullian had copies of the African Latin Version. He often translated the Greek for himself. Certainly Cyprian (about 258) had a practically complete Latin New Testament, for he quotes it abundantly. It seems probable that as early as 150 A.D. some translation of the Greek into Latin was made in North Africa. Most of the mss. that survive agree substantially with the quotations of Cyprian, but it seems doubtful if the Latin version was ever considered official. Individuals made their own translations with much freedom. The mss. that give the African Latin Version are not very numerous. They agree with Tertullian and Cyprian in supporting, as a rule, the Western text. The two chief African Latin mss. for the Gospels are *k* and *e*.

k (*Codex Bobiensis*), once at Bobbio, now at Turin. Probably fifth century, possibly fourth. Rough uncials with numerous blunders. One column to the page. Agrees now with D (Western), now with ℵ B (Neutral). It has only the short ending to Mark's Gospel. It has now only Matt. i: 1–iii: 10; iv: 2–xiv: 7; xv: 20–36; Mark viii: 8–11, 14–16; viii: 19–xvi: 9.

e (*Codex Palatinus*), now at Vienna (one leaf at Dublin). Fifth century. In gold and silver letters on purple vellum. Two columns to the page. The ms. contains now Matt. xii: 49–xxiv: 50; xxviii: 2–20; Mark i: 20–iv: 8; iv: 19–vi: 9; xii: 37–40; xiii: 2–3, 24–27, 33–36; Luke i: 1–viii: 30; viii: 48–xi: 4; xi: 24–xxiv: 53; John i: 1–xviii: 12; xviii: 25–xxi: 25.

There are African readings in other Latin Gospels like *c* and *gat*.

There is only one African Latin ms. for portions of Acts, the Catholic Epistles and the Apocalypse. That ms. is called *h* (*Fleury Palimpsest*). At Paris. Probably fifth century. Palimpsest. It has portions of the Gospels, of the Catholic Epistles, and of the Apocalypse.

The text agrees with that of Cyprian, of Tyconius, and of Primasius who gives a nearly complete text of the Apocalypse with commentary.

For the Pauline Epistles there is *r*, according to Souter (*Text and Canon*, p. 39), though Warfield calls this ms. European (*op. cit.*, p. 67).

But *m* (*Speculum wrongly attributed to Augustine*), eighth century, has church lessons from all the New Testament save Third John, Hebrews, Philemon. Gregory denies that it contains the three heavenly witnesses in 1 John v: 7–8 (*Canon and Text*, p. 410). Priscillian is the first who gives it in the fourth century. He uses the African Latin. For discussion of the African Latin Version see Wordsworth, Sanday, and White, *Old Latin K. Old Latin Biblical Texts* (Vol. II, 1886); Leclercq, *L'Afrique Chrétienne* (2 vols., 1904); Von Soden, *Das Lateinische Neue Testament in Afrika zur Zeit Cyprians* (1909); De Bruyne, *Quelques documents nouveaux pour l'histoire du texte africain des Évangiles* (Revue bénédictine, 1910); Berger, *Le Palimpseste de Fleury* (1889); Ziegler, *r, Italafragmente der paulinischen Briefe* (1876); Burkitt, *Old Latin and the Itala* (1896); Hoskier, *The Golden Latin Gospels* (1910); Buchanan, *Old Latin Biblical Texts* (1907).

(b) *The European Latin*

It is not certain when the European Latin version arose, probably the third century. Novatian in the middle of this century quotes a text like that of *a* (Souter, *op. cit.*, p. 41). Irenaeus (Latin translation) has the European Latin text. It was used also by

Lucifer of Cagliari for John and by Jerome for Luke. It is not clear what is the relation between the African and the European Latin versions. Von Soden holds that they had a separate origin while Burkitt thinks that the European grew out of the African. Souter (*op. cit.*, p. 40) notes that both versions have the same slip in Mark ix: 15 *gaudentes* (προσχέροντες for προστρέχοντες). It is true that the early European mss. show more likenesses to the African mss. than do the later ones. The bulk of the Old Latin mss. belong to the European Version.

For the Gospels we have *a, b, c* (mostly), *d, ff* (or *ff*²), *h, i, q, r* (?).

For the Acts there are *d, e, gig, m, p*.

For the Catholic Epistles we have *ff, m*.

For the Pauline Epistles we have *d, g*.

Some remarks are called for about some of these mss.

a (*Codex Vercellensis*), at Vercelli, fourth century, is the best of the European Latin mss. and ranks next to *k*, the best of the African Latin. It is in double columns and is more like the African Latin than any of the European mss.

b (*Codex Veronensis*), at Verona, fifth century, occupies, according to Souter, a central position in the European mss., and is the type followed most by Jerome in the Vulgate. In silver letters on purple vellum.

d is the *Latin of Codex Bezae* (*D*) as *e is of E* (Codex Laudianus) and *g of G*.

q (*Codex latinus Monacensis*), seventh century, gives the European text modified by a Greek ms. It used to be assigned to the so-called Italian Latin revision. It formerly belonged to the abbey of Freising in Bavaria. Often it shows a different text from that of the Old Latin mss. Souter mentions *f* (the other ms. of this supposed revision) "though it is not an Old Latin European ms." (*op. cit.*, p. 43). It really gives the Vulgate text.

p seems to show that the Spanish Latin texts were revised from the African Latin. Buchanan (*Old Latin Biblical Texts*, 1907) has attached an exaggerated importance to some of these Spanish texts of the Old Latin. But they are useful in helping to get at the African Latin and the European Latin texts.

Gig is from *gigas* because the largest of all mss. and it is kept at Stockholm. It belongs to the thirteenth century. It contains Acts and the Apocalypse.

See editions of these European Latin texts by Wordsworth and White, Buchanan, Berger, De Bruyne, Staerk, Weihrich.

As a rule, the European mss. follow the Western text, now and then the Neutral.

(c) *The Vulgate.*

It was the confusion in the Old Latin mss., both African and European, that led Pope Damasus (366 to 384) to ask Eusebius Hieronymus (Jerome) to make an authoritative version of the Latin Bible. He was well equipped for the task. The Gospels appeared in 383 and the rest of the New Testament by 386. He used, of course, some of the best Old Latin mss., like *a*, *b*, *g*, *k*, and he says he also used Greek mss. It seems probable that the Greek mss. were of the Neutral rather than of the Western type, for the Vulgate is much more Neutral than the Old Latin. But the Vulgate mss. themselves continued to make use of the Old Latin mss. and to make changes here and there in the work of Jerome. In the case of *f* it is ninety per cent. like Jerome (Souter, *op. cit.*, p. 49) and is therefore apparently a mere variant Vulgate ms. But, well as Jerome did his work, he met with intense opposition. "Dean Burgon's opposition to the English revision of 1881 seemed to us serious, but it was mere child's play beside the antagonism shown in the fourth century" (Gregory, *Canon and Text*, p. 411). By the ninth century there was less opposition, but the Anglo-Saxons copied the Old Latin mss. and the Codex Colbertinus (Old Latin *c*) was written in the eleventh or twelfth century at Languedoc and *Gigas* in the thirteenth. Pelagius in 409 used the Vulgate text for his commentaries, but Augustine used the Old Latin save the Vulgate in the Gospels (See Souter, *Pelagius's Expositions of Thirteen Epistles of St. Paul*, 1922). Continual efforts were made to revise the Vulgate back to the Old Latin (Berger, *Histoire de la Vulgate*, 1893). The first great work of Gutenberg's printing-press was the Latin Vulgate (1440 to 1445). It was not till the Council of Trent in 1546 that the term Vulgate was attached to Jerome's translation. The Clementine Vulgate of 1592 was brought out to displace that of Pope Sixtus V in 1592, which was full of errors though endorsed and enjoined by him. Wordsworth and White have published a critical edition of the Vulgate (1889-1905) and Abbot Gasquet is producing an official revision under Roman Catholic auspices. The literature on the Vulgate is very extensive. The number of mss. of the Vulgate in existence is estimated all the way from 8,000 to 30,000. The Vulgate mss. are usually designated by the first syllable of the name like *am* for Amiatinus. But that is not true of *f* which is now counted as a ms. of the Vulgate. One must beware of thinking that the Clementine Vulgate is the true Vulgate text. It has been corrupted by long use. Hence there are numerous Syrian readings in the Clementine Vulgate, though few in the original Vulgate. The true Vulgate text is found in the critical edition of Wordsworth and White, *Novum Testamentum Domini Nostri Jesu Christi Latine*. A good description of the more important mss. of the Vulgate is given by Kenyon, *Textual Criticism of the N. T.*, pp. 225–240, and by Jacquier, *Le Texte du N. T.*, pp. 195–207). Codex Amiatinus belongs to the eighth century and was written in England. It is now in Florence and is a magnificent manuscript. See Dom Chapman's *Notes on the Early History of the Vulgate Gospels* (1908), and A. Gramatica, *Bibliorum sacrorum juxta Vulgatam Clementinam nova editio* (1914); Harnack, *Zur Revision der Principien der Neutestamentlichen Textkritik: Die Bedeutung der Vulgate für den Text der Katholischen Briefe* (1916); von Dobschütz, *Zur Textkritik der Vulgate* (1894). H. J. White has published *Selections from the Vulgate*, (1919). Henslow has a striking book on *The Vulgate the Source of False Doctrines* (1909). It is difficult to overestimate the influence of the Vulgate on all modern versions until the critical text came to the front.

5. Secondary Versions

The secondary versions (the Aethiopic, Gothic, Armenian, Slavonic, Persian, Georgian, Arabic, Friesic, Anglo-Saxon) are of far less importance and need hold us for but a moment. Three of the number outrank the rest and deserve separate treatment.

The Armenian (arm) belongs probably to the fourth century, with two translations. One, by Mesrop, was from the Greek, the other by Sahak, was from the Syriac. After the Council of Ephesus in 430 both of them revised their work with the help of Greek mss. from Constantinople. This is the text represented in the mss. and is usually Syrian, sometimes Western. One ms. of the Armenian suggests that Mark xvi: 9-20 was added by Ariston Eritzu, a Presbyter, who may be the Aristion of Papias. The Armenian Version lacks Philemon, but has the spurious Third Corinthians. The version is not well edited save the Apocalypse by F. C. Conybeare.

The Aethiopic (aeth) likewise has two recensions, one in the fifth, the other in the twelfth century. Very little is known about this version and it is not considered valuable for textual criticism. For instance, in Acts xx: 15 ἄντικρυς is translated as a proper name. The text is often Western. See Littmann *Geschichte der äthiopischen Literatur*.

The Gothic (goth) Version is due to the conversion of some of the Goths before they invaded the Roman Empire. Their second bishop, Ulfilas, translated the Bible into the Gothic language for his people before they learned Latin. It seems to have been made in the fourth century. It is the oldest Teutonic literary monument and it is a pity that much of it is lost. We have no mss. of the Acts, the Catholic Epistles, the Apocalypse.

The *Codex Argenteus* at Upsala is in silver letters on purple vellum and belongs to the sixth century. It contains fragments of the Gospels. There are other mss. of the Gospels and some fragments of the Pauline Epistles. Ulfilas was an Arian, but the version has no special marks of his heresy. See Streiberg, *Die gotische Bibel* (1908).

The other versions (Arabic, Slavonic or Slavic, Persian, Georgian, Theotish, Bohemian, Francica, Anglo-Saxon) are all late and are of no critical importance. They add nothing to our knowledge of the original text. They simply show that Christianity has spread far and wide to make so many versions worth while. Gregory, *Prolegomena*, pp. 801–1128, gives a full list of the mss. of the various versions known at that date (1894), as does Nestle in his *Einführung in das griechische N. T.* (3rd ed., 1909, 4te Aufl., 1923, by Dobschütz), and Jacquier in his *Le Texte du N. T.*, 1913, pp. 117–295. Rendel Harris has an interesting article on *The Romance of the Versions* in his *Sidelights on N. T. Research* (1908).

In illustration of the use of the versions in the evidence presented by Tischendorf the student may read again Luke ii: 14 about εὐδοκίας and εὐδοκία and let him read also in Tischendorf the evidence concerning ἐν τῷ φανερῷ in Matt. vi: 4 and 6.

CHAPTER VII

THE FATHERS

1. *Introductory Remarks*

It might seem that we could do without what the early writers have to say since we have almost a plethora of Greek mss. (uncials, minuscules, lectionaries) and of versions (important and unimportant). If it were an ordinary book, this would be true, even if it were Shakespeare, Dante, or Homer. But Gregory considers that in the case of the New Testament it would be "a crime to fail to approach the last witness, to omit the last question that could be put, in order to gain a ray of light upon its history, in order to solve a problem touching the form of its original text" (*Canon and Text of the N. T.* p. 419). The quotations from the fathers are fragmentary in most cases and little of the vast amount has been preserved.

But we are confronted by obvious difficulties in the use of the early writers. The text of these writers is not always correct. The mss. that preserve the sermons of Chrysostom may differ as radically as those that give the Latin Vulgate or the Greek New Testament. Hence each one of the early writers demands critical study and editing in order to determine precisely what he really did say when he quotes a passage from the New Testament. Scribes may have modified a New Testament passage in Origen as in Irenaeus to suit the text which they knew or which they preferred just as scribes sometimes did when they made copies of the Greek New Testament. We need "scientific editions" (Gregory) of the early fathers, but we cannot wait for them to go on with our study. A beginning has been made by such works as Hautsch, *Die Evangelienzitate des Origenes* (1909); Barnard, *The Biblical Text of Clement of Alexandria in the Four Gospels and the Acts of the Apostles* (1899); Burkitt, *S. Ephraem's Quotations from the Gospel* (1901); Chapman, *Barnabas and the Western Text of Acts* (1913); Souter, *A Study of Ambrosiaster* (1905); Souter, *Pelagius's Expositions of Thirteen Epistles of St. Paul* (1922); Rönsch, *Das Neue Testament Tertullians* (1871); Gifford, *Pauli Epistolas qua forma legerit Joannes Chrysostomus* (1902). Von Soden also did a vast amount of work on the fathers.

The fathers were not always careful to make precise and exact quotations. The use of the roll made it difficult to quote as did the continuous text with no separation of words. The codex book helped very much. But even when a loose quotation is made, one can often tell whether a passage is used or not. The writer would not always have a copy of the New Testament book with him as books were costly. Hence he would often rely upon his memory as preachers may do now. Some passages are not referred to at all by any writers, but the argument from silence is very precarious. The verses that are most frequently quoted may be quoted in a great variety of ways by the same writer, showing that exactness was not his aim.

It is only in the case of *express* quotations that a father's evidence counts for much as to the text, that is, where he distinctly says that he is quoting a passage from a book. And even then, if the quotation stands alone or differs from the text of the Greek mss. and versions, it has to be viewed with scepticism. If the writer affirms that the reading quoted by him actually stands in a Greek ms. (or mss.) lying before him, then his quotation will have the worth of that Greek ms. (or mss.), if it has been correctly copied and correctly preserved.

It is not the opinion of a writer as to what the correct text is that we care for, but the fact that he presents a certain reading. It matters nothing at all whether the writer is orthodox or heretical. It is the witness that he bears to the existence of a certain reading in a given Greek ms. that matters.

When a writer is writing a commentary and follows a Greek text, it may be assumed that his quotations are made with more than ordinary care, as in the case of Origen and Chrysostom. Some of the commentators in Latin or Syriac may have used a Greek text besides that in their own language. Some of the Greek writings are preserved to us in a translation as portions of Irenaeus, Origen, Theodore of Mopsuestia. In such a case we sometimes have a different text in the Greek and in the Latin translation as in Origen and Irenaeus.

Warfield (*op. cit.*, p. 74) remarks that, if we had only the citations from the early writers, we could reproduce substantially the teaching, but not the text of the New Testament.

The fathers help in textual criticism chiefly because the dates of their activities are fairly well known. Hence they serve to help in dating readings and types of text related to them. In quoting the fathers the figures in Tischendorf refer to volumes and pages.

The writers came from different parts of the world and travelled a great deal, so that it is difficult to locate them in a geographical way. Still, most men probably clung to the text of their first love. It is best, on the whole, to treat men according to the language employed by them instead of by countries or by centuries. There are chiefly three languages used in quotations (Greek, Syriac, Latin).

2. *The Chief Greek Writers*

These are the most important because they uniformly make use of Greek mss. They alone are direct witnesses for they quote the Greek New Testament — they and the Latin and Syriac writers who can be proved to have used Greek mss. As a rule, the Latin and Syriac writers are only indirect witnesses. Little help is gained from the Greek Apostolic Fathers for the text, though their evidence is important for the use of the New Testament books. The quotations from and references to the New Testament in these writers (Epistle of Barnabas, Didache, First and Second Clement, Ignatius, Polycarp, Shepherd of Hermas) are fully presented in *The New Testament in the Apostolic Fathers* (1905), a book produced by a committee of the Oxford Society of Historical Theology. The quotations are made with much freedom as the apparent citation of Matt. xxii: 14 in the Epistle of Barnabas and of Luke vi: 36–8 and xvii: 1–2 in First Clement. Souter (*op. cit.*, p. 76) notes that in First Clement i: 3 the use of οἰκουργεῖν apparently supports the better mss. in Titus ii: 5 which give οἰκουργούς instead of οἰκουρούς. There is a good deal in the Didache from the Sermon on the Mount, but its date is not yet settled.

Marcion has received fresh study in recent years, but his text is still more or less obscure, since we only know it from references and quotations in the orthodox writers like Tertullian and Epiphanius who opposed his heresies and from a Latin translation of the prologues to the Epistles and the chapter headings found in many mss. of the Vulgate (Burkitt, *The Gospel History and Its Transmission*, 1911) and in certain mss. of Pelagius's *Expositions of the Epistles of St. Paul* (Souter). He was a native of Pontus, but lived in Rome from 140 onward. He issued an edition of Luke's Gospel and of the Pauline Epistles. He omitted the Pastoral Epistles and had the rest in this order: Galatians, First and Second Corinthians, Romans, First and Second Thessalonians, Laodiceans (Ephesians), Colossians, Philippians, Philemon. His text was apparently mutilated, *e.g.*, without chapters 15 and 16 of Romans. But some scholars hold that Paul issued two editions of this Epistle, one for Rome (complete), one for general use without i: 7–15 and the last two chapters. Souter (*Text and Canon*, p. 77) suggests that many petty variations in the Western text may be due to Marcion. At any rate his text of the Epistles is very much like that in the Old Syriac, the Old Latin, and D.

Justin Martyr came from Samaria to Rome and wrote in the middle of the second century. Hence he, like Marcion, cannot be classified clearly as belonging to the east or to the west. A fairly full outline of Gospel story can be gotten out of Justin's writings, but he quotes very freely and hence he is of small value for the precise text. However, he is a good witness for the existence of a passage. His type of text is Western like the Old Syriac, the Old Latin, Tatian's Diatessaron, the "Clementine" Homilies, and D. Souter (*op. cit.*, p. 78) notes the presence in Justin of the Light at the baptism of Jesus (Matt. iii: 16) as in Tatian's Diatessaron and the Old Latin mss. *a* and *g*, and of "Thou art" for "This is" in Matt. iii: 17 (Luke iii: 22) D, *a* of Old Latin, Irenaeus, Augustine.

Irenaeus was born in or near Smyrna about 140 and died about 202. As a youth he heard Polycarp, but he went to Rome where he heard Justin Martyr. He became Bishop of Lyons, where about 185 he wrote his chief work, Ἔλεγχος καὶ ἀνατροπὴ τῆς ψευδωνύμου γνώσεως. The Greek mss. that he used, of course, represented a much earlier text than A.D. 185. The whole of it has been preserved in a careful Latin translation of doubtful date. Some (like Kenyon) hold the translation to be nearly contemporary with the Greek original and that it was used by Tertullian in his treatise *Adv. Valentinianos*. Souter agrees with Hort (*Introduction*, p. 160) that the translation belongs to the second half of the fourth century and presents his arguments after careful study in the *Novum Testamentum S. Irenaei* (1923) edited by Sanday and Turner. Numerous quotations from the New Testament are made in this Latin translation. Often the Latin follows the Greek original, but Souter (*Text and Canon*, p. 80 f.) observes that in a long citation the translation frequently copied a Latin version. So in Matt. v: 22 Souter notes that the best ms. of the Latin Irenaeus (Claromontanus of the ninth century) has *pascitur* for *irascitur* just like the Old Latin *k*. He shows also that in Acts the agreement is often with *h* or with D *d* while in the Epistles of Paul the translator seems to have used a text like that employed by Augustine and in the Apocalypse his text is like the Vulgate.

The Greek text of Irenaeus is preserved in citations by Greek writers, especially by Epiphanius, where we have to face the question whether the real text of Irenaeus is given or that most familiar to the writer. There is one Greek papyrus fragment from Oxyrhynchus which revives the hope that the full Greek text may yet be found. This fragment gives σὺ εἶ for οὗτός ἐστιν in Matt. iii:17 like D. Souter argues that this fragment shows a remarkable likeness to D or to its Greek ancestor, but is better in points. At any rate Irenaeus is a witness for the Western type of text.

Clement of Alexandria was a contemporary of Irenaeus, though the dates of his birth and death are not known, probably 155 and 215. He was a Greek with a Roman name, Titus Flavius Clemens, possibly a freedman. He studied in Greece, Italy, and the east and was a convert to Christianity from Stoicism. He became a presbyter of the church in Alexandria and about 190 head of the Catechetical School there, succeeding his teacher, Pantaenus, but was forced out by persecution about 202. He shows a wide acquaintance with Greek literature and probably had access to the Alexandrian library. His quotations from the N. T. are not very carefully made. He shows the use of the Western type of text in the main as is proven by

Barnard's *The Biblical Text of Clement of Alexandria in the Four Gospels and the Acts of the Apostles* (1899). His chief work is his Στρωματεῖς or *Miscellanies*.

Origen was born A.D. 185 and died 253. He was reared as a Christian and the persecutions of 202–3 which killed his father and removed Clement of Alexandria from the headship of the Catechetical School there opened the way for him. He was only eighteen years old when appointed. He visited Rome in 213. In 215 he was compelled to leave Alexandria and went to Caesarea in 215, back to Alexandria in 219 and then in 231 to Caesarea again till his death in 253. The most of his works were written in Caesarea. He was the first textual critic of the New Testament and no scholar has exerted so much influence on the text as he. His Hexapla of the Old Testament had much influence on the Septuagint text. There is no evidence that he prepared such a work on the New Testament, but he wrote commentaries on most, possibly all, the New Testament books in which his text is given. Not all of his works are preserved. Some are still in the original Greek and some are in Latin translations (mostly the work of Rufinus). Rufinus sometimes altered the New Testament of Origen to show that he was less of a heretic than people supposed (Gregory, *Canon and Text*, p. 427). Critical texts of the Greek remains of Origen have been issued and made accessible to modern students of this greatest ancient Biblical scholar. As a matter of fact, his views and preferences for texts do not interest us anything like as much as his references to Greek mss. which he consulted. These mss. would be a hundred years or more older than ℵ and B. The type of text used by Origen varies in different books. In the Gospels his text is now Western, now Neutral, sometimes Alexandrian. "Perhaps the best way to describe the situation would be to say that Origen's favourite roll varied very seldom from the readings supported by B and D in common" (Souter, *Text and Canon*, p. 83). In the Pauline Epistles the text is more nearly Neutral, especially in Romans, a Greek ms. of which has been discovered belonging to the tenth century (Goltz, *Eine textkritische Arbeit des 10 bezw. 6 Jhdts* (1899). Kenyon (*Textual Crit. of the N. T.*, p. 253) even raises the question whether Origen is not largely responsible for the preservation of the Neutral type of text. In one case he is clearly responsible for an Alexandrian reading of the scholarly correction type, for he says so himself. This is the reading βηθαβαρᾷ instead of βηθανίᾳ in John 1:28. Origen, as quoted by Tischendorf, expressly says that βηθανία is the reading of practically all the mss., σχεδὸν ἐν πᾶσιν τοῖς ἀντιγράφοις κεῖται. He is not ignorant of this fact, οὐκ ἀγνοοῦμεν, but all the same he is convinced that it is not necessary to follow the mss., ἐπείσθημεν δὲ μὴ δεῖν βηθανία ἀναγινώσκειν. Why? Because he has made a visit there, γενόμενοι ἐν τοῖς τόποις ἐπὶ ἱστορίαν τῶν ἰχνῶν Ἰησοῦ, and has found no evidence of a Bethany except the one near Jerusalem. So Origen confessedly altered the text from Bethany to Bethabara. The only other early evidence for Bethabara given by Tischendorf is syr[cu]. Since Origen wrote in Caesarea, this ms. of the Old Syriac could easily have gotten the reading from Origen. It was taken up by K and some of the minuscules and got into the Textus Receptus, though ℵ A B C W it vg boh (cop) syr^sch and syr^p(txt) read βηθανίᾳ. The Greek margin of the Harclean Syriac (p) praises both readings. The works of Origen were for long preserved in the library of Pamphilus in Caesarea.

Hippolytus calls for only a word. He flourished about 220 in Rome and in Sardinia. He wrote much, but only a little has survived in the Greek. He appears to have used the Western type of text in the Gospels and Pauline Epistles, but the Neutral type in the Apocalypse. The Jerusalem ms. (tenth century) of the *De Antechristo* has been edited by Bonwetsch (1902) and "completely antiquates Tischendorf's reports of Hippolytus's readings, especially in chapters xvii. and xviii. of the Apocalypse" (Souter, *Text and Canon*, p. 82).

Pamphilus of Caesarea (died 309) did not write much, but he founded a great theological library at Caesarea which included the works of Origen. He was a disciple of Origen. It is possible that both ℵ and B were copied in this library, though most likely in Egypt, but both mss. were at any rate once in Caesarea if the correctors can be trusted (See Bousset, *Textkritische Studien zum N. T*).

Eusebius of Caesarea lived from about 270 to 340. For the last twenty-seven years he was Bishop of Caesarea. He was a pupil and protégé of Pamphilus and had full access to his library. He became the great historian of the early centuries and has preserved much for us from the early writers. Some commentaries are lost, but six volumes in Migne's *Patrologia* survive (the *Chronicle, Historia Ecclesiastica, Preparatio Evangelica, Demonstratio Evangelica*). He usually gives the

Western text like D in the Gospels, but his citations are not accurate. It was to Eusebius that Constantine applied for fifty copies of the Greek Bible to be made at Caesarea for Constantinople.

Cyril of Jerusalem (315–386) in his Catechetical Lectures used the Western text.

Athanasius was Bishop of Alexandria from 328 to 373. Much of his work survives. He used chiefly the Neutral text.

Basil the Great of Caesarea in Cappadocia, Bishop there, was born 329 and died 379. He wrote sermons, epistles, treatises.

Gregory of Nyssa (died about 395) was a brother of Basil and wrote commentaries and treatises. Quoted as Nyss.

Gregory of Nazianzus (died 390) was a great preacher and for a time Bishop of Constantinople. These are the three great Cappadocian Fathers. They all have the same type of text as the purple uncials N, O, Σ, Φ (chiefly Syrian).

Epiphanius was bishop of Salamis in Cyprus from about 368 to 402, but he came from Palestine. He wrote mainly against heresies.

Chrysostom (died in exile in 407) was born at Antioch about 347. He labored there till 398 when he became Patriarch of Constantinople. His works fill thirteen volumes in Migne's *Patrologia*. He uses chiefly the Syrian type of text, and occasionally the Western. Von Soden considers him the chief reviser of his K (Κοινή) text (Syrian of Westcott and Hort). He does not quote the Apocalypse or the smaller Catholic Epistles.

Cyril of Alexandria (died 444) used a text mostly Neutral, sometimes Alexandrian.

Cosmas Indicopleustes (sixth century) had a late Alexandrian text like L in the Gospels, but a Neutral text in the Acts.

Theodore of Mopsuestia (died 429) wrote commentaries on the lesser Epistles of Paul, but we have them only in a Latin translation.

Andreas (seventh century) wrote on the Apocalypse.

3. *The Chief Latin Writers*

The works of the Latin writers have been better preserved in mss., some of which are almost contemporary with the originals. Souter laments that these early mss. for the most part "lie unopened in the libraries of Europe, or are looked into only by the palaeographer and the cataloguer" (*Text and Canon*, p. 85). Hence the printed editions are largely unreliable, except the Vienna edition, as they were made from one or two late mss. that the printer happened to have. The Latin fathers are often useful for giving dates for readings and for the sense of a passage rather than for the precise language. Only the leading ones are listed here.

Tertullian (died 222) had been an advocate and became the great controversialist of the early Latin Christians of North Africa. In 203 he left the orthodox church for the Montanist sect. He wrote chiefly in Latin, but sometimes in Greek. He was not a technical scholar like Clement of Alexandria and Origen and quoted loosely. It is not always clear whether he is quoting a Latin version or translating the Greek himself. His text is most like that of D among the Greek mss. and less like B, distinctly Western. "The hypothesis that Tertullian used a manuscript in the main resembling *b* of the Old Latin satisfies most elements of the problem" (Sanday, *Gospels in the Second Century*, 1876, p. 342). The Vienna *Corpus Scriptorum Ecclesiasticorum Latinorum* gives the important material. Rönsch has discussed the problems also in *Das Neue Testament Tertullians* (1871).

Cyprian (died 258) was Bishop of Carthage. He was a pagan lawyer and was only converted in 245 and became Bishop at once. He was a great ecclesiastic and quotes freely and accurately from the New Testament. The Vienna *Corpus* gives his writings, but in the *Testimonia* the editor, Hartel, followed the least important of the mss. (Sanday, *Old Latin Biblical Texts*, ii, p. xliii). In the Gospels Cyprian follows Old Latin *k* and in the Acts and Apocalypse Old Latin *h* (Souter, *op. cit.*, p. 87). Von Soden discusses Cyprian in *Das lateinische Neue Testament in Afrika zur zeit Cyprians* (1909).

"*Ambrosiaster*" is now held to be *Isaac*, a converted Jew and enemy of Pope Damasus. He flourished in Rome and Spain the close of the fourth century (Souter, *Study of Ambrosiaster*, 1905). He made a commentary on the Pauline Epistles (not Hebrews) with an Old Latin text kin to *d* and *g*, that also used by Ambrose, "and may have been the very text which Jerome took as the basis of the Vulgate" (Souter, *Text and Canon*, p. 88). The Gospel text is more like the Old Latin *b* and that of the Apocalypse like *gigas* and Primasius.

Priscillian (died 385) employed a text like that of *m*

(the speculum) in the Catholic Epistles and more like *gigas* in the Apocalypse.

Ambrose of Milan (died 397) has the same text as "Ambrosiaster" in the Pauline Epistles and in the Gospels more like the Old Latin *ff*. He quotes mainly from the Greek rather than from the Latin Bible.

Jerome (*Hieronymus*, died 420) was a textual scholar like Origen. He travelled and knew so many Greek mss. that he did not follow a single type of text. As already shown (see *Vulgate* in Chapter VI), the type of text in the Vulgate is now Western like the Old Latin, Neutral like B, or even Syrian like Chrysostom (though seldom so). Souter (*op. cit.*, p. 89) thinks that in Luke Jerome used Old Latin *a*, in Acts a text like *gig* and *p*, and in the Epistles of Paul one like *d*, *m*, Lucifer and Ambrosiaster.

Augustine (died 430) lived in North Africa. But in 383 he came to Rome and became Professor of Rhetoric in Milan. Under the influence of Ambrose he was converted in 386. He returned to North Africa and became Bishop of Hippo in Numidia. Burkitt (*Old Latin and the Itala* 1896, pp. 57-59) shows that, while Augustine began by quoting the Old Latin and kept that habit up for short quotations, for long quotations he used the Vulgate of Jerome.

Pelagius in a commentary on the Pauline Epistles (cf. Souter's *Introduction to Pelagius's Thirteen Epistles of St. Paul*, 1923) about 409 is "the oldest British writer of whom any work has survived" (Souter, *Text and Canon*, p. 89). Souter says that his text agrees constantly with the Vulgate mss. Fuldensis or Amiatinus.

Primasius (sixth century) was Bishop of Hadrumetum in Africa. His commentary on the Apocalypse employed the text of *h*, used also by Cyprian and Augustine two hundred years before.

Cassiodorus (sixth century) was prime minister of Theodoric, but withdrew about 540 to his estate in the south of Italy. Here he established a theological seminary with a good library. In his *Institutiones Divinarum et Saecularium Lectionem* he tells of the Latin Bible there, including both the Old Latin and the Vulgate. "It has been proved beyond all doubt that our *Codex Amiatinus* in the Gospels is descended from the New Testament part of his copy of the Vulgate" (Souter, *Text and Canon*, p. 91). But he used now the Old Latin text like *d*, now the Vulgate like *am* as Pelagius did, though the Gospels changed his text to the Old Latin *d*.

The Venerable Bede (died 735) used some of the Latin Bibles of Cassiodorus in his commentaries. But "his biblical text is greatly disguised in the bad edition of Dr. Giles" (Souter, *op. cit.*, p. 92). On Acts Bede used E and often compares the Old Latin and the Vulgate.

4. *The Chief Syriac Fathers*

The list of important names is not great. Tatian's *Diatessaron* (second century) was in Syriac, as we have seen. Though he was an Assyrian, he wrote an Apology in Greek.

The *Acts of Judas Thomas* was written in Syriac and it has the quotations from the Old Syriac (Burkitt, *Evangelion da-Mepharreshe*, ii., pp. 101 ff.). "In no other work are the traces of the Old Syriac so clear" (Souter, *op. cit.*, p. 92).

Aphraates (fourth century) was Bishop in the Monastery of Mar Matthaeus near old Nineveh. Twenty-two of his *Homilies* (dated 337, 344, 345) survive in Syriac. Most of them are also in the Armenian where they are quoted as by "*Jacob of Nisibis.*" He made constant use of Tatian's *Diatessaron* and has points of contact with the Old Syriac, not with the Peshitta.

Ephraem Syrus (died 378) wrote sermons, treatises, commentaries, and a commentary on Tatian's *Diatessaron*. Burkitt (*Ephraem and the Gospel*, 1894; *S. Ephraem's Quotations from the Gospels*, 1901; *Evangelion da-Mepharreshe*, ii., pp. 112 ff.) has proven that Ephraem did not use the Peshitta, but some form of the Old Syriac besides the *Diatessaron*.

Isho'dad of Merv was Bishop of Hadatha about 850. He wrote commentaries compiled chiefly from Tatian's *Diatessaron* and Theodore of Mopsuestia on the Gospels (Edition in Syriac and English by Mrs. Gibson, 1911). For a complete list of the fathers quoted by Tischendorf, see Gregory's *Prolegomena*, pp. 1131–1230. See also a fairly full list in the Dobschütz revision of Nestle, pp 114–117.

The student will do well to read again Luke ii: 14 in Tischendorf for the evidence of the Fathers concerning εὐδοκίας and εὐδοκία.

Read also Tischendorf on Matt. vi: 13 and note how the quotations from Gregory of Nyssa (Nyss), Caesarius of Nazianzus (Caes) the brother of Gregory of Nazianzus, Euthymius Zigabenus (Euthym, twelfth century), Cyril of Jerusalem (Cyr^{hr}), and Maximus (fifth century) show the origin of the doxology in public worship. The form varies with each one. The earliest known forms appear in the syr^{cu}, the sah, and k of the Old Latin. W (Washington ms.) has the full form in the fourth century. It arose early as a Western addition (liturgical).

CHAPTER VIII

TRANSCRIPTIONAL EVIDENCE OF SINGLE READINGS

We now turn from the matter of criticism to the method of criticism.

1. *Two Methods in the Criticism of Readings*

The manuscripts (Greek, versions, fathers) are used first to advise us of the condition of the text. They give us the material of criticism, the external evidence. They do not show us how to value the evidence. When the mss. agree, we may feel sure that we have the true text, unless there is something in the context that makes it impossible to accept the evidence. Then one has to resort to conjectural emendation. But in the New Testament the mss. often vary a great deal and give divergent readings. One group of mss. support one reading, another group another. Sometimes three readings or even more are found instead of two. The problem now is to know how to decide between the different readings as presented by the mss. in Tischendorf's *critical apparatus*. There are two methods of attacking the problem as wrought out by Hort in his masterly *Introduction*. These two methods are internal evidence and external evidence. In the external evidence appeal is made to the evidence of single documents, of groups of documents, and most of all to families or classes of documents (genealogical evidence).

In actual practice appeal should first be made to the external evidence of the documents by first coming to understand the value of internal evidence of single readings. It will be seen that we have to consider the internal evidence of single readings, the internal evidence of single documents, the internal evidence of groups of documents, the internal evidence of classes of documents. That way of putting it appears paradoxical, but it is literally true that the scientific use of the external evidence (documents) turns on the application of the principles of internal evidence as seen in single readings. But the two methods must agree in result if one is to have confidence in his conclusion. At first the two methods may seem to conflict, but in the end they usually are in accord. If they really disagree, one had best go over the problem afresh. If the disagreement seems hopeless, one can only suspend judgment and wait for more light.

2. *Two Kinds of Internal Evidence of Single Readings*

By single readings we are to understand problems like εὐδοκίας or εὐδοκία in Luke ii:14, the doxology in Matt. vi: 13, etc. Internal evidence means looking at the problem of divergent readings independently of the weight of the evidence of the documents (external evidence). The two kinds of internal evidence are *transcriptional* and *intrinsic*. Transcriptional evidence aims to look at the problem from the standpoint of the scribe who copied the ms. Intrinsic evidence looks at the matter from the standpoint of the author who wrote the book (or who made the address). It is best to begin with transcriptional evidence and then to consider intrinsic evidence. The two lines of evidence must be kept distinct. It can be seen at once that in order to make a wise use of these two lines of evidence the critic must have some knowledge of the habits of scribes for one thing, and be familiar with the character of the book in question and the characteristics of the author. "A few hours of careful scrutiny of a series of acknowledged errors actually occurring in our codices will do more towards fitting us for the exercise of this nice process than any length of time spent in *a priori* reasoning" (Warfield, *Textual Criticism*, p. 91). The peril of all criticism is that one will give his instinctive impression without due consideration of all the data. The external evidence should first be heard. Then appeal should be made to internal evidence of single readings (first transcriptional, then intrinsic). By this method one puts off to the very last his own personal prejudices or predilections or preferences. He is shut off from saying at once, "It seems to me." Intrinsic evidence has to be satisfied, of course, but it comes last. The present chapter deals with the use of transcriptional evidence of single readings.

3. *Unintentional or Accidental Errors of the Copyist*

The corruptions due to the scribe are of two kinds (intentional and unintentional). By far the largest number are accidental or unintentional slips on the part of the scribe due to various causes. It must be borne in mind also that not one, but many scribes have copied the mss. that lie behind the documents that are before us. Each copying brought errors of its own, some of one sort, some of another, sometimes directly opposite to each other. In a series of errors it is often a fine point to discern the probable order of their origin. The various readings that one finds in mss. are either additions, omissions, or substitutions, but this classification does not carry one very far. What the student wishes to know is how various readings got started. The most of the slips made by scribes are due to errors of the eye, of the ear, of the memory, of the judgment, of the pen, of the speech. These are natural weaknesses of the flesh common to us all.

(a) *Errors of the Eye*

One of the simplest was a misreading of the ms. The ancients, as we have seen, ran the words together and the copyist had to catch up the separate words with his eye. It was easy to make a slip. Souter (*Text and Canon*, p. 113) cites an example in English, "Have you seen *a bun dance* on the table?" So in 1 Tim. iii: 16 some mss. have ὁμολογοῦμεν ὡς instead of ὁμολογουμένως.

The similarity between some of the Greek letters made it easy to misread a word. This was especially true in the uncials as with Α, Δ, Λ; Ε, C; Θ, Ο; Ν, Η; Ν, Π; ΕΙ, Η; Π, ΤΙ; Υ, Β. So in Mk. v: 14 some mss. have ἀνήγγειλαν for ἀπήγγειλαν.

Abbreviations in particular were subject to such misreading. So in Rom. xii: 11 some mss. read καιρῷ (κ, ρω) for Κυρίῳ ($\overline{\text{Κρω}}$). It is possible that in 1 Tim. iii: 16 some scribes mistook OC for $\overline{\Theta\text{C}}$. Another scribe would be led to change the OC to O for grammatical gender. And in Acts xvii: 25 the reading κατὰ πάντα may come from misunderstanding Κ ΤΑΠΑΝΤΑ.

Another error of the eye is the omission of words or

sentences that are alike or identical. If the words omitted have a like ending, it is called *homoeoteleuton*. In 1 John ii: 23 we have πᾶς ὁ ἀρνούμενος τὸν υἱὸν οὐδὲ τὸν πατέρα ἔχει, ὁ ὁμολογῶν τὸν υἱὸν καὶ τὸν πατέρα ἔχει. The two clauses end precisely alike with τὸν πατέρα ἔχει. Some mss. omit the whole second clause because the eye of a scribe lit on the second ending. In the same way a whole verse (Luke xviii: 39) is omitted in some mss. and a clause in John vi: 39 by C. ℵ.*

In the same way the eye may pick up the same word twice and repeat it (*diplography*). Thus is explained the reading Ἰησοῦν βαραββᾶν (Matt. xxvii: 17) in some minuscules, Origen, Harclean Syriac. In ΥΜΙΝ a scribe picked up ΙΝ again as ΙΝ (Ἰησοῦν).

The eye may wander (wandering eye) and mix up the order of words as in 1 Cor. i: 2 or carry on the wrong case as in Rev. i: 1 where some mss. read τοῦ ἀγγέλου αὐτοῦ τοῦ δούλου αὐτοῦ for τῷ δούλῳ αὐτοῦ.

(b) *Errors of the Ear*

When a manuscript was copied from dictation, as was common in the publishing houses, such errors were frequent. In particular, in the *Koiné* itacism led to a great variety of spellings as the papyri abundantly show, as well as the New Testament mss. Finally, as in the modern Greek, η, ῃ, ι, ει, υ, υι, οι, all had the long ῑ sound. To the ear they would all sound alike. Hence we observe the greatest whimsicalities in the use of these vowels in some documents. In the New Testament mss. one notes εἰ and ἥ (Heb. vi: 14), τιμήσῃ and τιμήσει (Matt. xv: 5), εἴδετε and ἴδετε (Phil. i: 30), ἴαται and εἴαται (Mark. v: 29). The confusion sometimes made different

EVIDENCE OF SINGLE READINGS

words as in εἰ and ἦ (II Cor. ii : 9), χριστός and χρηστός (I Pet. ii: 3). One of the commonest is the confusion between η and υ as in ἡμεῖς and ὑμεῖς in Acts xvii: 28. This confusion has been observed as early as 300 B.C. and after the third century was quite prevalent. But the early New Testament mss. generally preserve the spelling of the first century A.D., the old spelling. But they are not always trustworthy on this point. The scribe of ℵ shows a decided preference for ι and the scribe of B for ει.

There were other confusions also as αι and ε, especially in imperatives and infinitives. So we find ἔγειρε and ἔγειραι (Mark iii : 3), ἔρχεσθαι and ἔρχεσθε (Luke xiv : 17), ζηλοῦσθε and ζηλοῦσθαι (Gal. iv: 18). In Matt. xi: 16 ἑτέροις and ἑταίροις are confused.

The confusion between ο and ω is quite common (pronounced rapidly alike). The mss. give ἰάσομαι and ἰάσωμαι (Matt. xiii : 15), ἔχωμεν and ἔχομεν (Rom. v: 1; Heb. xii: 28). "There is no ms. of the New Testament that does not at times confuse ο and ω; consequently, the testimony of every ms. is liable to suspicion on this point, and our decision turns largely on intrinsic evidence" (Warfield, *op. cit.*, p. 104).

As an example of itacistic spelling take these examples from a letter from Alexandria, A.D. 22, P. Oxy. 294 (Milligan's *Greek Papyri*, p. 35): ἔχι for ἔχει, εἶνα for ἵνα, ποιήσις for ποιήσεις (line 12) and for ποιήσῃς (line 14).

(c) *Errors of Memory*

The scribe may forget what he saw on the roll or codex or what he heard. He actually writes something else because of a *lapsus memoriae*. The use of common synonyms is sometimes thus explained like εἶπεν and ἔφη (Matt. xxii : 37), ὀμμάτων and ὀφθαλμῶν (Matt. ix : 29), even ἐκ and ἀπὸ (Acts xii : 25). The small changes in the order of words may be due to this cause τοὺς στάχυας καὶ ἤσθιον and καὶ ἤσθιον τοὺς στάχυας (Luke vi : 1). Rapid writing and a treacherous memory can play strange tricks. So also the memory may almost unconsciously conform a passage in one of the Synoptic Gospels to a similar passage in another. The same thing would hold true of quotations from the Old Testament which are sometimes added to from the memory as in Matt. xv: 8 Luke iv: 18; Acts vii: 37.

(d) *Errors of the Judgment*

The commonest of these are the misreading of abbreviations due to dim writing or poor eyesight (See Errors of the Eye). Besides, marginal glosses were sometimes incorporated into the text under the misapprehension that they were part of the text. Such crude interpolations account for many additions in a ms. like D. Thus it is probable that the story of the angel disturbing the water crept into the text (John v: 4) as well as the story of the woman taken in adultery (John vii: 53–viii: 11). "What a sleepy or stupid scribe could do in this direction is illustrated by such a reading as δείξασθαι ἡμᾶς ἐν πολλοῖς τῶν ἀντιγράφων οὕτως εὕρηται καὶ οὐ καθὼς ἠλπίσαμεν, which stands in a minuscule copy at II Cor. viii : 4, 5" (Warfield *op. cit.*, p. 100). A good many minuscules added δέξασθαι ἡμᾶς before καὶ οὐ καθὼς ἠλπίσαμεν which Paul wrote. Then a scribe put on the margin beside δέξασθαι ἡμᾶς the words ἐν πολλοῖς τῶν ἀντιγράφων οὕτως εὕρηται. Then the sleepy scribe put the comment into the text to the utter undoing of Paul.

(e) *Errors of the Pen*

There are the careless omissions of letters in spelling and many repetitions. Some of these slips can be explained in several ways. But Warfield (*op. cit.*, p. 101) seems to be right in saying that, when ℵ writes εἰς τὰ ἅγια twice in Heb. ix: 12 and B repeats ἔφυγον οἱ δὲ κρατήσαντες in Matt. xxvi: 56 and 57 we have a simple slip of the pen, mechanical repetition. Sometimes a slip like this makes a difference in sense as when ἔλαβον in Mark xiv: 65 becomes ἔβαλον and then ἔβαλλον in H.

(f) *Errors of Speech*

Every scribe had his own habits of spelling (orthography) and pronunciation and of grammar (accidence and syntax). Some of these habits come out in his writing in spite of himself. The prolepsis in D, E, H, L, P in Acts xvi: 3 is correct Greek, but it destroys the proper emphasis, as Warfield notes, when the proper ᾔδεισαν γὰρ πάντες ὅτι Ἕλλην ὁ πατὴρ αὐτοῦ ὑπῆρχεν is changed to ᾔδεισαν γὰρ πάντες τὸν πατέρα αὐτοῦ ὅτι Ἕλλην ὑπῆρχεν. It has been pointed out that ℵ loves ι and B ει. So the scribe of A loves synonyms, Warfield observes. The scribe of ℵ wrote a rapid hand, while B was slow and careful and more reliable. *Humanum est errare.* It is not possible to bring all examples of *incuria* under a rule. Warfield (*op. cit.*, pp. 106 f.) gives a list of such *incuria* in the text of ℵ for Hebrews. He suggests that the scribe took "a sly nap when he was writing the tenth chapter."

4. *Intentional Errors*

It may be admitted at once that most of the conscious changes that copyists made were prompted by the best of motives and with the sincere conviction that they were correcting an error that had previously crept into the text. Some of this work was done by the copyist himself. Some of it was done by the official corrector who revised the copied ms. before it left the publishing house. This official corrector corresponded to our modern official proofreader. Some of his corrections would be justified when he corrected mere slips of the copyist or obvious errors of the text that had escaped the copyist. But often what at first glance seemed like an error was in reality the true text. These intentional errors, as has already been said, are few in number when compared with the unintentional ones. Sometimes the same slip can be explained from either standpoint.

(a) *Linguistic or Rhetorical Changes*

One of the commonest of these orthographical variations is seen in the variations between the o and the α forms for the second aorist active indicative as in ἦλθον or ἦλθαν. There are variations in spelling and euphony like λήμψομαι or λήψομαι, ἐνκακεῖν or ἐγκακεῖν, ἐμβαίνω or ἐνβαίνω. The papyri illustrate these variations in great abundance and different scribes have their own idiosyncrasies.

The spelling of proper names (persons and places) furnishes much diversity as Καφαρναούμ or Καπερναούμ, Ἰωάννης or Ἰωάνης, Βοές or Βοός or Βοόζ.

EVIDENCE OF SINGLE READINGS 157

Grammatical corrections are not infrequent as when κράξας and σπαράξας (natural gender of the man and so masculine) are changed (Mark ix: 26) to κράξαν and σπαράξαν to agree with πνεῦμα (grammatical gender). Likewise the grammar is smoothed out when ἐλθόντος αὐτοῦ (genitive absolute) is changed to ἐλθόντι αὐτῷ in Matt. xxi: 23. So also in Matt. xv: 32 some mss. change ἡμέραι τρεῖς into ἡμέρας τρεῖς because of the difficulty in construing the nominative here. See also the change of ἡ λέγουσα to τὴν λέγουσαν in Rev. ii: 20 in apposition with τὴν γυναῖκα Ἰεζάβελ. These are usually superficial corrections not really called for by the sense of the passage.

(b) *Clearing up Historical Difficulties*

Instances of these appear in the (Mk. 1:2) change of τῷ Ἡσαΐᾳ τῷ προφήτῃ into τοῖς προφήταις, the omission of υἱοῦ βαραχίου in Matt. xxiii: 35, the omission of Ἰερεμίου in Matt. xxvii: 9, the change of ἕκτη into τρίτη in John xix: 14 because of τρίτη in Mark xv: 25. But this last example is a good instance of the failure of such efforts, because John is speaking of the trial before Pilate and Mark of the beginning of the Crucifixion. We have noticed also that in John i: 28 Origen purposely changed βηθανίᾳ of the mss. to βηθαβαρᾷ to remove the geographical difficulty.

(c) *Harmonistic Corruptions*

Some of these were unconscious and unintentional, as we have seen. But some were made on purpose to make a passage in one Gospel agree with one in another. The assimilation of the so-called Lord's Prayer in Luke xi: 2-4 to agree with the longer form in Matt. vi: 9-13 is seen in some mss. So also εἰς μετάνοιαν of Luke v: 32 appears in some mss. for Matt. ix: 13. In the Acts some mss. make Acts ix: 5 and 6 agree with Acts xxvi: 14 and 15. So also quotations from the Old Testament may be occasionally enlarged in some mss. as appears apparently in Matt. xv: 8 (from Is. xxix: 13) to conform to the Septuagint translation.

(d) *Doctrinal Corrections*

Warfield (*op. cit.*, p. 96) is doubtful concerning real cases of doctrinal corrections. "Even the Trinitarian passage in 1 John v: 7 and part of 8 may have innocently got into the text." Yes, but it is under suspicion, since Erasmus found it in no Greek ms. for his first edition and only put it in for his chief edition under the promise to do so if a Greek ms. containing it were produced. The one that was produced was very late (sixteenth century), apparently made to order to prove the doctrine of the Trinity in this passage, "a forged entry in a sixteenth century ms. now at Dublin" (Souter, *op. cit.*, p. 95). Warfield holds that the most likely instances are the passages where fasting has been coupled with prayer in some mss. as in Mark ix: 29; Acts x: 30; 1 Cor. vii: 5. But there are others that are not above suspicion. In the change from ὅς to θεός (OC, $\overline{\Theta C}$) in 1 Tim. iii: 16 Tischendorf cites the case of Macedonius, Bishop of Constantinople, who is said by Liberatus (sixth century) and by Hincmarus (ninth century) to have been expelled by the Emperor Anastasius for changing ὅς to θεός, *qui* to *Deus*, in 1 Tim. iii: 16. The change was probably made before the time of

Macedonius by others, but it may have been unknown to him. The question of the deity of Christ was apparently involved also in the readings υἱός or θεός in John i: 18 as well as τοῦ θεοῦ or τοῦ κυρίου in Acts xx: 28. See also the variations in the question in Matt. xix: 17. The Arian controversy divided the world into two bitter camps and one must not overlook this fact. The variations in 1 Cor. xv: 51* may be also due to rival theories of the resurrection or to failure to understand Paul's language: πάντες οὐ κοιμησόμεθα, πάντες δὲ ἀλλαγησόμεθα. Some mss. place οὐ before ἀλλαγησόμεθα. Some even change κοιμησόμεθα to ἀναστησόμεθα. It must be borne in mind also that Irenaeus, Clement of Alexandria, and Tertullian accused the heretics of tampering with the text. The case of Marcion is well known and we know how he treated the text of Luke and of Paul's Epistles. J. Rendel Harris (*Sidelights on New Testament Research*, pp. 29 ff.) accuses Marcion of removing the Infancy Sections from the Gospel of Luke and also any reference to Christ's having been brought up in Nazareth (Luke iv: 16) which is absent even in Codex Bezae. Harris not only finds Marcionism in D, but Encratism also in Tatian's change of "locusts and honey" to "milk and honey." Harris also finds the problem of Ebionite and Adoptionist views discussed in the second century. "This is not the place to discuss the point at length, but it may suffice to show that Dr. Hort cannot be right in divesting the various readings of New Testament mss. of dogmatic significance or in assuring us of the universal *bona fides* of the transcribers" (Harris, *op. cit.*, p. 34). Berger (*Histoire de la Vulgate*, p. 8) says: "La dogmatique elle-même a sans doute une grande part de responsabilité dans la corruption du texte de la Bible Latine." Harris adds a closing word: "But to Dr. Hort the scribes were all angels, as far as theology was concerned." I agree that Harris has here scored on Hort, a difficult thing for any man to do. But we must not go to the other extreme from Hort and Warfield and see doctrinal perversion at every turn. It was rare, but it was a fact to be reckoned with. The loss of the doctrine of the Trinity from 1 John v: 7 and 8 and from 1 Tim. iii: 16 led Burgon and Miller to "accuse the codices ℵ and B with sceptical tendencies, and especially with minimizing the Divinity of our Lord; but the evidence adduced in support of this charge is wholly inadequate" (Kenyon, *Text. Crit.*, p. 317). Prejudice in favor of a true doctrine should not blind one's eyes to actual facts about the mss.

(e) *Liturgical Corruptions*

These are common enough in the lectionaries or service books, where they deceive no one. However, some mss. (minuscules mainly) have been adapted "for public reading by such changes as inserting 'And turning to His disciples. He said,' at Luke x: 22 (the beginning of the lesson) or of 'But the Lord said,' at Luke viii: 31, or the change of 'His parents' into 'Joseph and Mary,' at Luke ii: 41, and the like" (Warfield, *op. cit.*, p. 96).

5. *The Canons of Criticism*

It is not possible to reduce all phases of transcriptional evidence to stiff rules of procedure. "All 'canons of criticism' are only general averages, and operate like a probability based on a calculation of chances" (Warfield, *op. cit.*, p. 107). Certainly no one is entitled to do such delicate balancing who has not equipped himself with knowledge and who does not possess also trained common sense. One must needs be a scholar, but scholars differ like other people. No one is infallible, not even Hort, but Westcott and Hort have produced the text that on the whole commends itself most to modern scholars.

One who has adequate knowledge needs to proceed cautiously in the use of transcriptional evidence. He must be able to contrast real with apparent excellence and to bear in mind that the changes made by transcribers are with rare exceptions due to first impressions, to first thoughts (Hort, *Introduction*, p. 28). The reading thus hastily chosen by a scribe may have the semblance of superiority, but with real inferiority. The modern critic has also to watch his own feelings and prejudices. If transcriptional probability stands alone, it does not usually stand at all.

But broad generalizations are useful if we do not press them too rigorously.

(a) The chief canon is that the reading must be preferred that explains the origin of the others.

(b) As a rule, the more difficult reading is likely to be genuine. It probably bothered the scribe and led to a change.

(c) The shorter reading is more likely to be genuine. Scribes more often added than they omitted words and phrases.

(d) The reading more characteristic of the author is more likely correct. This is not an easy canon to apply but scribes often have a wooden tendency to weed out an author's peculiarities.

(e) Hort (*op. cit.*, p. 25) warns us of our need of another canon, viz., that a scribe may be moved by a variety of impulses. Different scribes responded to different impulses. Decision in such cases may be precarious and calls for caution in the critic.

These canons will help the student in the application of transcriptional probability to single readings.

6. *Examples for the Application of Transcriptional Evidence*

In Matt. vi: 4 and 6 it is plain to see that a scribe would add ἐν τῷ φανερῷ to correspond with ἐν τῷ κρυπτῷ.

In Luke ii: 14 the reading εὐδοκίας would puzzle the scribe and lead to the easier εὐδοκία.

In Matt. vi: 13 it is plain that the Doxology was added as a climax in the liturgical use of the Lord's Prayer in public worship. It was used in various ways in different places and finally one form prevailed.

Now read in Tischendorf the evidence on John vii: 8 concerning οὐκ and οὔπω and see on which side transcriptional evidence speaks. Which is the reading that did cause trouble among the early writers? Which reading best explains the origin of the other? Beyond a doubt, the answer is that οὐκ is the harder reading and explains the change to οὔπω. But then even B has οὔπω. Yes, and therefore we need to go further and learn more.

CHAPTER IX

INTRINSIC EVIDENCE OF SINGLE READINGS

1. *The Second Kind of Internal Evidence*

This is the second phase of internal evidence of single readings (Hort *Introduction*, pp. 20–2). Warfield (*op. cit.*, pp. 84–90) and Lake (*Text of the N. T.*, p. 8) treat it before transcriptional evidence. It is true, as Hort says (p. 20), that "the first impulse in dealing with a variation is usually to lean on Intrinsic Probability, that is, to consider which of two readings makes the best sense, and to decide between them accordingly." But that is an "impulse" that should be held in abeyance, not a critical judgment to be followed. It is better to begin with the transcriptional evidence, to look at the two or more readings in dispute from the standpoint of the copyist, to see which better explains the origin of the other. That is often an easy process, and it is certainly more objective. It is also a good preparation for the appeal to the intrinsic evidence, which is a separate and independent line of argument.

2. *The Precise Nature of Intrinsic Evidence*

Intrinsic evidence looks at the several readings from the standpoint of the author and decides which reading makes the best sense in the particular context and in harmony with the author's known style and habits of speech and thought. One actually tries the various readings by these tests and reaches a tentative conclusion as to which makes the best sense in this passage.

3. *The Danger in Intrinsic Evidence*

The obvious peril is that the modern critic will decide what is "best" to him, not what is best to the author. "Authors are not always grammatical, or clear, or consistent, or felicitous" (Hort, *op. cit.*, p. 21). No one has put this point so well as Warfield (*op. cit.*, p. 85): "The danger that attends the use of the method grows out of our tendency to read our own standpoint into our author, instead of reading ourselves back into his. It is easy to become an improver instead of remaining a simple editor, and it is often very difficult not to make an author speak our thoughts, if not even our own language. It cannot, however, be too strongly insisted upon that any attempt to estimate intrinsic probabilities by the rule of what appears to us to be the best reading is simply an attempt to corrupt the text and train it to festoon the trellises of our own desires." The rule of "it seems to me" (δοκεῖ μοι) is the one that comes first and is the poorest of all. The hard fight made against the critical text of Westcott and Hort (the Canterbury Revisers' text in substance) and in favor of the *Textus Receptus* grew out of prejudice in favor of the text to which people were used. Sermons were upset by the readings of the old mss. that now displaced those of the late mss. to which they had become accustomed.

4. *Serious and Sympathetic Study of the Author*

Before one is prepared to give a sound opinion on intrinsic evidence, he must steep himself in the times of the author and assimilate himself to his thought and style. This is a delicate historical process, beyond a doubt, as Warfield insists, but not an impossible one. Walter Savage Landor in his *Imaginary Conversations* has let his own imagination reproduce possible converse between great characters that meet for the first time in the other world. He has done it with great skill and in essential harmony with the known traits of each speaker. That is not merely a stroke of genius. It is the result of intimate knowledge of each author here pictured.

5. *Fine Mental Honesty Required*

The critic must be willing for the author to say what he may prefer that he had not said. "Intrinsic evidence in the hands of some critics means nothing else than a ruthless elimination of everything exceptional or even distinctive in an author's style" (Warfield, *op. cit.*, p. 86). The business of the textual critic is not to correct grammar, to remove obscurities, or to clarify the logic, but simply to restore what the author actually wrote. We must be able to distinguish between what Paul said and what we wish he had said.

6. *The Golden Canon of Intrinsic Evidence*

"No reading can possibly be original which contradicts the context of the passage or the tenor of the writing" (McClellan). Put in another form, this means that intrinsic evidence has more negative value than positive force. In actual use we shall see that external evidence of the documents is appealed to first, then internal evidence. Since transcriptional evidence should come before intrinsic evidence the last piece of evidence brought forward is the intrinsic evidence. This is as it should be. This is the way to avoid deciding by one's prejudices and predilections. Get all the other evidence and draw a tentative conclusion. Then appeal to intrinsic evidence. Often we shall see that intrinsic evidence is not a deciding factor one way or the other. For instance, if all the documents gave ἐν τῷ φανερῷ in Matt. vi: 4 and 6, probably no question would ever be raised about the propriety of this phrase in contrast with ἐν τῷ κρυπτῷ. Intrinsic evidence would not object. And yet, now that it is undoubtedly an addition to the true text, we can see a fine appropriateness in the mere promise of reward, but without the note of publicity. See also Matt. vi: 13. If the external evidence and transcriptional evidence justified the Doxology as a part of the Lord's Prayer, certainly intrinsic evidence would not raise any objection.

But there are cases where intrinsic evidence positively refuses to agree to the reading approved by external evidence of the documents and even by transcriptional evidence.

It is like getting married. The girl has to say "Yes." When intrinsic evidence clearly rejects a reading, we may know such a reading is wrong. Take as an instance Ἕλληνας or Ἑλληνιστάς in Acts xi: 20 and read the evidence as presented by Tischendorf. Here B reads Ἑλληνιστάς against Ἕλληνας (AD) while ℵ has Εὐαγγελιστάς (a mere slip for Ἑλληνιστάς). Westcott and Hort follow B (the Neutral) as against D (the Western). Transcriptional evidence apparently favors

Ἑλληνιστάς, a rare word except in Acts, but the scribe could be easily puzzled by the use of Ἕλληνας here before the campaign in chapters 13 and 14. So transcriptional evidence here is not so clear as Hort thinks it is (*Introduction: Notes on Select Readings*, p. 93). But Hort (*op. cit.*, p. 94) admits the force of intrinsic evidence here: "'Ἕλληνας has *prima facie* intrinsic evidence in its favour, as being alone in apparent harmony with the context." Hort seeks to break the force of this admission, but unsuccessfully. The context, as any one can see, does demand Ἕλληνας. The Neutral class is not always right. Transcriptional evidence is indecisive. Here intrinsic evidence positively turns the scales in favor of Ἕλληνας as correct.

Another good example occurs in Acts xii: 25. Here there are three readings (read Tischendorf) ἐξ Ἰερουσαλήμ (A, many minuscules, syr[sch et p txt] sah cop), ἀπὸ Ἰερουσαλήμ (D E, many min. s, vg), εἰς Ἰερουσαλήμ (א B H L P, many mins., syr[p mg]). The Neutral class reads εἰς, the Western ἀπό, the Alexandrian and Syrian ἐξ (but note sah cop). Transcriptional evidence favors εἰς as the hard reading that would bother a copyist. The case seems clear and Westcott and Hort boldly place εἰς in the text with ἐξ in the margin. But in the *Notes on Select Readings*, p. 94, Hort admits that εἰς "cannot possibly be right if it be taken with ὑπέστρεψαν (xi. 27 ff.)." Hort suggests a dislocation of words and that εἰς Ἰερουσαλήμ came between τὴν and διακονίαν. But why not admit that the Neutral reading is here wrong and the Western ἀπό right? There is little to choose between ἀπό and ἐξ (Alexandrian correction followed by the Syrian class).

7. Intrinsic Evidence Generally Reënforces the Best Attested Reading

The copyist usually acted on his hurried first thought and failed to see the deeper harmony beneath the surface. When tested by all lines of evidence, it is usually the case that they all agree. Intrinsic evidence is appealed to last, but it often corroborates the conclusion already reached in a striking and convincing manner.

A good illustration is seen in Matt. vi: 1 δικαιοσύνην or ἐλεημοσύνην (read Tischendorf). It may be granted that if all the documents read "alms," intrinsic evidence would acquiesce. But, since the best documents (Neutral and Western vs. Syrian and possibly Alexandrian) read "righteousness," we at once see that this reading suits the context best. In chapter v: 21–48 preceding Jesus had shown the superiority of his teachings concerning "righteousness" (verse 20) to that of the scribes on six points (murder, adultery, divorce, profanity, retaliation, enemies). Now in vi: 1–8 he shows the superiority of his conception of "righteousness" likewise to the practice of the Pharisees in three respects (alms 2–4, prayer 5–15, fasting 16–18). Probably some stupid copyist failed to see the inner relation of δικαιοσύνην to these three subdivisions and changed it in vi: 1 to ἐλεημοσύνην like verse 2. So there transcriptional evidence argues for δικαιοσύνην. So then all the lines of evidence (external and internal) support δικαιοσύνην for vi: 1.

In Luke xv: 21 (read Tischendorf) ℵ B D U X and 20 minuscules give the last part of verse 19 (the speech of the returning boy). But A L P and 13 other uncials,

INTRINSIC EVIDENCE OF SINGLE READINGS 169

most minuscules, it vg cop syr^{sch et hr} do not give it. Here D stands apart from the usual Western company. ℵ B D are usually correct, but not quite always so. Transcriptional evidence favors rejection as a scribe would easily put it in from verse 19. Intrinsic evidence is decidedly against it. While it is a fine trait in the son to want to say this, it is a noble one in the father to interrupt him before he says it. Such a subtle point suits the context admirably. Westcott and Hort put the clause in the text, but bracket it. They hesitate to go against ℵ B D, but do not feel certain.

In like manner one can see that in Luke ii: 14 εὐδοκίας really suits the context better than εὐδοκία, for God's peace is only among ἀνθρώποις εὐδοκίας.

In John vii: 8 οὐκ at first seems flatly to contradict the facts in the context, for Christ did go up to the feast (vii: 10). The documents are pretty evenly divided here (formal study of classes comes later), but transcriptional evidence, as we have seen, strongly supports οὐκ, for a number of the fathers faced the difficulty in this hard reading in various ways with no knowledge of οὔπω (first) as the true text. The second οὔπω is genuine. But the point in the advice of the brothers of Jesus was that he should not work ἐν κρυπτῷ (vii: 4) as he had been out of Galilee for some time, but φανέρωσον σεαυτὸν τῷ κόσμῳ. Now John takes pains to explain that, when Jesus did go, he went, οὐ φανερῶς, ἀλλὰ ὡς ἐν τῷ κρυπτῷ. He asserted his independence, went later, and went in a different way (privately, not publicly). Hence οὐκ really suits the context better than οὔπω. Westcott and Hort put οὔπω in the text (after B) and οὐκ in the margin.

170 INTRODUCTION TO TEXTUAL CRITICISM

There are many other examples that illustrate the force of intrinsic evidence finely like the rejection of εἰκῆ in Matt. v: 22; the reading γινομένου in John xiii: 2, for the feast was still going on; the reading ἀσπασάμενοι in Acts xxv: 13 (effective aorist κατήντησαν and simultaneous use of aorist participle). The change to future participle in Acts xxv: 13 came from failure to see this. There are a few possible instances in the κοινή of the aorist participle where purpose can be meant, but the constative use of the aorist is usually sufficient. See an article, The Aorist Participle for Purpose, in the April, 1924, *Journal of Theological Studies*. Once more, the reading "kingdom and priests" in Rev. i: 6 is supported by intrinsic evidence over "kings and priests."

Skill in the use of both transcriptional and intrinsic evidence will come by practice. Both of these kinds of internal evidence must be used in each reading. But they come after the use of external evidence to which we must now give attention.

CHAPTER X

THE EVIDENCE OF SINGLE DOCUMENTS

1. *External Evidence More Important than Internal Evidence*

We have been dealing with internal evidence of single readings (both transcriptional and intrinsic). But it is precarious and dangerous to "trust exclusively to our own inward power of singling out the true readings from among their counterfeits, wherever we find them" (Hort, *Introduction*, p. 31). Neither in theory nor in practice is internal evidence of readings the primary guide. "The first step towards obtaining a sure foundation is a consistent application of the principle that knowledge of documents should precede final judgment upon readings" (*ibid.*). The documents themselves apprise us of the difference in readings and absolutely the first step after obtaining this information is to know how to value the evidence of the documents themselves. The problem is how to use the evidence of the mass of documents.

2. *Steps in the Use of External Evidence*

(a) *Not the Number of the Documents*

That was the crudest form of criticism. It is employed now by many of the defenders of the *Textus Receptus*. On almost any point the *Textus Receptus* can poll a large majority of the minuscules and even of the uncials. If we knew that we had all the mss., which we do not, we should still be unable to decide the true text by a majority vote. As a matter of fact, the great majority of the mss. are late. The few of the fourth century may give us the true text rather than the many of the eleventh century. The more copyings that we have the more chances for errors. The mss. of the fourth century may be the very antecedents of those of the eleventh. It is clear then that it is wholly unreliable to count mss. Even one ms. may be right in a given reading against all the rest.

(b) *Not Always the Oldest Manuscripts.*

This is obviously a far better canon than the preceding one of the most documents. Lachmann made a distinct advance in urging this canon. He used only early documents, those of the first six centuries, and ignored all the later ones. But it is not always the oldest document that gives the oldest text. A document of the fifth century may be copied from another of the fifth, while one of the seventh may be copied from one of the third or even of the second. "After all, it is not the mere number of years that is behind any ms. that measures its distance from the autograph, but the number of copyings" (Warfield, *op. cit.*, p. 110).

(c) *The Age of the Text More Important*

Tregelles has the honor of advancing this canon which he called comparative criticism. This is a really scientific method and carries us to reasonably safe results. A list of readings is made from dated sources, known to be ancient, like versions and quotations.

THE EVIDENCE OF SINGLE DOCUMENTS

Each manuscript can then be tested by this list. "If a ms. contains a considerable proportion of these readings which on grounds of transcriptional probability are older even than these, it is demonstrated to contain an old text. If, on the other hand, a ms. fails to contain these readings, and presents instead variants which according to transcriptional probability appear to have grown out of them, or which can be proved from dated citations to have been current at a later time, its text may be assumed to be late" (Warfield, *op. cit.*, p. 113). So Tregelles divided the documents into two great classes, those that give an early text, and those that give a late text. The early type of text is presumably better than the late one. But it often happens that the oldest documents differ among themselves as when ℵ D read οὐκ and B W οὔπω in John vii: 8. Besides, if we get the text of the fourth century we cannot assume that we have the original text unless it can be shown that no errors of copying crept in during the second and third centuries. As a matter of fact, the Western type of text, which can be traced to the third and even to the second century, has numerous glaring errors. So then we need to go a further step.

(d) *The Best Text the Real Goal*

Westcott and Hort have shown that it is the actual excellence of the text contained in documents that really matters. What we desire is not the text of the most mss., nor the text of the old mss., nor merely an old text, but the best text, the original text if possible. Once this point has been made, it seems strange that it took so long to see it. But, in order to get the best

174 INTRODUCTION TO TEXTUAL CRITICISM

text, we must know how to weigh the evidence of the documents themselves, for, as we have seen, external evidence comes first in time and in importance. Westcott and Hort apply the term Internal Evidence of Documents to the method which they have proposed for deciding on the best text.

3. *Principles of Internal Evidence of Single Readings Applied to the External Evidence*

This apparent paradox is easily cleared up. We saw the use of Internal Evidence of Single Readings by means of Transcriptional and Intrinsic Evidence. Precisely so Westcott and Hort propose that both Transcriptional and Intrinsic Evidence be applied to each of three forms of the External Evidence (a) The Whole of a Single Document (b) Groups of Documents (c) Classes or Families of Documents. When this has been done, we are ready to approach the external evidence in a scientific manner.

4. *The Internal Evidence of Each Document as a Whole*

In order to get a proper view of the character of a single document like ℵ or B, one can take a single reading in ℵ or B and weigh the probabilities in each instance from the standpoint of transcriptional and intrinsic evidence. Suppose, for instance, that in the case of B the disputed readings in the Gospels should be found by this process to be nine-tenths good and one-tenth bad. The character of B would thus be so well established that one would wish to go back and review the one-tenth in the light of the now known character of B. He might now be led to revise his opinion of the one-tenth and consider half of these readings as good also instead of doubtful. This process can be applied to ℵ and to each Greek ms. (uncial and minuscule), to each version, and to each father. This is a laborious process, to be sure, but it is a necessary step in order to get definite results. By this process one is able to form an opinion of the comparative opinion of each ms. So ℵ, B, D, and all the rest may be compared with each other after the value of each is known. Thus we can appeal to the value of the text in each document and not merely to the age of the text or of the ms. Warfield (*op. cit.*, p. 138) goes astray in my opinion when he says: "Suppose we are testing the value of B. Is it valid to take account of the readings for which B ℵ witness? Certainly not, in order to obtain a value to assign to B when it stands alone." But it is not B when it stands alone that we are chiefly concerned with in learning the worth of B, but B in every disputed reading. The presence or absence of other documents cuts no real figure in the matter. Certainly the scribe of B made use of various documents, but we must treat B as a whole, not the few cases where it stands alone.

So in the case of ἐν τῷ φανερῷ in Matt. vi: 4 and vi: 6 all the best uncials save W reject it. It is plainly an Alexandrian-Syrian addition, for W L Δ are here Alexandrian. Much the same situation applies to the doxology in Matt. vi: 13 which W also has, though rejected by ℵ B D. A and C have lacunae in these passages. But there is a doxology as early as the second century (Afr. Lat. k syr ^{cu} sah) and in the Didache. It appears first in shorter forms. Later the fathers give it in longer forms, but differently and as a climax in the public rendition of the Lord's Prayer.

In Luke ii: 14 ℵ A B D W read εὐδοκίας, five primary uncials. C has a lacuna here. The weight of these great uncials is very great in a case like this.

5. *If the Best Documents Disagree*

It is by no means always true that all the best and oldest documents agree. Often they disagree as in John vii: 8 where ℵ D read οὐx and B W read οὔπω. Here also the oldest versions are divided. It is plain in a case like this that some other process is called for in order to handle a case like this. Some method of grouping the documents must be found when they split into hostile camps. It must be borne in mind that errors occur in each one of the documents that we possess. No one of them is absolutely free from corruptions. The best of them all, B, sometimes has (like ℵ) crass blunders as ὑπὸ τὴν λυχνίαν in Mark iv: 21 for ἐπὶ τὴν λυχνίαν, mere mechanical repetition of ὑπὸ from the preceding instances, ὑπὸ τὸν μόδιον, ὑπὸ τὴν κλίνην. We argue in the same way that B is wrong in reading Ἑλληνιστάς instead of Ἕλληνας (Acts xi: 20). Both ℵ and B wrongly read εἰς in Acts xii: 25 instead of ἀπὸ or ἐξ.

The best example of such crass error in good mss. like ℵ B C L occurs in Matt. xxvii: 49, where these mss. give what occurs in John xix: 34: ἄλλος δὲ λαβὼν λόγχην ἔνυξεν αὐτοῦ τὴν πλευρὰν καὶ ἐξῆλθεν ὕδωρ καὶ αἷμα. But they insert it here *before* Jesus is dead, for in Matt. xxvii: 50 the death of Jesus is recorded. A D W do not have it. This is one of the passages where the Western class is right against the Neutral and the Alexandrian.

The importance of single documents can be understood when we recall that the discovery of ℵ by Tischendorf revolutionized his whole conception of the text of the New Testament.

6. *Each Document May Be Copied from Several Manuscripts*

It cannot be assumed that a scribe always had only one document before him. We do know that F of Paul is merely a copy of G of Paul and E of Paul is a copy of D of Paul. A scribe may have copied one document in one Gospel, another in another Gospel, another in the Acts, another in the Pauline Epistles. Δ in Mark, for instance, represents a better text than in the other Gospels. A in the Gospels is not as good as elsewhere. B is far better in the Gospels and Acts than in the Pauline Epistles. And then the scribe may have had several documents for each Gospel and he may have copied now one, now the other. This mixture appears in many, probably most, documents. Here simultaneous use of different mss. occurs instead of a successive use.

CHAPTER XI

THE EVIDENCE OF GROUPS OF DOCUMENTS

1. Two Previous Lines of Argument

We have seen in Chapters VIII (Transcriptional Evidence of Single Readings) and IX (Intrinsic Evidence of Single Readings) the force of Internal Evidence of Single Readings, where each reading is looked at as a separate item. But we have also seen the second step (Chapter X) in the application of the same method of internal evidence (transcriptional and intrinsic) to one entire document in order to learn the worth of the document as a whole by testing all its readings that are in dispute. By this method we saw that B is the best single document with ℵ second. The use of single documents becomes more difficult when we have a great number of them. Some method of analyzing or of combining the documents is needed.

2. Testing a Group of Documents by Internal Evidence

Any given group of documents can be tested in precisely the same way by transcriptional evidence and intrinsic evidence. Each reading of this group can be examined, one at a time, and a definite idea formed of the value of this group.

We have already noticed ℵ B D Z rejecting ἐν τῷ φανερῷ in Matt. vi: 4 and 6 and rejecting the Doxology in Matt. vi: 13. In each case this group is correct. A further study of the readings of this group will confirm the opinion that this is a good group.

Another striking group worth studying is ℵ B L Δ in Mark vi to xi. The group occurs here repeatedly and it is nearly always right. It will be a useful exercise for a student to take his copy of Tischendorf and underscore every appearance of this group in those chapters in Mark and then apply transcriptional and intrinsic evidence to all these readings. Thus one will gain a definite idea of the value of this group here. A word of caution is needed to the effect that, when one is studying any given group, he pays no attention to other documents. He confines his attention to the group under consideration. The presence or absence of other documents has nothing to do with the group in question. Warfield (*op. cit.*, pp. 137 f.) goes too far, I think, when he says: "If B C D in Paul, for instance, is being tested, we must exclude all readings supported by ℵ B C D, because we do not know whether the common ancestor of ℵ B C D may not be another ms. from the common ancestor of B C D, and thus we may be confusing two mss. in our investigation." But that conception is an error, for we do not have to count all the mss. on each side for fear of another ms. not counted upsetting the whole plan. If we only take note of the readings where a given group stands alone, we shall have meager data for any group. Each ms. has a variety of ancestors. In a group it matters little where the genealogy comes in. And then many mss. may have the same ancestor for a given reading.

3. *A Group Represents an Old Document*

It is plain enough that ℵ B L Δ, for instance, in Mark vi to xi agree so often because in these readings they are following an ancient document. Agreement by accident in so many instances by this group is inconceivable. At bottom, therefore, we are reproducing an old and unknown document. "The value of Internal Evidence of Groups in cases of mixture depends, it will be seen, on the fact that by its very nature it enables us to deal separately with the different elements of a mixed ancestry" (Hort, *op. cit.*, p. 61). It is precisely the same line of argument as the internal evidence of single documents (Chapter X) rediscovered by the internal evidence of a group of documents. And, just as a single document may be mostly good and partly bad or mostly bad and partly good, so it is with a group of documents. Warfield (*op. cit.*, p. 128) notes that, as a rule, the group ℵ D K M Π 17** 389 p[scr] that supports οὐκ in John vii: 8 is a poor group. But it is sometimes right and that may still be the case here.

4. *A Group not the Addition of Single Documents*

It is quite important that one understand that one is dealing with a single unit, not with the added values of separate documents. ℵ B is not ℵ and B, but the common ancestor of ℵ and B on the readings in question. In the group ℵ B L Δ in Mark vi to xi, for instance, we do not have the value of ℵ plus B plus L plus Δ. We are not dealing here at all with the separate values of each document. Hence we have here a separate and additional line of argument that supplements, though independent of, the evidence of single documents. There is no confusion in these separate lines of argument. It is not reasoning in a circle, but a progressive method of dealing with the evidence. Each document has the value that it has, but the readings of a group represent a common ancestor for these readings, not the added value of each document. The internal evidence of single readings helps, but we need also the internal evidence of single documents. But we must be able to treat the documents as groups, not only as separate units

5. *Confining a Group to One Section*

A group may be good in one section of the New Testament and poor in another because different mss. were copied. The binary group ℵ B is the best throughout the New Testament. Next in value come B L, B C, B T, and throughout the New Testament. But ℵ D is suspicious, if B is absent. In the Apocalypse A C is the best binary group, but not so in the Gospels. B G in Paul's Epistles is a bad group, while B D is a good group. Hort (*Introduction*, pp. 207–263) has made a careful examination of the various binary groups with B or ℵ. One must know that the value of any group can only be learned by the actual testing of its readings. That is a slow process, but there is no other way.

6. *Confounding Two Groups*

The loss of one member of the group destroys the evidence of the group. ℵ B L is not ℵ B L Δ. The addition of another document destroys that group. ℵ B C L Δ is not the same as ℵ B L Δ. That is to say, in considering any single group, we ignore the presence or absence of all other documents as not pertinent to the group. If C anywhere agrees with ℵ B L Δ and we are studying ℵ B L Δ, we take no notice of that fact. But this is not all. The group in question can only be recognized by the readings witnessed by the group. Those that are witnessed by part of the group are not considered at all. The number of actual groups is not so great as one might imagine from the great number of documents. A striking instance of the separateness of groups that look alike is seen in B D and B G in Paul's Epistles, the first a good group, the second a poor one. If the group B D G occurs, it is also a bad one in Paul's Epistles. So also D G is a bad group in Paul's Epistles as is ℵ D G. But ℵ B D G is a good group.

7. *No Perfect Group*

Since no single document is free from corruptions, it is not to be expected that any group of documents will be. But some groups undoubtedly represent an older and better ms. than any that we now possess. In Luke ii: 14 the group ℵ B D W reads εὐδοκίας. That is a good group. It rejects the story of the angel in John v: 4. In Matt. xxvii: 49 the group ℵ B C L insert a clumsy addition from John xix: 34 and put it in the wrong place. It is genuine in John and spurious in Matthew, though supported by one of the strongest possible groups. But it is wrong in the reading in Matt. xxvii: 49. Intrinsic evidence of single readings will not allow it. Transcriptional evidence of single readings explains its origin as a clumsy addition from John xix: 34. This is one of the slips of a good group. We can argue in the same way about John vii: 8. B L is a better group as a rule than ℵ D, but internal evidence here supports οὐκ, not οὔπω. Οὐκ is the hard reading as the quotations from the Fathers show. And yet οὐκ does make sense in the light of the context and so intrinsic evidence allows it. If the student will read in Tischendorf the evidence concerning John v: 4, he will get a fine illustration of the force of the combined evidence (both internal and external). The best single documents (ℵ, B, C, D, W) omit it. The best group omits it. The internal evidence confirms this rejection. A scribe probably added the story as an explanation of ταραχθῇ in verse 7. Intrinsic evidence agrees to the omission. It is not demanded by the context.

8. *Where a Group Falls Short*

Take B ℵ. When they agree, we know that we have the common ancestor of both. But suppose B and ℵ disagree in a reading. Which has followed that ancestor and which has diverged after another ms? The group process cannot help us. Besides, why is it that certain documents so often run together like D, Afr. Lat., Old Syr., Iren., Tert., Cypr.? or like B Boh Orig? or like E F G H K, minuscules, late versions and late fathers? or like C L Orig.? The group process cannot answer. But we need an answer to these important and pertinent questions. Hence we turn to the Internal Evidence of Classes (Chapter XII) for a solution of this vital problem

CHAPTER XII

THE EVIDENCE OF CLASSES OR FAMILIES OF DOCUMENTS

This is the great modern weapon for attacking the manuscript evidence. It is the Genealogical Method. Identity of reading implies identity of origin.

1. *Includes All the Documents*

A group is any given number of documents that one cares to consider together. This is done without regard to genealogy. The argument from groups simply recognizes a bunch of documents that agree in certain readings and whether a good or a bad group. But one sees all the while that this agreement is due to genealogy. So the whole mass of documents is divided into classes. The mss. of the New Testament form a single great class separate from all other mss. Hence it is not surprising to find the same principle of kinship in large classes of the New Testament mss. Community in readings argues community of origin. This applies to bad readings as clearly as to good readings.

2. *One Document May Equal a Thousand*

Suppose you have a thousand and one documents of a book. Suppose of a thousand of them that they are copied from the same ms. while the one shows its independence. At bottom you have two documents, one the independent document, the other the immediate ancestor of the thousand. The one may be as good or even better than the thousand. Suppose you have ten documents and they fall into three groups by actual likeness. In reality you have three documents to deal with instead of ten. If two of these groups agree against one, they are correct, unless mixture has confused the genealogy. That will be explained directly.

3. *The Actual Number of Classes or Families*

Instead of an indefinite number there prove to be only four types of text as already shown in Chapter V. These are the Syrian Class (the α text), the Neutral Class (the β text), the Alexandrian Class (the γ text), the Western Class (the δ text). These names stand for actual genealogical relations shown in the mss. themselves. Dr. Hort gives the proof for this classification with great skill in his *Introduction*. This theory is the great contribution of Westcott and Hort and it has stood the test of time in the past generation with certain modifications.

4. *Relations of the Classes to Each Other*

The latest is the Syrian Class. This is shown by the fact that readings that are only Syrian are supported by late Fathers. No early Fathers give them. It is proven also by the fact that the Syrian Class often follows one of the Pre-Syrian Classes, now the Western, now the Neutral, now the Alexandrian. If a reading occurs only in the Syrian Class and is rejected by all the Pre-Syrian Classes (Western, Neutral, Alexandrian) we know at once that it is wrong. Take the addition to I Cor. vi: 20 καὶ ἐν τῷ πνεύματι ὑμῶν ἅτινά ἐστι τοῦ θεοῦ.

This reading is supported only by the Syrian Class. All the Pre-Syrian Classes reject it. Here, as generally, the Alexandrian Class agrees with the Neutral and in this case with the Western also. But in Luke xxiii: 45 the reading τοῦ ἡλίου ἐκλιπόντος is supported by the Neutral and Alexandrian Classes while the reading καὶ ἐσκοτίσθη ὁ ἥλιος is Western and Syrian. Only occasionally does the Alexandrian Class go against the Neutral.

The relation of the classes to each other is well presented by this diagram.

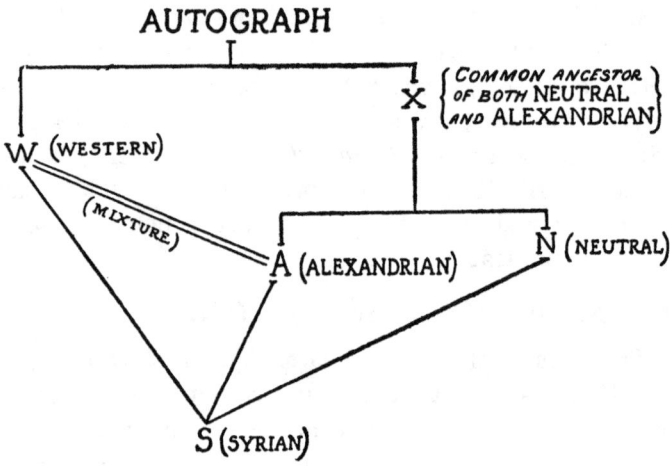

When the Syrian Class stands alone, it is manifestly a late addition and is wrong. There are no purely Syrian readings earlier than the fourth century or late third. When the Syrian copies, as it usually does, one of the preceding classes, it adds nothing, of course, to the value of the evidence. If the Alexandrian Class

CLASSES OR FAMILIES OF DOCUMENTS 187

stands apart from the Neutral and the Western Classes, it is, of course, wrong. The Neutral and the Western can only agree in the autograph. An example of this classification occurs in Luke ii: 14 where the Neutral and the Western combine in reading εὐδοκίας. The Alexandrian correction εὐδοκία was followed by the Syrian Class and so got into the *Textus Receptus* and the King James English Version. When the Neutral and the Western classes disagree, these two classes have to be weighed against each other. At bottom the real test is that between the Neutral and the Western Classes. If the Alexandrian Class agrees with the Western against the Neutral, we should likewise have the autograph but for mixture between these two classes, a point to be explained directly. It is shown that in some instances the Alexandrian Class copies the Western instead of the ancestor of the Neutral. A good example of this is the long ending added to Mark xvi: 9–20 which is supported by the Western and Alexandrian and Syrian Classes and rejected by the Neutral Class.

5. *Conflate Readings*

Hort argues (*Introduction*, pp. 90 to 119) that the purely Syrian readings are shown to be later than the Pre-Syrian readings by the evidence of the Fathers, of Conflate readings, of internal evidence of the readings themselves. Hort calls attention to the fact that an overwhelming proportion of the variants in the Acts and Pauline Epistles common to late uncial Greek mss. and the great mass of the minuscules are identical with the readings followed by Chrysostom in his Homilies.

Chrysostom died 407 A.D. and spent most of his life in Antioch except the last ten years (Constantinople). "The fundamental text of late extant Greek mss. generally is beyond all question identical with the dominant Antiochian or Graeco-Syrian text of the second half of the fourth century" (*ibid.*, p. 92). This is the Syrian type of text. When it stands alone, it is invariably shown to be wrong as in the addition to 1 Cor. vi: 20 above. The scribe would bring in "spirit" there to take the strain off of the "body" (interpretation), but Paul is really pressing the point of bodily purity. Hence transcriptional and intrinsic evidence combine against the Syrian addition.

But the plainest proof of the lateness or "posteriority" of the Syrian class is seen in what Hort calls "Conflate" readings. These are instances where the Pre-Syrian Classes have two readings (usually Neutral *vs.* Western) and where the Syrian class combines the two instead of following now one, now the other. Hort only cites eight of these, but thinks that there are others. The eight are found in Mark vi: 33; viii: 26; ix: 38; ix: 49; Luke ix: 10; xi: 54; xii: 18; xxiv: 53 (Hort, *op. cit.*, pp. 93–107). It is not necessary to discuss them all. Two of the simplest are here given.

Mark ix: 49

(a) πᾶς γὰρ πυρὶ ἁλισθήσεται ℵ B L Δ 1–118–209, 61, 435, al⁹ cop^cdd sah arm ^codd. Neutral and Alexandrian.

(b) πᾶς γὰρ θυσία ἁλὶ ἁλισθήσεται D, 2 min.s, (a) b c ff i (k) vg^codd (cf. Luke vii: 13). Western.

(c) πᾶς γὰρ πυρὶ ἁλισθήσεται καὶ πᾶσα θυσία ἁλὶ ἁλισθήσεται. A C W N X E F G H K M S U V Γ Π, all min.s save 15, f q vg syr ^utr cop ^codd aeth arm ^codd. Syrian.

CLASSES OR FAMILIES OF DOCUMENTS 189

Here it is perfectly plain that the Syrian class has combined the two earlier readings.

Luke xxiv: 53

(a) εὐλογοῦντες τὸν θεόν ℵ B C* L cop syr^hr. Neutral and Alexandrian.

(b) αἰνοῦντες τὸν θεόν D a b e ff vg^codd Aug. Western.

(c) αἰνοῦντες καὶ εὐλογοῦντες τὸν θεόν A W C³ X F H K M S U V Γ Δ all min.s, c f q vg syr^utr arm aeth Syrian.

This is the simplest of all the examples. The Syrian class has simply combined the two earlier readings.

Another good example not given by Hort is in Matt. x: 3 where the Western class reads Λεββαῖος, the Neutral Θαδδαῖος, the Alexandrian and Syrian have both.

One of the best instances of conflation is not given by Hort. It occurs in Acts xx: 28. The Western and Alexandrian classes read τοῦ κυρίου A C* D E 15 min.s sah cop syr^p ^mg arm Ir^int Did, and the Neutral class has τοῦ θεοῦ ℵ B 10 min.s, vg syr^p txt Ign ^Greek Epiph, etc. The Syrian Class reads τοῦ κυρίου καὶ θεοῦ C³ H L P al plus¹¹⁰ Theoph. Chrysostom uses now θεοῦ and now κυρίου.

It may be wondered if single documents do not sometimes show conflate readings. They do, as Hort shows. For instance in Acts vi: 8 E₂ reads πλήρης χάριτος καὶ πίστεως, combining the Neutral and Western πλήρης χάριτος and the Syrian πλήρης πίστεως. It is the kind of thing that constantly tempted the copyist. Hort (*op. cit.*, p. 94) notes an instance in D in John v: 37 and in ℵ in Luke xvi:30 and John xiii: 24.

The most difficult case of an apparent conflate reading is not discussed by Hort at all. It is in Luke x: 42. There are four readings:

(a) ἑνὸς δέ ἐστιν χρεία A C* et 3 W P Γ Δ Λ Π unc⁹ al pler f g¹ q vg syr cuet sch et p txt Chrys Aug.

(b) ὀλίγων δέ ἐστιν χρεία 38 arm sy hr.

(c) ὀλίγων δέ ἐστιν χρεία ἢ ἑνός ℵ B C² L 1, 33, cop syr p mg aeth Or. Bas. Hier.

(d) *Omit.* D a b c e ff² i l syr sin Amb. Now the Western evidence is divided, as one can see between (a) and (d). The Neutral apparently supports (c) which looks like a conflate reading combining (a) and (b).

The support for (b) is very slight, hardly justifying a classification and apparently later than any of the others.

The support for (a) is Western and Syrian.

The location of the Alexandrian class is not certain, apparently with (c) the Neutral.

The omission in (d) can be explained on the ground of difficulty to understand, but note the African Latin e and the syr sin besides D. Is it a Western non-interpolation? Internal evidence, both transcriptional and intrinsic, argues for (a) as explaining the others and yet making sense. There is actual need of only one dish instead of so many. In that case, the Western class is right as represented by European Latin, Vulgate, Syriac of Cureton, Peshitta, and Harclean text and Augustine. The Syrian class here simply followed the Western instead of the Neutral and was right in doing so. Hort would probably say that, just as conflate readings appeared sporadically in single documents, so we have this one instance of it in the Neutral class. This example does not really militate against the argument of Hort when rightly understood. If this is a conflate reading, it simply shows that no class was absolutely immune against it. But it does not disprove the examples of conflation that prove that the Syrian class is later than the other classes (Neutral, Alexandrian, Western) and made use of them. But it would tend to show that the Western Class was earlier than the Neutral but for the separate strata shown here in the Western Class.

Burgon and Miller objected to the theory of Westcott and Hort that they ignore the possibility that the late mss. represent lost originals earlier than ℵ B and the rest. The obvious answer is that no purely Syrian readings have been found that are supported by early Patristic evidence. The Syrian readings that have such support are also either Western or Neutral.

Burgon and Miller also objected that there is no record of such a Syrian revision as Westcott and Hort suppose. They argue it in *The Traditional Text* and in *The Oxford Debate on Textual Criticism*. But Hort does not insist that the revision was made all at once, though Lucian (died 311 A.D.) did make a similar revision of the Septuagint. Hort suggests at least two stages in the Syrian revision, that seen in the Peshitta Syriac and then that in the later Greek mss. Lake (*Text of the N.T.*, p. 69) notes that Chrysostom may differ from Origen or from Irenaeus, but never from both of them. He had or made an eclectic text. Chrysostom shows, what conflation shows, that somebody made a revision of the text. The revision is called Syrian.

If it be urged that perhaps the Neutral text is also a revision, the answer is to agree to that. It is probably

192   INTRODUCTION TO TEXTUAL CRITICISM

more true than Hort supposed that the Neutral text is itself a revision, but it at any rate usually avoided the numerous corruptions seen in the Western text and comes nearer to the original than any other form of the text now accessible to us. The Western text was widespread in the second century A.D., but it was a careless text, while the Neutral is a careful and adequately correct text.

6. *Mixture*

The documents that have conflate readings show mixture in its simplest form. They simply combine the two preceding readings (Neutral and Western). Mixture occurs in various ways. A scribe may have two manuscripts spread out before him. One may represent one type of text and one another. He may combine them as in conflate readings. He may follow now one, now the other, as the Syrian class usually does. Hence the mass of Syrian readings are also either Neutral or Western. The scribe may have only one document before him, but he may be familiar with another and follow it now and then. Sometimes marginal corrections are made as in the syr^p with Greek marginal readings now and then. As a matter of fact we have very few documents that do not show mixture. D, D$_2$, G$_3$ seem purely Western everywhere. Probably also the Old Syriac (syr^{sin} syr^{cu}) and the African Latin are purely Western. But the African Latin sometimes agrees with the Neutral against the Old Syriac and the Old Syriac agrees occasionally with the Neutral against the Old Latin. B has no Syrian readings and is almost purely Neutral in the Gospels and Acts, but has a

CLASSES OR FAMILIES OF DOCUMENTS 193

Western element in Paul's Epistles. ℵ has no Syrian readings, but has both Western and Alexandrian readings on a Neutral base. W is often Neutral, but sometimes Western and Alexandrian and even Syrian. A has a Syrian base in the Gospels, but a Neutral base elsewhere with Western and Alexandrian elements. C has Alexandrian, Neutral, Western, and even Syrian readings as has L. Δ is fundamentally Syrian except in Mark where it is Alexandrian-Neutral. The Bohairic (cop) and Sahidic (sah) versions were originally Neutral-Alexandrian with Western admixture, but have a Syrian addition. The Peshitta is usually Syrian.

In particular, we must observe the mixture in the mss. of the Alexandrian class. There are no documents that are always Alexandrian. This class usually agrees with the Neutral. But sometimes the documents follow the Western class. For this reason a combination of Alexandrian and Western documents may be only Western whereas a combination of Western and Neutral documents will give us the original. The example given above in Acts xx: 28 illustrates this point where the Western and Alexandrian classes read τοῦ κυρίου, the Neutral τοῦ θεοῦ, the Syrian both (conflate). The Alexandrian here shows mixture with the Western. The reading τοῦ κυρίου is at bottom Western as opposed to Neutral τοῦ θεοῦ.

Mixture arose early. It is widespread in the fourth century. The Fathers quote now one type of text, now the other. Hort explains why the Syrian type of text finally triumphed over the others. Antioch was the ecclesiastical parent of Constantinople, which was the centre of Greek Christendom. The Syrian type of text prevailed here in the day of Chrysostom. During the imperial persecutions there had been wholesale destruction of the Greek mss. of the New Testament that contained the Pre-Syrian types of text. In the West the Greek language largely died out. The ravages of the barbarians and later of the Mohammedans did much to dispose of the early texts. The early types of text were not wholly destroyed, for many minuscules preserve Pre-Syrian readings.

The presence of mixture in the documents complicates the critical process, but does not render the task impossible at all. One simply needs to be on his guard to see the bearings of all the facts.

7. *Recognizing the Classes*

This is the practical side of the problem. When one turns to a passage in Tischendorf, he does not find the genealogical classification of Westcott and Hort. The documents fall into two divisions, if there are two readings, or into three or into four as the case may be. The student has to learn the *praxis* of criticism by actual use.

The simplest plan is to look first for the Syrian Class. This class is supported by late uncials (some or all as the case may be), by the minuscules (all or many as it turns out), by late versions, by late Fathers who often quote a passage in different ways. The point is that the Syrian Class has no early testimony at all. It is all late, though not all the late documents may be Syrian.

Next find the Western Class. Hunt for D or D_2. Usually with D or D_2 one will find the African Latin and the Old Syriac (syr^{sin} syr^{cu}), if in the Gospels, perhaps Tertullian, Irenaeus, Cyprian. Often other documents will join these like the European Latin, Vulgate, Sahidic, Augustine. Sometimes the Western documents disagree as the Old Syriac with the Old Latin or with D. The Western Class of documents in the second century was widely used in both east and west. Readings would start in one section that were not adopted in another. This class shows more corruptions than any other and more variations and individual idiosyncrasies in the mss. Many Western readings survive in many documents.

Next find the Neutral Class. B is the most frequent representative of this text, almost wholly so save in Paul's Epistles (mixture again). Along with B one will usually find ℵ and W, with often the Bohairic Version (cop or mem) and Origen. There are frequent traces in other documents like A C L, minuscules like 1, 33.

The Alexandrian Class is left for the last. Nearly always this class appears with the Neutral or with the Western. Sometimes it is not nearly clear where it is. As a matter of fact it matters very little. A few times it is found opposed to the Western and the Neutral. It is seen more frequently in the Gospels in C L Δ ℵ (in Mark), 33, Bohairic, Origen, Cyril of Alexandria.

Now turn to Luke ii: 14 and find each of the classes. At once one sees that the Syrian Class (late uncials, mass of minuscules, late versions (syr^{utr} arm aeth) and late Fathers (a host of them) read εὐδοκία. The Western Class is easily recognized by D it vg Ir^{int} Aug as supporting εὐδοκίας. The Neutral Class supports the same reading ℵ A B W Or. The Alexandrian Class is evidently represented by L Δ (C is wanting here) Ξ cop Cyr for εὐδοκία. It is plain, therefore, that the Syrian has simply followed the Alexandrian grammatical correction of the hard reading εὐδοκίας to the smoother εὐδοκία. But it is also plain that the Western and Neutral can only unite in the original. Therefore εὐδοκίας is the true reading. This is confirmed by transcriptional and intrinsic evidence.

8. *Weighing the Evidence of the Classes*

The principles of internal evidence of single readings can be applied to classes as to whole documents and to groups of documents. The readings supported by each class are tested by transcriptional and by intrinsic evidence and the results added together give the worth of the class. By this test no one class is always right. No one class is always wrong. Only, if the Syrian Class is opposed by the three Pre-Syrian Classes, it is wrong. We saw that in I Cor. vi: 20. The same thing appears in Matt. vi: 4 and 6 where ἐν τῷ φανερῷ is supported by the Alexandrian and Syrian Classes. But the Syrian text is not a bad text. It is a smoother and purer text than the corrupt Western which had won so large a place for a century, practically the *Textus Receptus* of the Christian world from 250 to 350 A.D. For practical purposes the Syrian text is "competently exact" (Warfield, *op. cit.*, p. 160), is free from the gross faults of the Western text, and well suited for popular use. "But, considered as a witness of what was in the original New Testament, it passes out of court simply because it is a good editorially-framed revision of the text, and not a simple copy of it" (*ibid.*).

The Western is the most corrupt text of the New Testament in existence. It shows addition, interpola-

CLASSES OR FAMILIES OF DOCUMENTS 197

tion, paraphrase, assimilation. The age when the Western text was dominant did not care for accuracy. But in the Gospels in particular there are Western non-interpolations that challenge attention. That is to say, the Neutral Class itself had some additions made to it.

The Alexandrian text shows scholarly corrections in form and syntax and petty modifications. "These variations would appear to have had their origin in Alexandria, and to belong to a partially degenerate form of Pre-Syrian non-Western text" (Souter, *Text of the N. T.*, p. 125).

The Neutral text is the authentic text according to Westcott and Hort, except in Western non-interpolations, which readings they consider of much worth. It is doubtful if the Neutral text stands quite as high today as opposed to the Western text as when Hort wrote. But this type of text still outranks any other. It is probably itself an effort to get back to the original text. It represents honest and careful copying with only the errors incidental to such work. The Neutral text has the presumption in its favor, though it is not always right. If it is right nine times out of ten variations, it is wrong one time out of ten. This one-tenth calls for careful scrutiny. There is enough doubt left to call for the closest scrutiny and the use of all forms of evidence before one reaches a final conclusion in each instance.

9. *The Proper Procedure*

The following plan is suggested to students as the right method in the use of the evidence as given by Tischendorf.

(a) See clearly the point at issue and whether the documents give two readings or three.

(b) Appeal first to the External Evidence.

Do it in the following order.

Get the evidence of classes. Begin with the external evidence and this phase of the external evidence. Find the classes and draw a tentative conclusion. Get the evidence of groups. This is independent of classes, but is confirmatory and worth noting. Note the evidence of single documents. This is also confirmatory.

(c) Appeal now to the Internal Evidence.

Do it in this order.

Look at the transcriptional evidence first. What would influence a scribe here? Which reading more easily accounts for the other (or others)? The reading that puzzled the scribe is most likely to be correct. Often the quotations from the Fathers show this trouble with a reading as about οὐκ in John vii: 8. Finally appeal to intrinsic evidence. The reading must make sense in this context. Usually intrinsic evidence will agree with the transcriptional and with the external evidence. Take Luke ii: 14 again. The Neutral and the Western classes read εὐδοκίας. This combination goes back to the original. The Alexandrian and the Syrian classes read εὐδοκία, a scholarly correction of the Alexandrian Class followed by the Syrian. Hence εὐδοκίας is the original reading. The evidence of groups confirms this finding. The group ℵ A B D W outweighs any group for εὐδοκία. The argument from single documents is in the same direction, for five primary uncials support εὐδοκίας. Transcriptional evidence confirms εὐδοκίας, for this is precisely the reading that would

CLASSES OR FAMILIES OF DOCUMENTS 199

bother a copyist as it does us. But the reading does make sense, for men who are the subjects of God's good pleasure are precisely those who do have God's peace. So intrinsic evidence consents to it. The case is made out.

It only remains now to put into practice these principles. The following chapter has to do with the *praxis* of textual criticism. One learns how to do a thing by doing it. The way to learn how to decide between readings is to study the evidence.

CHAPTER XIII

THE PRAXIS OF CRITICISM: ILLUSTRATIONS OF THE VARIOUS CLASSES

It is not practicable for the average student to work through Tischendorf for the entire New Testament. But it would richly repay any one to do so. There are, however, a number of outstanding examples of important and interesting readings that we can study before undertaking so formidable a task. Practice makes perfect in this science as in all other things. Much help can be obtained from Hort's *Notes on Select Readings* (Appendix 1 to his *Introduction*, pp. 1–140).

1. *Readings Supported by Only One Class*

It will be simple to look at some of these in order to sharpen the class alignment in one's mind. The examples will be taken from those where we have only two readings. The triple readings will follow later.

(a) *The Syrian*

Mark 1: 2 has a good example. Here only the Syrian Class gives ἐν τοῖς προφήταις while all the three Pre-Syrian Classes (Western, Neutral, Alexandrian) read ἐν τῷ 'Ησαίᾳ τῷ προφήτῃ. It will not be possible to argue the matter with each of these examples. The student will have to do that. But it is obvious that the change was made to the plural because both Malachi and Isaiah are quoted by Mark. Isaiah was mentioned as the more prominent and important.

In Mark i: 10 ἀπὸ τοῦ ὕδατος is Syrian (harmonistic correction to agree with Matt. iii: 16). Pre-Syrian Classes have ἐκ τοῦ ὕδατος.

In John xii: 7 τετήρηκεν has only Syrian support and it is an effort to remove the difficulty in ἵνα τηρήσῃ.

In Rom. v: 1 ἔχομεν has only Syrian witness, the Pre-Syrian Classes all having ἔχωμεν. There was no confusion among the old documents here about the pronunciation of ω and ο. There has been a curious failure of modern American scholars to understand the force of the tense of ἔχωμεν. Paul did not write σχῶμεν (ingressive aorist subjunctive) for "make peace", but ἔχωμεν (present subjunctive, linear action) for "keep on enjoying peace" (cf. the imperfect εἶχεν εἰρήνην in Acts ix: 31). That is the point of the exhortation. It is not a repetition of δικαιωθέντες, but assumes that.

In 1 Cor. vi: 20 we have already seen that the addition has only Syrian support and is therefore wrong, as is true of all these purely Syrian readings.

In 1 Cor. vii: 5 τῇ νηστείᾳ is a Syrian addition.

In 1 John ii: 23 the Syrian Class has omitted a line ὁ ὁμολογῶν τὸν υἱὸν καὶ τὸν πατέρα ἔχει because of ending like the previous line (homoeoteleuton).

In 1 John iii: 1 the Syrian Class omits the striking Johannean phrase καί ἐσμεν.

These examples give a fair impression of the Syrian type of readings.

(b) *The Western*

In Matt. v: 32 a few Western documents (D 64 a b k cdd ap Aug) omit καὶ ὃς ἐὰν ἀπολελυμένην μοιχᾶται. This is a typical Western omission except that it is not supported by all the Western documents. There are frequent variations within the Western documents. A reading would start in one branch and not spread to all.

In Matt. viii: 12 the Western Class reads ἐξελεύσονται, the other classes have ἐκβληθήσονται.

D has a long addition to Matt. xx: 28 that appears also in Φ (Codex Beratinus), Syr^{cu}, Old Latin mss. with many variations, and one or two Vulgate mss. It is a plain Western addition and is very much like Luke xiv: 8–11. One may see also in Tischendorf the curious passage in D in place of Luke vi: 5 (D puts verse 5 after verse 10). This passage in D about the man working on the Sabbath day may be a true saying of Jesus, but it is certainly not a genuine part of Luke's Gospel. It illustrates well how such additions came to mss. of the Western Class in particular. The addition reads thus: τῇ αὐτῇ ἡμέρᾳ θεασάμενός τινα ἐργαζόμενον τῷ σαββάτῳ, εἶπεν αὐτῷ· ἄνθρωπε, εἰ μὲν οἶδας ὃ ποιεῖς, μακάριος εἶ· εἰ δὲ μὴ οἶδας, ἐπικατάρατος καὶ παραβάτης εἶ τοῦ νόμου.

The Western Class omits Luke v: 39 and Westcott and Hort bracket it as they do Matt. xxi: 44 and the last clause in John iv: 9 for the same reason. They attach more weight to these Western non-interpolations than to the Western additions. It is at this point that the Western Class shows up best.

Acts viii: 37 is a Western addition that grew out of ecclesiastical custom in connection with baptism.

In Acts xv: 20 the Western Class omits καὶ τοῦ πνικτοῦ and thus changes the demands made of the Gentile Christians to purely moral regulations. The Western Class then adds the negative form of the Golden Rule to this verse.

THE PRAXIS OF CRITICISM 203

These examples show also how in the Gospels, especially in Luke, the Western text is sometimes a shorter text, while in the Acts it is usually a longer text. Blass has suggested the theory that Luke made two editions of his Gospel and of the Acts (the shorter second in the Gospel, the shorter first in the Acts). But the theory is still in dispute.

(c) *The Neutral*

In Mark vi: 20 the Neutral Class reads ἠπόρει, while the Western, Alexandrian, and Syrian Classes have ἐποίει.

In Mark ix: 29 the Neutral Class (א B k) rejects καὶ νηστείᾳ which is supported by the Western, Alexandrian, and Syrian. It is to be noted that the African Latin k sometimes has Neutral readings.

A good example is found in Luke xi: 2. The Neutral Class (א B L Vg) rejects ἡμῶν after πάτερ while the Western (D Old Latin Syr^{cu}), Alexandrian (C Δ cop Or), and Syrian (A with late uncials, minuscules, Syr^{utr}) classes have it. So in the same verse the Neutral Class rejects the clause γενηθήτω τὸ θέλημά σου ὡς ἐν οὐρανῷ καὶ ἐπὶ γῆς, a harmonistic addition to agree with Matt. vi: 10 and supported by Western, Alexandrian and Syrian classes.

Acts xv: 34 is rejected by the Neutral Class (possibly also Alexandrian). It is supported by the Western, probably the Alexandrian (C cop) and certainly the Syrian, classes.

In Eph. i: 1 ἐν 'Εφέσῳ is rejected by the Neutral Class alone (א B 67 Origen), while the Western, Alexandrian, and Syrian classes give it. But the Neutral class is certainly right, for it was apparently a circular letter to the churches of Asia (province). Paul in Col. iv: 16 refers to the letter to Laodicea (apparently our Ephesians). Tertullian and Epiphanius say that Marcion called the Epistle to the Ephesians the Epistle to the Laodiceans. The chances are that the church in Ephesus made a copy for its own use and put in the words "in Ephesus". This copy has come down to us, while the original copy left the space blank as ℵ B have it.

(d) *The Alexandrian*

In Matt. xiv: 15 οὖν after ἀπόλυσον is given by the Alexandrian Class while the Neutral, Western, Syrian omit it. A reading supported only by the Alexandrian or by the Alexandrian and the Syrian is bound to be wrong, for the Neutral and Western can only meet in the original. In Matt. xv: 32 there is an Alexandrian correction (ℵ min.s Or) which changes the difficult reading ἡμέραι τρεῖς to ἡμέρας τρεῖς.

In John i: 28 there is a curious situation. βαθηνία is given by ℵ* ABC*W (five primary uncials) EFGHLM-SVX ΓΔΠ al plus[130] it vg cop syr sch et p txt et hr arm arr Cyr. D is wanting here, but one sees here the typical representatives of all four classes and yet the *Textus Receptus* (and King James) has βηθαβαρᾷ supported by ℵ cb (βηθαραβᾷ. So also syr p mg) C² K T^b U ΛΠ corr 1.22.33.69 al plus[30] (many in the margin) syr sin syr cu Origen, Epiphanius. The late Syrian evidence is divided, but the *Textus Receptus* followed some of these minuscules. Certainly the Neutral, Western and most of the Syrian documents read Bethany. The

combination of Neutral and Western settles it anyhow.
C W Δ Cyr may mean also the Alexandrian or only
further witnesses for the Neutral ℵ B cop. The earliest
witnesses for Bethabara are the syr^{sin} syr^{cu} and Origen.
It is not clear whether there is any connection between
them. Ordinarily syr^{sin} syr^{cu} are Western with the Old
Latin. We miss D here. But Origen tells us expressly
that practically all the ancient mss. known to him read
Bethany. He quotes none for Bethabara. But he says
that in his visit to Palestine he found no trace of a
Bethany beyond Jordan, but only the Bethany near
Jerusalem. Hence he reads Bethabara in opposition to
the mss. Here is the first New Testament textual
critic known to us who consciously decides against the
external evidence on internal grounds. We seem to
catch Origen in the act of altering the text. It did not
spread very widely at first. The syr^{sin} syr^{cu} either got
it from Origen or started it on similar grounds. Origen
lived in Caesarea a long time. Some would place both
syr^{sin} syr^{cu} before Origen, but this reading has to be
considered on that point. At any rate whether we call
Bethabara Alexandrian in origin or Western, it is
manifestly a correction, Origen himself being the witness
about himself, and therefore wrong. The same reasoning that influenced Origen may have led the Old Syriac
to say Bethabara. In Judges vii: 24 the name Bethbara
occurs. Perhaps this fact may have led to the change
from Bethany. It is beside the mark to argue that
nearly two hundred years afterwards no village of the
name of Bethany could be found over Jordan.

The article ἡ with ἑορτή in John v: 1 is another Alexandrian reading (ℵ C L Δ). The Neutral and Western classes reject ἡ. It is a manifest effort to make ἑορτή mean the Passover. The Syrian evidence divides here as often.

In John xix: 14 the Western, Neutral, and Syrian classes rightly read ἕκτη, but the Alexandrian Class has a foolish attempt to make it agree with Mark xv: 25. But John is talking about the trial before Pilate while Mark is speaking of the crucifixion. John clearly uses Roman time.

2. *Examples with Two Classes for Each Reading*

Attention cannot be called to all the examples, but only to enough to give facility to the student. The student is expected with each example given to apply all the processes of external and internal evidence and to reach a conclusion of some sort in the light of the evidence as a whole.

In Matt. vi: 4 and 6 the mss. divide almost exactly for and against ἐν τῷ φανερῷ. The Neutral and Western classes oppose the insertion while the Alexandrian and Syrian give it. The insertion is due to the Alexandrian class (W L Δ) to balance with ἐν τῷ κρυπτῷ. In verse 4 Tischendorf has omitted AΠ al pler in favor of the addition. W has it in both verses.

In Matt. vi: 13 the Doxology is not found in the Neutral and Western classes while the Alexandrian (W L Δ again) and the Syrian classes give it. But there is some early Western evidence for a shorter form of the Doxology in syr[cu], k (African Latin), and the Sahidic. But this is not all. Several of the Fathers (Gregory of Nyssa, Caesar of Nazianzus, Euthymius Zigabenus, Cyril of Jerusalem) likewise give doxologies which differ from each other and say that they were used at the close of the liturgical service when the Lord's Prayer was used as a climax. Thus we seem to see the origin of the Doxology in this public use. Gradually the one that we know drove out the others.

In Matt. ix: 13 the Alexandrian and Syrian classes add εἰς μετάνοιαν against the Neutral and Western.

In Matt. xxiv: 36 οὐδὲ ὁ υἱός is read by the Neutral and Western classes (ℵ B D 13. 28. 86. 124. 346, most Old Latin mss., syr^{hr} aeth arm Ir Hil Amb Chrys). This looks like a typical Neutral Western combination that could only unite in the original. The words are omitted by the Alexandrian Class (W L Δ cop) and by the Syrian Class also. It is omitted also by the syr^{sin} (syr^{cu} is defective here) syr^{utr}, and by the Sahidic, showing that the omission was early and partly Western. The only thing that makes one pause about accepting the words as genuine is the fact that in Mark xiii: 32 all the mss. give οὐδὲ ὁ υἱός. It would be easy to add the words here in Matt. xxiv: 36 because of Mark. This argument from transcriptional evidence convinces Broadus (see footnote in Comm. on Matthew) that the Neutral and Western classes are wrong here or even that ℵ B may be Western in this case. But it is quite possible for an Alexandrian scribe to have considered οὐδὲ ὁ υἱός superfluous in Matt. xxiv: 36 because of μόνος here which is not in Mark. It is repetition, but of a kind to impress the point. On the whole one hardly seems justified here to go against the Neutral and Western evidence for οὐδὲ ὁ υἱός.

In Mark vi: 22 the Neutral and Western classes read αὐτοῦ while the Alexandrian and Syrian have αὐτῆς τῆς.

The girl may have had the name Herodias as well as Salome (Josephus).

In Mark ix: 24 the Western and Syrian classes add μετὰ δακρύων, the Neutral and Alexandrian classes opposing.

In Mark ix: 44 and 46 the repetition of ix: 48 is supported by the Western and Syrian classes while the Neutral and Alexandrian reject it. All classes support verse 49.

In Luke ii: 14 we have already seen that the Neutral and Western classes read εὐδοκίας while the Alexandrian and Syrian have changed this hard reading to εὐδοκία.

In Luke iv: 44 the Neutral and Alexandrian classes have τῆς 'Ιουδαίας in the general sense for all Palestine which the Western and Syrian have changed to τῆς Γαλιλαίας because they took 'Ιουδαίας in the narrow sense exclusive of Galilee. W here reads τῶν 'Ιουδαίων.

In Luke vi: 1 δευτεροπρώτῳ is read by the Western and Syrian classes while it is rejected by the Neutral and Alexandrian classes. It is an unintelligible word. It is probably a bungling attempt to relate this Sabbath to that in vi: 6 ἑτέρῳ σαββάτῳ, one scribe giving πρώτῳ, another δευτέρῳ, another carelessly combining both words.

In Luke xxiii: 45 the Neutral and Alexandrian classes support τοῦ ἡλίου ἐκλιπόντος while the Western and Syrian give καὶ ἐσκοτίσθη ὁ ἥλιος perhaps changing because they wrongly made ἐκλιπόντος mean "eclipse" of the sun, which was impossible at the Passover, time of the full moon. But the word does not have to have this technical idea. "The sun failing" is enough.

In Luke xxiv: 17 the Neutral and Alexandrian reading καὶ ἐστάθησαν σκυθρωποί is a great improvement over the Western and Syrian καὶ (ἐστὲ) σκυθρωποί.

In John i: 18 the Western and Syrian classes read υἱός while the Neutral and Alexandrian give θεός. It is evident that the difficult μονογενὴς θεός was changed to the more usual ὁ μονογενὴς υἱός. It is to be noticed also that μονογενὴς θεός simply combines in one phrase verses 1 (pre-existent Deity) and 14 (Incarnation). Certainly this combination suits the Virgin Birth narratives in Matthew and Luke.

The whole verse in John v:4 is wanting in the Neutral and Western classes. It is supported by the Alexandrian (L cop Cyr) and the Syrian classes. It has some Western support (Old Latin, Tertullian). We have seen frequent influence of the Western on the Alexandrian mss. Probably this explanation of ταραχθῇ in verse 7 as being due to the periodic visit of the angel spread from North Africa to Alexandria. Didymus adds to the story that the angel came only once a year. But it is clearly not a part of the Gospel of John. The periodicity of this miracle made it troublesome for interpreters. But they are now relieved of this burden.

In John vii: 8 it is clear that the Neutral and Syrian read οὔπω while the Western has οὐκ. The position of the Alexandrian class is in doubt, probably with the Western and found in ℵ cop Cyr., though W L Δ read οὔπω. But even so the Alexandrian frequently copies the Western (mixture). The Neutral is more frequently right than the Western. But transcriptional evidence argues strongly for οὐκ since the Fathers struggle over the difficulty of οὐκ (Jerome, Epiphanius, Cyril) and seem ignorant of οὔπω. Intrinsic evidence will allow it as we have seen, for it really concurs with verses 4 and 10, rightly understood.

In John vii: 53 to viii: 11 we have one of the most famous of all the disputed passages. The Neutral and Alexandrian classes reject it while the Western and Syrian give it. But here again syr^{sin} and syr^{cu} do not have it, and Tertullian is ignorant of it, showing probably that the story arose in the West and did not reach the eastern branch of the Western class of documents. It is to be noted also that some of the documents that give it put asterisks by it to indicate doubt. Some also comment on the fact that many old documents did not have it. Others that have it use the system of canons and sections that do not provide for it. Still others place it at the end of John's Gospel. Some even put it at the close of Luke xxi. It is clear that it is not a genuine part of the Gospel of John. And yet the incident has every mark of reality. It is probably a true story like many others that are not in our Gospels (*cf.* John xx: 30 and xxi: 25).

In John xiii: 2 the Neutral and Alexandrian classes (ℵ B W L X Or) have γινομένου while the Western and Syrian give γενομένου. But the context shows (see verse 4 ἐγείρεται ἐκ τοῦ δείπνου) that the supper was still going on. So that γινομένου is correct.

In Acts ii: 47 the Western and Syrian classes add τῇ ἐκκλησίᾳ, which the Neutral and Alexandrian classes reject.

In Acts xxv: 13 ἀσπασάμενοι is supported by the Neutral and Alexandrian classes and possibly even by the Western. The Syrian reads ἀσπασόμενοι with some Western support (e has salutandum). D is wanting here, but vg arm give future. There is no doubt at all that ἀσπασάμενοι is correct, the effective aorist. There is some evidence in the papyri of a possible use of the aorist participle to express purpose like the future participle, but it is not necessary to appeal to that possible idiom here.

3. *Examples of Three Readings*

Sometimes more than three readings occur, as in John vi: 69, where there are seven readings (variations of ὁ ἅγιος τοῦ θεοῦ. In Col. ii: 2 Dobschütz (*op. cit.*, p. 134) notes fourteen variations of τοῦ θεοῦ χριστοῦ. There are five in 1 Thess. iii: 2 and eight in Acts ii: 30.

All the examples of conflation belong here, the eight given by Hort (Mark vi: 33; viii: 26; ix: 38; ix: 49; Luke ix: 10; xi: 54; xii: 18; xxiv: 53) and Luke x: 42 and Acts xx: 28, examples discussed in Chapter XII under Conflation. These need not be discussed again, but there are others worth noticing.

The first one to notice may puzzle us a bit. It is in Matt. xix: 16. B D Origen read σχῶ, W C Δ and a dozen other late uncials with most of the minuscules and Basil and Chrysostom and Cyril of Jerusalem have ἔχω, while ℵ L some minuscules e syr [cu et p mg] cop Or Bas Ir [int] give κληρονομήσω as in Mark and Luke. The Alexandrian and Syrian classes read ἔχω. But where are the Neutral and the Western? B D go together while ℵ L e syr [cu] flock together. The Neutral seems divided as well as the Western. Origen gives σχῶ in his text and κληρονομήσω in his commentary. If B is Western with D, then the Neutral is found in ℵ L Or. But σχῶ has the best of the internal argument.

In Matt. xxiv: 20 the Neutral and Alexandrian classes have σαββάτῳ, the Syrian ἐν σαββάτῳ, the Western σαββάτου (but d has *sabbato*).

But in Mark iii: 29 we have a simple case. The Neutral and Alexandrian classes read ἁμαρτήματος, the Western ἁμαρτίας, the Syrian κρίσεως.

In Mark vii: 4 the Western and Syrian read βαπτίσωνται, the Neutral ῥαντίσωνται, the Alexandrian βαπτίζονται (L al., but Δ E F al. βαπτίζωνται and K N X al. βαπτίσονται). The words βαπτίσωνται and ῥαντίσωνται are not here used interchangeably. The point is which gave the scribes most trouble. The Western and Syrian classes read also καὶ κλινῶν, while the Neutral and Alexandrian reject this addition. Was the addition due to knowledge of Jewish custom about their pallets or was it dropped because of supposed difficulty about dipping beds? It is a nice point to argue.

In John ix: 4 there is a beautiful illustration of the classes in a triple reading:

    ἡμᾶς————με
    ἡμᾶς————ἡμᾶς
    ἐμὲ————με

But the documents do not agree in the support of the first and second words. The Syrian class consistently supports ἐμὲ————με.

The Neutral class reads ἡμᾶς————με.

The Western documents are divided over the first ἡμᾶς (D sah) and the first ἐμὲ (it vg syr^{sin}).

The Alexandrian documents seem to support ἡμᾶς————ἡμᾶς (ℵ W L cop Cyr).

But in that case the true way to put it is that for the first ἡμᾶς the Neutral and Alexandrian classes combine

THE PRAXIS OF CRITICISM

with some Western support. For the second ἡμᾶς there is only Alexandrian support, while the Neutral here goes with the Western and the Syrian. Internal evidence argues strongly for ἡμᾶς ——με, as the one that explains the origin of the others and yet as making the best sense also. Jesus associates the disciples with Him in His mission.

In Acts xv: 18 the Neutral and Alexandrian have simply γνωστὰ ἀπ' αἰῶνος. The Western has γνωστὸν ἀπ' αἰῶνος τῷ κυρίῳ τὸ ἔργον αὐτοῦ. The Syrian has γνωστὰ ἀπ'αἰῶνος τῷ θεῷ πάντα τὰ ἔργα αὐτοῦ.

In I Cor. xi: 24 the Syrian class reads κλώμενον while the Western has θρυπτόμενον (D) or διδόμενον (f vg sah cop arm). But the Neutral and Alexandrian classes have only τὸ ὑπὲρ ἡμῶν. This is undoubtedly correct and explains the others. In Luke xxii: 19 διδόμενον appears. It was natural for it to appear in I Cor. xi: 24. D changes it to θρυπτόμενον. The Syrian class uses the more familiar κλώμενον. And yet we know that the body of Jesus was not broken (John xix: 33). "Broken body" is not genuine here, but preachers keep on using it in the observance of the Lord's Supper. It is not the true text and it is not true in fact.

But the most striking instance of this point is in I Tim. iii: 16. The Syrian class reads θεός, the Western ὅ, while the Neutral and Alexandrian have ὅς. B is wanting here, giving out at Heb. ix: 13, but ℵ A C F G sah cop Or Cyr give these two classes. The classification is plain enough in spite of some doubt about the reading in C a palimpsest document. This example is interesting for we can see how from ὅς both ὅ and θεός arose. In the uncials they would appear thus OC O ΘC.

The scribe who had ὅς may have been disturbed by the lack of grammatical agreement in gender between μυστήριον and ὅς. Hence he would change it to ὅ. But Greek has also natural gender and Christ as the μυστήριον is masculine so that after all ὅς can be correct. Besides it is quite possible that this sentence is a fragment of an early Christian hymn and Westcott and Hort so print it. Hence there is no real difficulty in ὅς.

But OC and ΘC look exactly alike save two little marks. These could easily be imagined to be there as specks on the parchment, especially if the scribe was on the lookout for a Trinitarian proof text. It so happens that Tischendorf quotes from Liberatus the narrative of the expulsion of Macedonius, Bishop of Constantinople, by the Emperor Anastasius, for changing O to Θ in this very passage: "Hunc enim immutasse, ubi habet OC, id est *qui*, monosyllabum Graecum, littera mutata o in θ vertisse et fecisse ΘC, id est *deus*, ut esset; *Deus apparuit per carnem*". Here then we have positive proof that such a thing could be done, for it was done. The critical text thus loses I Tim. iii: 16 as a proof text for the Deity of Jesus as it does I John v: 7 and 8. But it gains θεός applied to Jesus in John i: 18. But, apart from doctrinal controversy, we all want the original text whether it suits our notions or not.

The outstanding example is Mark xvi: 9–20, the most important variant reading in the whole New Testament. The Neutral class stops with verse 8. The Western, Alexandrian, and Syrian classes support the long ending. But we know that there is frequent mixture between the Alexandrian and Western classes. That is probably true here. The Alexandrian follows the Western. The Syrian follows the Western-Alexandrian. At bottom, then, we have Western versus Neutral. The Neutral is more frequently right than the Western, So the evidence of classes argues for rejection. The evidence of groups is to the same effect, ℵ B or A C or D W. The argument from single documents is to the same conclusion. Three Armenian mss. also have no ending. One, the earliest, (at Edschmiadzin) gives the long ending and attributes it to Ariston (probably the Aristion of Papias). W has the long ending but with a strange addition to verse 14. The cursive Greek ms. 22 has τέλος after verse 8, but adds that in many mss. the passage 9–20 is found and gives it. But this is not all. Some documents give a shorter ending instead of the long one as in 274 (margin to verse 7), k. But a number of mss. have both the short and the long ending. So L, Ψ, 0112, 099, 579, two Bohairic mss., the Harklean Syriac (text has the long ending, the Greek margin the short one). These mss. really testify against the long ending by giving both. So a curious situation arises. We have no ending beyond verse 8 in ℵ B, the short ending alone in 274 and k, the short ending with the long ending in L, Ψ, 0112, 099, 579, two Bohairic mss., Harklean Syriac, the long ending in the Western-Alexandrian and Syrian classes, an addition to the long ending in W. These are the outstanding facts. If we now apply the arguments from internal evidence we find the following situation which is peculiar. Transcriptional evidence raises the question as to how we are to explain the variety of readings here presented. Did the Gospel end at verse 8? Was a leaf torn off? Would a scribe deliberately tear it off? Would a scribe try to fill out an ending better than verse 8? The fact of the two endings shows that such efforts were made. Hence transcriptional evidence argues against the genuineness of either of the two additions. What does intrinsic evidence say? If the Gospel ended with verse 8, it is difficult to believe that Mark meant to do that. He may have been interrupted. He may have died. He may have written another ending that has been lost. It is argued by some that the style of xvi: 9–20 is quite different from that of the rest of Mark's Gospel. But that is not decisive. It is pointed out by others that these verses are after all a real summary of what is in Matthew 28. If so, Aristion may very well have done it. Certainly the shorter ending has no value nor has the Apocryphal addition in W. But intrinsic evidence does agree here with the other lines of evidence. It does not demand the long ending. If the external evidence and transcriptional evidence supported it, probably intrinsic evidence would acquiesce. So the passage as it stands seems condemned as not a genuine part of the original Mark.

4. *Neutral Interpolations*

It is well known that the Western class, like the Syrian, makes many additions to the original text. These are generally rejected like the Syrian additions. As we have seen, if a reading is only Syrian, it is rejected by modern scholars out of hand. The same thing is true if it is only Alexandrian or even Alexandrian and

Syrian. If it is only Western or Western and Syrian, it is suspected and the Neutral (or Neutral and Alexandrian) preferred. But there are Western readings that call for more serious consideration. There are some Western non-interpolations, as Hort calls them (*Introduction*, pp. 175–179), which are undoubtedly correct. This is but another way of saying that there are some Neutral (and Alexandrian) interpolations. It is not claimed that the Neutral class is always right, but that it is much more frequently so than any other class.

It is important now to look at some of the Neutral interpolations. Curiously enough these are nearly confined, according to Hort (p. 175), to the last chapters of Luke. He admits one in Matt. xxvii: 49, a very glaring example. But it is passing strange that Westcott and Hort should actually put this passage in their text, although in brackets. This is mere slavery to the Neutral class, to ℵ B C L. Here the Neutral and Alexandrian (ℵ B C L) classes insert from John xix: 34 (a manifest and blundering harmonistic addition), the story of the piercing of the side of Jesus. But it is inserted before Jesus dies. That is told in Matt. xxvii: 50. The Western and Syrian classes do not have this addition and they are clearly right. Intrinsic evidence agrees with transcriptional evidence in rejecting it. Undoubtedly here the Western class gives the true reading while the Neutral and Alexandrian classes have fallen into error. The persistence of this error in so large a group of the very best documents (ℵ B C L) shows what literal copyists they were as a rule. They went on putting these words in without seeing the incongruity in the very next verse. If it played them false here it probably stood them in good stead in most other passages. It may be remarked that W goes with the Western and Syrian classes here in rejecting this passage. The question may properly be raised whether the Alexandrian class is represented here by C L with the Neutral or by W Δ with the Western class.

The Western class rejects Matt. xxi: 44 and Westcott and Hort bracket this verse in their text. It is supported by all the other classes.

In Luke xv: 21 a very nice question is raised. The great mass of the documents here reject ποίησόν με ὡς ἕνα τῶν μισθίων σου. These words are genuine in xv: 19. But ℵ B D U X al[20] gat mm tol bodl cat[ox119] put it in here. W rejects it. Ordinarily we would go with ℵ B D in the Gospels, but not necessarily so in Paul's Epistles. Was the phrase copied in from verse 19? Or was it dropped because of a feeling that it was a finer trait for the son not to be allowed by the Father to finish his speech? And is this a Western or a Western and Neutral reading? If Neutral and Western, we are disposed to stand by it. Westcott and Hort bracket it.

The last part of Luke xxii: 19 and all of verse 20 are wanting in the Western class. Westcott and Hort bracket also this passage.

In John iv: 9 the Western class rejects the sentence about the Jews having no dealings with the Samaritans. Westcott and Hort bracket it. But it is given by A B C L W etc.

5. *Possible Western Readings in B in the Gospels*

Hort denies this, though he admits it in the Pauline Epistles. But Westcott and Hort do not always follow

B in the Gospels nor even always ℵ B. In Mark iv: 21 ℵ B read ὑπὸ τὴν λυχνίαν, an obvious *lapsus pennae* because of ὑπό twice before. Westcott and Hort actually put ὑπό in the margin here.

But in Matt. xi: 23 B has only Western support for καταβήση (cf. Luke x: 15) except W instead of καταβιβασθήση. It is probably correct here, but if B is Neutral here, it stands without other Neutral support unless W is here Neutral.

In Matt. xviii: 17 B D W read εἰπέ while ℵ L give εἰπόν. Westcott and Hort print εἰπόν.

In xix: 9 B cop Or have only Western support for παρεκτὸς λόγου πορνείας (as in Matt. v: 32) while ℵ C W (sixteen other uncials) 150 min.s g² vg syr^{utr} read μὴ ἐπὶ πορνείᾳ. Westcott and Hort follow ℵ C W and put the reading of B D at the bottom of the page in a note. If we have Neutral and Western combined here, that should give us the original. Has B here a Western reading or is it Neutral here? Why desert B at this verse if not Western?

In xix: 22 B has only Western (divided) support for τοῦτον (bracketed by Westcott and Hort), while C D W al pler ff² q vg cop syr^p Or have only τὸν λόγον but ℵ L Z Chrys have no addition.

In Matt. xix: 24 Westcott and Hort follow ℵ C L W etc. for εἰσελθεῖν against B D G it vg for διελθεῖν.

In Matt. xxvii: 28 Westcott and Hort follow A L Δ N al omn sch cop syr$^{utr\ et\ hr}$ in reading ἐκδύσαντες against B D 157 a b c ff² g ἐνδύσαντες.

In Matt. xxviii: 19 Westcott and Hort again follow ℵ Δ W al omn it vg Ir in reading βαπτίζοντες against B D βαπτίσαντες.

In Mark i: 40 B D G 8 min.s a b c ff² g¹ omit καὶ γονυπετῶν. Westcott and Hort bracket it.

In Mark vi: 14 B has ἔλεγον (D ἐλέγοσαν) with 6. 271. a b ff² mt Aug. rather than ἔλεγεν supported by ℵ A C L al pler c f g¹ l q vg cop syr^utr.

We can close with Luke xxiii: 34. This verse is omitted by B D W 38. 435. a b d syr^sin sah cop^dz. But it is in all the other documents of importance including ℵ A C L Δ al longe pler c e f ff² l vg cop^w syr^cu et utr et hr Ir. Westcott and Hort bracket it. But here B stands with the Western class unless W is here Neutral with B. If it is a Western non-interpolation, where does B come in if it does not here have a Western reading? Note also that it is in the African Latin e and the syr^cu and Irenaeus besides the Neutral and Alexandrian classes, if B is here Western. But the usual Western documents are divided. Certainly this beautiful saying is like Christ. He said it, one is bound to feel. And it is an open question whether it is a part of Luke's Gospel or not. At any rate it is not in B and D.

CHAPTER XIV

THE FUTURE OF THE STUDY

1. *Confirmation of the Theory of Westcott and Hort*

These scholars did not claim that they had produced the original text, but that it was the oldest and the best text known to us now in the present state of research. The purely Syrian text has been set aside. The *Textus Receptus* can never be reëstablished to critical favor unless revolutionary discoveries are made. The attacks of Burgon and Miller (*The Revision Revised*, 1883; the *Traditional Text of the Holy Gospels Vindicated and Established*, 1896; *The Causes of the Corruption of the Traditional Text of the Holy Gospels*, 1899; *A Textual Commentary upon the Holy Gospels*, Part I, Matt. i–xiv, 1899; *The Oxford Debate on Textual Criticism*, 1897) were vigorous, but they have failed to stand against the facts. Independent investigators have come practically to the same conclusion about the text as that reached by Westcott and Hort.

Bernhard Weiss has published a series of studies on the Text of the New Testament in Gebhard and Harnack's *Texte und Untersuchungen* which is mainly an examination of the principal Greek mss. Weiss does not treat the Versions and Fathers, but he shows conclusively the superiority of B to all other Greek mss. in spite of its being disfigured by obvious blunders in transcription like ὑπό for ἐπί in Mark iv: 21. These

volumes of B. Weiss appeared in the following order:
Apocalypse, 1892; Catholic Epistles, 1892; Pauline
Epistles, 1896; Gospels, 1899; his Text of the Gospels,
1900.

Eberhard Nestle in 1901 published a resultant Greek
text with some critical apparatus that is in practical
agreement with the conclusions of Westcott and Hort.

Von Soden worked on his own lines, but his text
published in 1913 with short critical apparatus does not
differ greatly from that of Westcott and Hort. The
Von Soden text is the Greek text used by Moffatt in
his *New Translation of the New Testament* (1914).

The modern handbooks for the study of New Testament textual criticism (by Warfield, 1886; by Lake, 1900; by Kenyon, 1901; by Nestle, 1899, revised by Dobschütz in 1923; by Souter, 1912; by Jacquier, 1913) all stand by the position of Westcott and Hort in broad outline. Lake says (*Text of the N. T.*, p. 73): "Although not perhaps universally received, the theory of Westcott and Hort is certainly the basis of most modern textual criticism". Kenyon (*Textual Criticism of the N. T.* p. 308) says: "Westcott and Hort's theory was epoch-making in the fullest sense of the term. In spite of certain criticisms and modifications, which appear to be well founded, and of which mention will have to be made below, this theory holds the field among the scholars of today".

Souter (*The Text and Canon of the N. T.*, p. 138) says: "It appears to the present writer that a great advance upon the text of Westcott and Hort in the direction of the original autographs is highly improbable, at least in our generation. If they have not said the last word they have at least laid foundations which make it comparatively simple to fit later discoveries into their scheme." With this judgment I heartily agree. New discoveries will be made and the more the better. The Washington manuscript (W) and the Sinaitic Syriac (syr^{sin}) were not known to Westcott and Hort. But these famous manuscripts have not overturned, but rather confirmed the broad conclusions on which they based their general theory. It is practically certain that progress will be made in the future, but it will be made in the direction so wonderfully outlined by Hort in his great *Introduction.* Souter has a most interesting chapter entitled *Progress in the Textual Criticism of the Gospels since Westcott* in the volume presented to Dr. A. M. Fairbairn on his seventieth birthday, *Mansfield College Essays* (1909). These include papyrus fragments that go back to the third century, W (the greatest of all, and of the fourth or fifth century), O (a purple uncial of Matt. 13-24 and of the sixth century), Ψ' (an uncial of the eighth or ninth century, latter part of Mark), the Sinaitic Syriac, more fragments of the Sahidic, the Arabic translation of Tatian's *Diatessaron*, the publishing of a photograph of ℵ so that it can now be studied better, 227 more leaves of N now discovered, publishing the text of 1 (and its allies 118, 131, 209) by Lake, more knowledge of the Ferrar Group (not only 13, 69, 124, 346, but also 230, 543, 788, 826, 828, 983, 1689, 1709), accurate publishing of k (*Codex Bobiensis*, edited by Wordsworth, Sanday, and White, *Old Latin Biblical Texts*, 1886), accurate edition of ff^2 (in *Old Latin Biblical Texts*, 1907, by E. S. Buchanan), new edition of the Vulgate by Wordsworth and Professor White (*Novum Testamentum Domini Nostri Iesu Christi Latine*, 1889-1898), edition of the *Peshitta Gospels* by Pusey and Gwilliam (1901), Horner's edition of the Bohairic Version (1898), the Berlin series of Ante-Nicene Greek Fathers (1897——), Barnard's *Clement of Alexandria's Biblical Text* (1899), Burkitt's *Ephraem's Quotations from the Gospels* (1901), and editions of other fathers.

But progress did not stop in 1909. In 1912 H. A. Sanders published the photograph of the Washington Manuscript with a full discussion of the character of the manuscript and the facts concerning it. In 1914 E. J. Goodspeed published *The Freer Gospels* in which the important readings of the Washington Manuscript were noted. Goodspeed had already published the *Newberry Gospels* (1902). He has gone on with *The Toronto Gospels* (1911), *The Bixby Gospels* (1915), *The Harvard Gospels* (1918), *The Haskell Gospels* (1918). Gebhard and Harnack have continued their *Texte und Untersuchungen*.

Edmunds and Hatch have published their *Gospel Manuscripts of the General Theological Seminary* (1918). In 1922 there appeared two notable works. One is Souter's *Pelagius's Expositions of Thirteen Epistles of St. Paul* (Vol. IX of *Texts and Studies*). The other is in *Old Latin Biblical Texts* no. vii. It is called *Nouum Testamentum Sancti Irenaei Episcopi Lugdunensis* and it is edited by W. Sanday, C. H. Turner, and A. Souter. Both books are works of great scholarship and will help very much in their respective fields.

Hoskier has published in two volumes, *Codex B and*

Its Allies (1914). He starts out by saying (p. 7): "It is high time that the bubble of Codex B should be pricked". He proceeds to prick it at great length, but he fails to overturn the general position of Westcott and Hort.

Dr. J. Rendel Harris (*The Expositor*, February, 1924, pp. 126 f.) holds that we can only be sure of a reading when we can explain the origin of the rest: "All the older rules about 'harder readings', 'shorter readings', 'earlier readings', and the like are out of date". Ah, yes, but whose "explanation" are we to accept? That one rule works sometimes and often it does not work at all.

In 1920 Prof. C. H. Turner, of Oxford, delivered his Inaugural Lecture on *The Study of the New Testament 1883 and 1920*. It is a most suggestive lecture. He says (p. 49): "So far as the work of the critical editors and of Hort in particular was directed to the substitution of the text attested by the oldest Greek mss. for the text attested by the mass of mediaeval mss., the issue has been settled once for all. The *textus receptus* is as dead as Queen Anne". But he goes on to say (p. 53): "Our task today is to inquire how far exclusive dependence on these few Greek witnesses should be modified by taking account of other equally ancient texts attested in the versions". To that problem we must now turn.

2. *The New Interest in Western Readings*

(a) *The Admission of Hort*

Hort admitted that Western non-interpolations (Neutral interpolations) had more value than any other

Western readings. But Westcott and Hort actually inserted the manifestly wrong reading in Matt. xxvii: 49. To be sure, they put double brackets around it, to indicate that they did not really think that the words belonged to the original text. But the failure to leave the words out of the text entirely indicates clearly that Westcott and Hort were too much under the spell of ℵ B and the Neutral class. The rival of the Neutral class was the Western class. The new discoveries have not put the Western class higher than the Neutral class. Bornemann did say that the Western text is the best text of the New Testament, but he has won no following of importance. Souter (*Text and Canon of the N. T.*, p. 140) gives the list of Hort's Western non-interpolations with single brackets and double brackets (for those considered clearly wrong).

1. Matt. vi: 15 (τὰ παραπτώματα αὐτῶν)
2. Matt. vi: 25 (ἢ τί πίητε)
3. Matt. ix: 34 (οἱ δὲ φαρισαῖοι—δαιμόνια)
4. Matt. xiii: 33 (ἐλάλησεν αὐτοῖς)
5. Matt. xxi: 44 (καὶ ὁ πεσὼν—λικμήσει αὐτόν)
6. Matt. xxiii: 26 (καὶ τῆς παροψίδος)
7. Matt. xxvii: 49 end [(ἄλλος δὲ—αἷμα)]
8. Mark ii: 22 (ἀλλὰ οἶνον νέον εἰς ἀσκοὺς καινούς)
9. Mark x: 2 (προσελθόντες φαρισαῖοι)
10. Mark xiv: 39 (τὸν αὐτὸν λόγον εἰπών)
11. Luke v: 39 (οὐδεὶς—χρηστός ἐστιν)
12. Luke x: 41f. (μεριμνᾷς—ἢ ἑνός)
13. Luke xii: 19 (κείμενα—φάγε, πίε)
14. Luke xii: 21 (οὕτως —εἰς θεὸν πλουτῶν)
15. Luke xii: 39 (ἐγρηγόρησεν ἂν καὶ)
16. Luke xxii: 19b, 20 [(τὸ ὑπὲρ ὑμῶν—ἐκχυννόμενον)]

17. Luke xxii: 62   (καὶ—ἔκλαυσεν πικρῶς)
18. Luke xxiv: 3   [(τοῦ κυρίου 'Ιησοῦ)]
19. Luke xxiv: 6   [(οὐκ ἔστιν ὧδε, ἀλλὰ ἠγέρθη)]
20. Luke xxiv: 9   (ἀπὸ τοῦ μνημείου)
21. Luke xxiv: 12   [(ὁ δὲ Πέτρος—τὸ γεγονός)]
22. Luke xxiv: 36   [(καὶ λέγει αὐτοῖς Εἰρήνη ὑμῖν)]
23. Luke xxiv: 40   [(καὶ τοῦτο εἰπὼν—πόδας)]
24. Luke xxiv: 52   [(καὶ ἀνεφέρετο εἰς τὸν οὐρανόν)]
25. Luke xxiv: 53   [(προσκυνήσαντες αὐτόν)]
26. John iii: 31, 32 (ἐπάνω πάντων and τοῦτο)
27. John iv: 9   (οὐ γὰρ—Σαμαρείταις).

Several things call for remark in this interesting list. One is that over half of them are in Luke's Gospel. Another is that two-thirds of those in Luke's Gospel are in chapters xxii and xxiv. And all that have double brackets are in these two chapters save one in Matt. xxvii: 49. In fact all are in Luke xxiv save xxi: 19b, 20.

Westcott and Hort are frankly puzzled about these Western non-interpolations. They have not hesitated to brush aside Syrian interpolations, Alexandrian alterations, Western interpolations and alterations. What shall they do with what looks like Neutral interpolations? Have we more knowledge today on this subject than Hort had? For one thing, two new documents have been discovered of prime importance, the Sinaitic Syriac which is Western and the Washington Codex (W) which often has Western readings. Let us push the problem further if we can.

(b) *The Date of the Western Text*

Patristic quotations help us in dating a type of text. Irenaeus in Gaul used the Western text. He wrote in

Greek and even the Latin translation really represents his Greek. Traces of the Western text are also found in Marcion (in the quotations by Tertullian and Epiphanius) and in Justin Martyr. Cyprian and Tertullian in North Africa used the Western Text. They wrote in Latin. Aphraates and Ephraem wrote in Syriac in the East and they used the Western text. They are later than the second century, but the Old Syriac is Western and that includes Tatian's *Diatessaron*, the Syriac of Cureton, and the Sinaitic Syriac. Barnard in his *Clement of Alexandria's Biblical Text* (1899) argues that Clement used the Western text in Alexandria in the second century. Hence Lake (*Text of the N. T.*, p. 78) concludes his able treatment of this subject thus: "If this theory be true, we can say that the Western text is everywhere found wherever we have any evidence for the text of the second century in Patristic quotations". But Lake does not mean that we find the same text everywhere, but only that we find Western readings in all parts of the Christian world in the second century.

The evidence of the early versions confirms the testimony of the early Fathers concerning the wide spread of the Western text in the second century. The Old Syriac in the East is Western. The African Latin in North Africa is Western. The Sahidic in Egypt has frequent Western readings and it is probably older than the Bohairic (Coptic).

There are no Greek mss. of the New Testament known to us of the second century. "The weak point in the external evidence for the 'Western' text was the comparative absence of support for it among the Greek uncial mss." (Turner, *The Study of the New Testament*, 1920, p. 55). D belongs to the fifth century. ℵ of the fourth century has occasional Western readings as has B (fourth century) in Paul's Epistles if not also a few in the Gospels. But now we have W which certainly has Western readings. Indeed, Turner (*op. cit.*, p. 56) says: "And W is an Egyptian Gospel-book of the Western type: it arranges the Gospels in the Western order, Matthew John Luke Mark, and in one part of St. Mark's Gospel it corresponds almost word for word with the important Old Latin Ms. *e*—next to *k* the best representative of the African text." He cites Mark i: 27. Turner also argues that W was written in Egypt. It is known also that Origen used a Western text of Mark while writing on Matthew and a Neutral text of Mark while writing on John. Thus we see in the case of Origen evidence of the Neutral and the Western text in Egypt before the end of the third century. Turner (*op. cit.*, p. 57) says that "The earlier of the two, so far as our evidence goes, was the Western, and if the emergence and popularity of one or the other was due to a definite recension, that recension must be what we have in ℵ B". He adds (p. 58): "In any case, the ℵ B recension can hardly be later than Origen". There is an Oxyrhynchus papyrus fragment of Matt. i: 1–20 ($\mathfrak{p}^1$, *Oxyrhynchus Papyri*, vol. I, p. 4) that gives a text strikingly like that of B, especially in orthography.

But, even if the Western text can be traced beyond our present Neutral text, it does not follow that the Neutral is a mere revision of the Western or that the

Western is the best. All the evidence goes to show that the Neutral and the Western have independent lines of genealogy to the original. It is true that the Neutral type of text has little support outside of Egypt (א B Bohairic Origen and W when it is Neutral), Palestinian Caesarea and Rome (Jerome's Vulgate). But we have seen that the preservation of any of the Pre-Syrian types of text is remarkable in view of the wholesale destruction of New Testament mss. during the imperial persecutions. We are not at liberty, therefore, to argue that the early silence proves the non-existence of the Neutral text.

(c) *Different Strata in the Western Text*

The discovery of the Sinaitic Syriac has done several things. One is to show that the Old Syriac and the African Latin do not always agree. There are Old Syriac interpolations and there are Old Latin interpolations. In Luke xxiv: 3 and xxiv: 52 the Old Syriac interpolation differs from that in א B (Neutral interpolation). But in Mark ii: 22; xiv: 39; Luke v: 39; Luke xii: 21 the Old Syriac agrees with the Neutral in retaining the passages. "The Old Syriac, then, was free from the interpolations characteristic of non-Western documents, and at the same time helps us to revise Westcott and Hort's list and to differentiate between the various items of it" (Souter, *Text of the N. T.*, p. 141). Burkitt (*Evangelion da-Mepharreshe*, Vol. ii, p. 232) says that "these insertions in our Old Syriac mss. appear to have been ultimately based on Greek mss. nearer akin to the 'Textus Receptus' than to the type represented by א and B". Burkitt gives in this work the best list of these Old Syriac interpolations as he does of the Old Latin interpolations in his *Old Latin and the Itala* (*Texts and Studies*, iv. 3). There are then two classes of these interpolations (the Old Syriac and the Old Latin).

Lake (*Text of the N. T.*, p. 80) notes that the same phenomena occur in Latin omissions and Syriac omissions. The Syriac are more numerous in proportion to the small ms. evidence than the Latin omissions. See the list of Syriac omissions in Mrs. Lewis's *The Sinaitic Palimpsest Retranscribed*.

Clearly then the Western text is not always a definite whole. It grew in different ways in different parts of the world. Thus we may find syr^{sin} and syr^{cu} opposed, as in Mark xvi: 9–20 (rejected by syr^{sin} while syr^{cu} has verses 17–20). So also in Luke ix: 55 syr^{cu} agrees with the Western and Syrian classes in giving οὐκ οἴδατε ποίου πνεύματός ἐστε, while syr^{sin} agrees with Neutral and Alexandrian in not having it. In Luke xxiv: 6, 12, 36 both syr^{sin} and syr^{cu} retain the words which D and the Old Latin omit.

It is quite possible that we may have to see in the very independence of syr^{sin} proof of a text antecedent to both the Western and the Neutral classes. The original text is what is desired, not necessarily the Neutral or the Western. Certainly the Old Syriac and the Old Latin often disagree with each other and with D. The Western corruptions (interpolations, alterations, omissions) arose gradually and did not become universal. Western readings of all these kinds appear in all parts of the world, but they do not all of them appear everywhere. It is not quite so easy now to quote the Western type of text. Often the usual representatives of this type of text (D syr^{sin} syr^{cu} k e sah Tert Cyp) will be found on different sides. So in John v: 4 D syr^{cu} sah f l q reject the verse with the Neutral class while a b c e ff^2 g vg Tert have it with the Syrian class.

There is evidently more yet to learn about the origin and relation to each other and to the originals of both the Neutral and the Western classes. Souter (*Progress in Textual Criticism since Westcott and Hort, Mansfield College Essays*, p. 363) says: "The combination of syr^{sin} and k would now generally be regarded as sufficient to upset the combination B ℵ or, in other words, the versions may sometimes have retained the correct text where all known Greek mss. have lost it. This is a principle of the highest importance and likely to be increasingly fruitful". The reason for the force of this combination is that it combines the early witness of the East and of the West. If syr^{sin} and k or e combine against not only ℵ B but even against syr^{cu} and D. we should certainly have a reading that would seem to antedate both the Neutral and the Western classes.

If it should be shown that the Neutral is itself a recension of the Western, then the Neutral would be placed in somewhat the same position as the Syrian and Hort's arguments against the Syrian would be used against the Neutral. But the evidence has not gone that way, though the Western type of text used by Clement puts it early. The variations in the Western text, as will be shown, also prove that the Western was not a definite and homogeneous text. It may

THE FUTURE OF THE STUDY 233

turn out after all that the "Western text" is simply the name to be given to the remnant of the local texts that survived the period of recensions. It must be remembered also that both the oldest known papyrus fragments of the New Testament, $\mathfrak{p}^1$ and $\mathfrak{p}^5$, of the third century, confirm the text of ℵ B. They are Neutral, not Western. The same thing is true of $\mathfrak{p}^{13}$ late third or fourth century.

(d) *The Origin of the Western Class*

The difficulties in the Western readings have given rise to many theories to explain the phenomena. There is at present no agreement among scholars on this subject.

Blass (*Evangelium secundum Lucam, Acta Apostolorum*) held that Luke wrote two editions of both the Gospel and the Acts. In the case of the Gospel Blass holds that Luke addressed the Neutral form (the longer) to Theophilus from Caesarea and the Western form (the shorter) to the Roman church. In the case of the Acts Blass holds that Luke wrote the Western form (the longer) for the Roman church and the Neutral form (the shorter) for Theophilus from Rome. It is ingenious certainly and won Nestle and Salmon to accept it. But the theory fails to take note of the strata in the Western text and few now hold to his idea of a double edition of Luke.

Dr. J. Rendel Harris suggests that most of the Western interpolations in the Acts are due to a Montanist scribe, as, for instance, in Acts xv: 29; xix: 1. He likewise argues that in Luke's Gospel he can trace readings to Marcion as the addition in Luke ix: 54, 55.

Dr. Harris urges also that some of the interpolations were made in the Latin side of a supposed bilingual original (Graeco-Latin).

Dr. Chase finds the variations in the Western text due to the influence of the Syriac in a bilingual original (Graeco-Syriac). He makes out a plausible case, as does Dr. Harris.

Lake (*op. cit.*, p. 88) sets Dr. Harris against Dr. Chase and is inclined "to consider that the theory of each is partially true and explains some readings, while neither entirely solves the whole problem".

Sir W. M. Ramsay suggests that the Western glossator in Acts reveals a knowledge of geography and customs and conditions of travel that proves the primitiveness and correctness of the additions in the Western text of Acts.

Resch argues for a Hebrew original as the explanation of most of the variations in the Synoptic Gospels. He holds that his Hebrew original was in use even after the present Gospels were written and accessible to copyists who used it.

It cannot be claimed that these theories make a great advance on the view of Westcott and Hort that the Western interpolations are a series of corruptions on the stock from which both the Neutral and the Western classes came. Some of these may preserve early and original traditions, but not a part of the original text. Westcott and Hort admit also Neutral interpolations on a much more limited scale which attacked the Neutral text after the Western had split off from the stock. In these cases the Western seems to preserve the original text while the Neutral interpolations may also be early traditions though not a part of the original text.

(e) *Changes Demanded by the New Knowledge of the Western Text*

Souter thinks that, if we ask how the text of the Gospels would be altered today by Westcott and in view of the discovery of the Sinaitic Syriac and of the Washington Manuscript, "the real extent of alteration would doubtless be small" (*Mansfield College Essays*, p. 363). He thinks it certain that in Matt. xi: 5 καὶ πτωχοὶ εὐαγγελίζονται is brought over from Matt. vii: 22 since it is wanting in k and syr^{sin}. He holds also that in Matt. xxv: 1 καὶ τῆς νύμφης would be changed from the margin to the text because here again syr^{sin} and it vg unite with D in giving it. But this is to me not so conclusive. Souter also suggests that John xii: 8 would go out because syr^{sin} and D do not have it. Once again I am not convinced because it vg have the verse along with Neutral and Alexandrian classes. It may be added that k and syr^{sin} very often agree with ℵ B. They represent here an uncontaminated strain of Western text that goes back to the original as do ℵ B. The syr^{sin} "does not contain a single one of the characteristically Western longer interpolations" (Valentine-Richards, *Cambridge Biblical Essays*, p. 529).

Turner (*Study of the N. T.*, p. 58) raises the same question of "a fuller recognition of the claim of the 'Western' witnesses to contribute their quota towards the restoration of the apostolic autographs". He admits that the antiquity and the universality of Western readings will not avail unless they can command also superior probability. "In textual criticism external and internal evidence are alike indispensable" (*ibid*). He calls attention to the fact that Westcott and Hort were the first editors to follow the Western traditions in Western non-interpolations and that in the margin they go farther than in the text. But I do not agree with Turner when he says that Westcott and Hort neglected the Western text. They attacked the problem with the light before them. We have a bit more light and we ought to see a bit clearer than they did. But the light points in the same direction now as then. Turner takes Mark as a sample and finds a few instances in which he would follow the Western text as against the Neutral like ὀργισθείς for σπλαγχνισθείς in Mark i:41, the omission of ἠκολούθησεν in Mark iii:7, ἔρχεται for ἔρχονται in Mark iii:31, omission of Τύρου καὶ Σιδῶνος in Mark vii:24, omission of προσελθόντες Φαρισαῖοι in Mark x:2, possibly the omission of the names of the women in Mark xvi:1 by D K. This is not a formidable list and something positive can be said against some of them.

But we know that ℵ B are wrong in Acts xi:20 Ἑλληνιστάς (Εὐαγγελιστάς, mere slip in ℵ) and that the Western reading Ἕλληνας is right here. So in Acts xii:25 ℵ B are wrong in reading εἰς and the Western ἀπό (or ἐξ) is right. The text of ℵ B is the best text on the whole that we have, but in places it has retained or added errors that do not appear in the Western text. The Western text is sometimes right against the Neutral, say one time in ten, but the Neutral is right against the Western, say nine times in ten.

The result is not to overturn the general position of

Westcott and Hort. We shall learn more with new discoveries and new research. The original text is what we all desire whether Neutral or Western. The Neutral is still far and away the best text that we know, but the Western is a shade better than Hort knew. The best critical text for today will give the Neutral type for the most part save where the Western is right or where both are possibly wrong.

In the matter of orthography the spelling of ℵ B, particularly B, has been remarkably vindicated by the papyri discoveries. The admirable discussion of Hort (*Introduction*, pp. 301–310, Appendix pp. 143–173) has rich amplification in the new discoveries. This point is presented at length in Mayser's *Grammatik der griechischen Papyri* (1906), Helbing's *Grammatik der Septuaginta* (1907), Thackeray's *Grammar of the O. T. in Greek* (1909), Moulton's *Prolegomena* (1906) and *Accidence* (1920) to his *Grammar of N. T. Greek*, and Robertson's *Grammar of the Greek N. T. in the Light of Historical Research* (4th ed., 1924).

3. *Conjectural Emendation*

We have seen that we have no Greek mss. of the New Testament earlier than the fourth century save some papyri fragments. We have seen also that the Western type of text in the second and third centuries was a corrupt text in many points. The Neutral text is a better text but we have as yet no way to get closer to the apostolic autographs than a century or a century and a half. The earliest versions go back to the end of the second century or the beginning of the third. We possess no Greek ms. and no early version that are free from errors of some kind. It cannot be assumed therefore that no errors were made by copyists during the hundred or two hundred years intervening between the autographs and our earliest documentary evidence. We are trying to restore the original text as far as that is possible. The effort has succeeded in a remarkable manner. But it is not claimed that no errors survive after the work has been done.

Hort calls these errors that apparently survive in all known documents "primitive errors". They are not very numerous and some of them may not be errors at all. We may not be able to understand the point. Certainly scholars today disagree quite a deal about them. Westcott and Hort mark sixty-five such "primitive errors" in the list of readings in the Appendix to their Greek New Testament. The list is as follows:

Matthew xv: 30; xxi: 28–31; xxviii: 7;
Mark iv: 28;
Luke xi: 35;
John iv: 1; vi: 4;
Acts iv: 25; vii: 46; xii: 25; xiii: 32, 42; xvi: 12; xix: 40; xx: 28; xxv: 13; xxvi: 28;
I Peteri : 7; iii: 21;
II Peter iii: 10; iii: 12;
I John v: 10;
Jude 1, 7 (two), 22f;
Romans i: 32; iv: 12; v: 6; viii: 2; xiii: 3; xv: 32;
II Corinthians iii: 3; iii: 17; vii: 8; xii: 7;
Galatians v: 1;
Colossians ii: 2, 18, 23 (two);
II Thessalonians i: 10;
Hebrews iv: 2; x: 1; xi: 4, 37; xii: 11; xiii: 21;

I Timothy iv: 3; vi: 7;
II Timothy i: 13;
Philemon 9;
Revelation ii: 12, 13; ix: 10; xi: 3; xiii: 10, 15, 16; xviii: 12; xix: 13.

Warfield (*op. cit.*, p. 209) says: "Our own judgment would greatly reduce this number". And so would mine. It is largely a matter of personal judgment how one looks at these confessedly difficult readings. In some cases it is highly probable that all the mss. known to us have been led astray. Hort (*Introduction*, p. 279) is particularly confident about II Peter iii: 10. He argues conclusively that εὑρηθήσεται supported by ℵ B explains the four other readings. "Yet it is hardly less certain by intrinsic probability that εὑρεθήσεται cannot be right: in other words it is the most original of recorded readings, the parent of the rest, and yet itself corrupt. Conditions of reading essentially the same, in a less striking form, occur here and there in other places". Those who wish to examine for themselves what Hort has to say on all these passages will be able to consult his *Notes on Select Readings*.

Warfield (*op. cit.*, p. 209) makes two good points on the subject. One is that conjectural emendation is not to be employed until all the methods of textual criticism have been exhausted and unless clear occasion for its use can be shown in each instance. The other point is that no conjecture can be considered that does not satisfy all the demands of both transcriptional and intrinsic evidence. "The dangers of the process are so great that these rules are entirely reasonable, and indeed necessary".

Nestle (*Text of the N. T.*, Hastings *D.B.*) insists that conjectural emendation is necessary in spite of the great mass of known mss., though it must be cautiously used. Blass in his *Evangelium secundum Matthaeum* put conjectural emendation in his text with a star (*) like προσέπαισαν vii: 25; ὀπίσω μου xvi: 23; εὑρήσει xvii: 27; ζωῆς xxii: 31; ἔλαβον—ἐξελθεῖν xxv: 1; αἶρε xxvi: 50; ἀζαφθανί xxvii: 46.

Dr. J. Rendel Harris thinks that "to Dr. Hort the scribes were all angels, as far as theology was concerned" (*Sidelights on N. T. Research*, p. 35). He thinks that some of the scribes made conscious as well as unconscious errors that have affected all our documents. Dr. Harris thinks also that "the text of Luke has been glossed from the Gospel to the Hebrews by some well-intentioned early scribe" (*ibid*, p. 103). One of the boldest of Dr. Harris's conjectures is that in 1 Peter iii: 19 some early scribe dropped out ΕΝΩΧ after ΕΝΩΚΑΙ because of its similarity. Certainly this emendation would greatly relieve this famous passage of the difficulty about the preaching to the spirits in prison if it was done by Enoch instead of Christ. It may be added that both Moffatt and Goodspeed have adopted this conjecture in their translations.

C. H. Turner does not hesitate to make conjectural emendations to get out of critical difficulties. For instance he makes such suggestions for the text of Mark iv: 29; viii: 26; ix: 9–13; x: 32 (*The Study of the New Testament*, pp. 61 f.).

Kenyon, on the other hand, thinks that "the sphere of conjecture in the case of the New Testament is infinitesmal; and it may be added that for practical purposes it must be treated as non-existent" (*Textual Criticism of the N. T.*, p. 17). That may sound extreme, but his remark that "a critic who should devote himself to editing the Scriptures on conjectural lines would be merely wasting his time" is more to the point. Dobschütz (*op. cit.*, pp. 140–2) thinks that some primitive errors exist and reminds us of Origen's change of Bethany to Bethabara.

Speculation is inevitable where so much is at stake as in the New Testament. But certainly sobriety of judgment is constantly needed. There is no way to account for the whims of every scribe and of every translator. Mrs. Lewis is much impressed by the curious reading in the Sinaitic Syriac for John i: 13: "Who (plural) was born, not in blood, and not of the will of the body", etc., "nor of the will of man, but of God". Burkitt remarks that some mss. of the Peshitta have a similar reading. Irenaeus and Tertullian know it also. Augustine has here *qui natus est*. Mrs. Lewis adds (*Light on the Four Gospels from the Sinaitic Palimpsest*, p. 134): "No one can now claim that the Fourth Gospel contains no allusion to the Virgin Birth". I agree to that, but I see it in verse 14, not in verse 13.

4. *The New Notation of Von Soden*

There is no discounting the amount of work that Von Soden put upon his task. It is now complete, fortunately, before his untimely death. It is entitled *Die Schriften des Neuen Testaments in ihrer ältesten erreichbaren Textgestalt* (I i, 1902; I ii, 1906; I iii, 1907; I iv, 1910; II, 1913). The volumes include about 3,150 quarto pages, a stupendous achievement.

He aimed to simplify the notation of mss. by dividing them into three classes disregarding the distinction between uncials and minuscules. His δ(διαθήκη) mss. contain all parts of the New Testament except that the Apocalypse need not be included. His ε(εὐαγγέλιον) mss. have only the Gospels. His α(ἀπόστολος) mss. contain the Acts and Epistles with or without the Apocalypse. But the working out of this system, simple as it seems, becomes exceedingly complex. For the δ mss. he uses 1 to 49 for those up to the ninth century, 50 to 99 for those of the tenth century, for the succeeding centuries numbers of three ciphers and with the cipher in the hundreds' place showing the century (121 the eleventh, etc.). Similar schemes are used for the ε and the α mss. For the later centuries the system is confusing and it wearies one to try to use it readily. Turner bluntly says: "I find it almost impossible to use with advantage" (*The Study of the N. T.*, p. 57). Souter (*The Text of the N. T.*, p. 132) holds the same view: "Further particulars of this ingenious system need hardly be given here, especially as the use of it is likely to be confined to the inventor's own edition". That seems certain to be its fate. It is so overdone and difficult that it is largely wasted labor. Dobschütz explains the scheme of von Soden for the benefit of German students.

He divides the mss. into three great groups which he calls K, H, I with subdivisions for K and I. His K text is practically the Syrian text of Westcott and Hort, his H text is Westcott and Hort's Neutral and Alexandrian texts, and his I text roughly answers to Westcott and Hort's Western text. Here again his apparent simplicity defeats itself for he finds eleven subdivisions of I. It is not deemed necessary to bother the student further with the manifold ramifications of Von Soden's textual theory as it is certain that it will not come into general favor. His actual Greek text does not differ greatly from that of Westcott and Hort though he reaches his conclusions in his own independent and tortuous way. See his *Griechisches Neues Testament: Text mit Kurzen Apparat* (1913).

5. *Unfinished Tasks*

These are many. The most needed single thing is the new edition of Tischendorf. But there are others. Turner (*The Study of the N. T.*, p. 52) longs for a new edition of Cyprian's *Testimonia*. It is to be hoped that he will supply that need himself. But many of the Greek writers need reëditing as Souter has shown (*Progress in Textual Criticism etc.*, *Mansfield College Essays*, p. 358). The relation between the Western and the Neutral classes needs to be better understood. New discoveries will come. Gregory's hope about the autograph copy of Mark's Gospel may or may not come true in Egypt. But progress will go on and it will go along the lines of Westcott and Hort.

6. *Streeter's Theory of Local Texts.*

This volume was in the press when Streeter's important volume, *The Four Gospels* (1925), appeared. I discussed his theory of classification in Chapter VI of *Studies in the Text of the New Testament* (1926). It is in the first half dozen chapters of *The Four Gospels* that Streeter makes the most important contribution to the

Study of Textual Criticism since the days of Hort. He proposes that Griesbach's term "Byzantine" be followed in the place of Hort's "Syrian Class." The same documents are involved. There is no objection to this change of nomenclature. He objects also to Hort's distinction between "Neutral" and "Alexandrian" as really begging the question by using "Neutral," and suggests that the name "Alexandrian" be applied to both. Certainly Hort's "Alexandrian" and "Neutral" come from a common ancestor as has been shown in this volume (p. 186). Hort's "Alexandrian" is a variation from his "Neutral" with occasional Western mixture. No single document always represents this type of text. But the main contribution of Streeter is the proposal to divide Hort's "Western" into a geographical Western and a geographical Eastern. We have seen already (pp. 230 ff.) that there are different strata in the so-called Western Class. It has been already known that there is a frequent cleavage with the Syr^{sin} and Syr^{cur} on one side and old Latin manuscripts like k e a b and D on the other. But Streeter insists upon a further division of the Eastern text into the Antiochian (the old Syriac as above) and the Caesarean text as found in θ (the Koridethi Uncial), Codex I and its allies, the Ferrar Group of Manuscripts (13, 69, 124, 230, 346, 543, 788, 826, 828, 983, 1689, 1709), the Paris Manuscript 28, No. 565 (Hort's 81, Tischendorf's 2^{pe}), No. 700. Perhaps 2358 may belong to this group. It is still unsettled whether Streeter's distinction between the Antiochian and the Caesarean texts will stand. Burkitt has raised serious objection (*Journal of Theol. Studies*, April, 1925). Meanwhile we are grateful for the bold path outlined by Streeter, even though we retain Hort's classification.

New books continue to be published bearing on the text of the New Testament, but the outstanding item is the "Proposed Edition of the New Testament with Full Critical Apparatus" to take the place of Tischendorf's *Novem Textamentum Graece*. The editor is Rev. S. C. E. Legg of London. He is assisted by a group of British scholars with a few in America and Germany. One wishes every success to this important enterprise. It will require years to bring it to fruition.

FACSIMILES OF EARLY TEXTS

L xx^{ogni} Factum est autem cum
turbae inruerent in eum
ut audirent uerbum d̄i
et ipse stabat secus stagnū
genesareth

CODEX AMIATINUS. LUKE V : I

c̄ia μαθητας τ̄ Μαρία δε ἑστήκει
ἀνασ̄τας Προς το μνημειον κλαιουσα εξω· ως
ἐν τ̄ ὄρορ οὖν ἔκλαιεν, παρέκυψεν εἰς το μνη
μεῖον· καὶ θεωρεῖ δύο ἀγγέλους
ἐν λευκοῖς, καθεζομένους, ε̄

MINUSCULE. IX OR X CENTURY. JOHN XX : II, 12
(BRITISH MUSEUM, ADD MS. II, 300)

ΠΕΝΥΜΙΝΚΑΙΕΞΕΛΘΟΥ
ϹΑΙΕΦΥΓΟΝΑΠΟΤΟΥ
ΜΝΗΜΕΙΟΥΕΙΧΕΝΓΑΡ
ΑΥΤΑϹΤΡΟΜΟϹΚΑΙΕΚ
ϹΤΑϹΙϹΚΑΙΟΥΔΕΝΙΟΥ
ΔΕΝΕΙΠΟΝΕΦΟΒΟΥΝ
ΤΟΓΑΡ

ΚΑΤΑ
ΜΑΡΚΟΝ

CODEX VATICANUS. MARK xvi : 8

ΠΑΡΑΚΑΛΩΔΕΥΜΑ·
ΑΔΕΛΦΟΙΑΝΕΧΕ
ϹΘΕΤΟΥΛΟΓΟΥΤΗϹ
ΠΑΡΑΚΛΗϹΕΩϹΚΑΙΓΡ
ΔΙΑΒΡΑΧΕΩΝΕΠΕ
ϹΤΙΛΑΥΜΙΝ

CODEX SINAITICUS.   HEB. xiii : 22

FACSIMILES OF EARLY TEXTS 253

CURETONIAN SYRIAC. MATT. XV : 20

ⲚⲦⲀⲎⲄⲎⲚⲒⲘ
Ⲛ̄ⲦⲀⲒⲦⲈ̄Ⲛ̄ⲤⲞⲠ·
ⲈⲦⲞⲨⲚⲀⲞⲨⲀⲰⲤ̄
ⲈⲨϢⲀⲚⲬⲰⲔⲈⲂⲞⲖ

SAHIDIC VERSION. V CENTURY. REV. xi : 6
(BRIT. MUS. MS. OR. 3518)

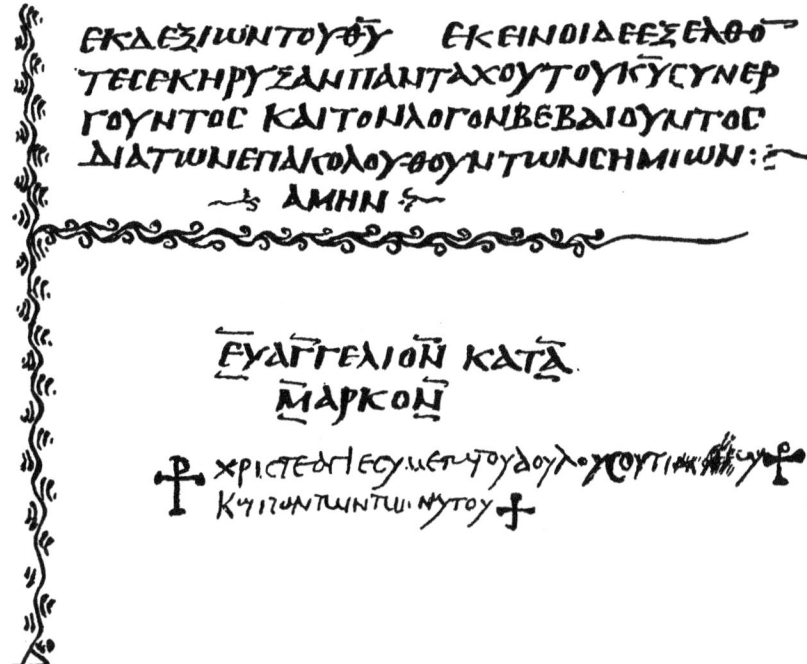

WASHINGTON CODEX. MARK xvi : 20

α
ΒΙΒΛΟΣΓΕΝΕΣΕΩΣΙΥ ΧΥ ΥΥ ΔΑΥ ΙΒ
ΑΒΡΑΑΜ ΑΒΡΑΑΜ ·―ΕΓΕΝΝΗΣΕΝΤΟΝ
ΙΣΑΔΚ ....ΓΕΛ.ΙΙΣΕΝΤ......ΙΑΚL
Δ=ΕΓ......ΝΗΣΕ.ΤΟΝΙΟΥΔΑΝ·
. ΕΛΦ..ΣΑΥΤΟΥΙΟΥΔ.....ΕΕΓ=ε,
ΣΕΝΤΟΝΦΑΡΕΣΚΝΤΟΝΖΑΡΕΕΚΤΗΣΘ .
Δ..ΦΑΡΕ ΔΕ ΕΓΕΝΔΗΣΕΝΤΟΝ ΕςωΜ

PAPYRUS p¹. III CENTURY. MATT. i : 1-3

ΠΡΟϹΕΧΕΤΕΕΑΥΤΟΙϹΚΑΙΠΑΝΤΙΤΩ
ΠΟΙΜΝΙΩ·ΕΝΩΫΜΑϹΤΟΠΝΑΤΟ
ΑΓΙΟΝΕΘΕΤΟΕΠΙϹΚΟΠΟΥϹ·
ΠΟΙΜΑΙΝΕΙΝΤΗΝΕΚΚΛΗϹΙΑΝ

CODEX ALEXANDRINUS. ACTS XX : 28

FACSIMILES OF EARLY TEXTS 261

ΜΑ : ΤΗΡΟΥΝΤΑΙ ΚΑΙΕΓΕΝΕΤΟΑΥΤΟΝ
ΕΝCΑΒΒΑΤШΔΕΥΤΕΡΟΠΡШΤШΔΙΑ
ΠΟΡΕΥΕCΘΑΙΔΙΑΤШΝCΠΟΡΙΜШΝ

CODEX BEZAE. GREEK. LUKE vi : 1

Seruantur etfactumest eum
inSabbatoSecundoprimo
abire persegetes

CODEX BEZAE. LATIN. LUKE vi : 1

A SELECTED BIBLIOGRAPHY

A SELECTED BIBLIOGRAPHY

ABBOT, EZRA, *Notes on Scrivener's 'Plain Introduction'.* Edited by Thayer. 1885.
  Critical Essays. 1888.
ALFORD, HENRY, *The Greek New Testament.* 4 Vols. with Prolegomena. 1849. 6th ed. 1868.
ALLEN, T. W., *Notes on Abbreviations in Greek Manuscripts.* 1889.
BAETHGEN, H., *Der griechische Text des Cureton'schen Syrers.* 1885.
BALJON, *Novum Testamentum Graece.* 1898.
BARNARD, P. M., *Clement of Alexandria's Biblical Text.* 1899.
  Text of the Gospels (Hastings' D C G. 1908).
BARTLET, J. V., (with committee of Oxford Scholars), *The New Testament in the Apostolic Fathers.* 1905.
BEBB, L. J. M., *Evidence of the Early Versions and Patristic Quotations.*
BENGEL, J. A., *Novum Testamentum Graece.* With various readings. 1734.
  Gnomon Novi Testamenti. Editio tertia. 1855.
BERGER, S., *Le Palimpseste de Fleury.* 1887.
  Histoire de la Vulgate. 1893.
  Notice et Extraits. 1895.
BENSLEY, R. L., J. RENDEL HARRIS, F. C. BURKITT, *The Four Gospels in Syriac transcribed from the Sinaitic Palimpsest.* 1894.
BEERMANN UND GREGORY, *Die Koridethi Evangelien* θ 038 *herausgegeben.* 1913.
BEZA, THEODORE, 'Η Καινὴ Διαθήκη. 1565 to 1598.
BIRT, T., *Das antike Buchwesen.* 1882.
  Die Buchrolle in der Kunst. 1907.

BIRKS, T. R., *The Text of the New Testament.* 1878.
BLASS, F., *Acta Apostolorum.* 1896.
    Evangelium secundum Lucam. 1897.
    The Philology of the Gospels. 1898.
    Notwendigkeit und Wert der Textkritik des Neuen Testaments. 1901.
BONUS, A., *Collatio Cod. Lewisiani evangeliorum Syriacorum cum Cod. Curetoniano.* 1896.
BONNASSIEUX, F. J., *Les Évangiles Synoptiques de S. Hilaire de Poitiers,* 1906.
BOUSSET, W., *Textkritische Studien zum Neuen Testament.* 1894.
BRANDSCHEID, F., *Novum Testamentum Graece et Latine.* 1906.
BUCHANAN, E. S., *Old Latin Biblical Texts* (No. V, 1907; No. VI, 1911).
    The Codex Harleianus 1772 of the Epistles and the Apocalypse. 1912.
    The Epistles of Paul from the Codex Laudianus. 1914.
    A New Text of the Apocalypse from Spain. 1915.
BUDGE, E. A. W., *Coptic Biblical Texts in the Dialect of Upper Egypt.*
The British Museum. 1911.
BURGON, J. W., *The Last Twelve Verses of the Gospel according to St. Mark.* 1871.
    The Revision Revised. 1883.
BURGON AND MILLER, *The Traditional Text of the Holy Gospels.* 1896.
    The Causes of the Corruption of the Traditional Text of the Holy Gospels. 1896.
BURKITT, F. C., *The Old Latin and the Itala.* 1896.
    Evangelion da-Mepharreshe. 1904.
    S. Ephraem's Quotations from the Gospels. 1901.
    Two Lectures on the Gospels. 1901.
    Ephraem and the Gospel. 1894.

Texts and Versions, New Testament. Encyclopaedia
Biblica. 1903.
Rules of Tyconius. 1894.
The Gospel History and Its Transmission. Third ed.
1911.
BRUYNE, DOM DE, *Quelques documents nouveaux pour l'histoire
du texte Africain des Évangiles.* Revue bénédictine.
T. XXVII, 1910.
CHAPMAN, DOM J., *Notes on the Early History of the Vulgate
Gospels.* 1908.
The Diatessaron and the Western Text of the Gospels.
Revue bénédictine. T. xxix. 1912.
Barnabas and the Western Text of Acts. Revue
bénédictine. T. xxx. 1913.
CHASE, F. H., *The Old Syriac Element in the Text of Codex
Bezae.* 1893.
The Syro-Latin Text of the Gospels. 1895.
CLARK, A. C., *The Primitive Text and the Gospel and Acts.*
1914.
CONYBEARE, F. C., *The Armenian Version of Revelation.* 1907.
CORSSEN, P., *Bericht über die lateinischen Bibelübersetzungen*
(Jahresbericht über die F. d. cl. Alt., 1899).
CRONIN, H. S., *Codex Purpureus Petropolitanus.* 1899.
CRUM, W., *Coptic Manuscripts Brought from the Fayyum.* 1893.
DEISSMANN, A., *Light from the Ancient East.* Tr. 1910.
Licht vom Osten. Vierte, völlig neuarbeitete Auflage. 1923.
DOBSCHÜTZ, E. VON, *Zur Textkritik der Vulgata.* 1894.
Ebrard Nestle's Einfuhrung in das griechische Neue Testament. Vierte Aufl. 1923.
DRUMMOND, J., *The Transmission of the Text of the New
Testament.* 1905.
DURAND, A., *Le texte du Nouveaux Testament.* Études. 1911.
Saint Jérôme et notre Nouveaux Testament. Recherches
de Sc. rel, Oct. 1916.

EDMUNDS AND HATCH, *The Gospel Manuscripts of the General Theological Seminary.* 1918.

ELZEVIR, A. AND B., ‘Η Καινὴ Διαθήκη.. 1624 to 1641.

ERASMUS, D., ‘Η Καινὴ Διαθήκη. 1516 to 1535.

FERRAR, W. H., AND ABBOTT, T. K., *A Collation of Four Important Manuscripts of the Gospels.* 1877.

GEBHARDT, O. VON, *Bibeltext des N. T. in Realencyclopädie.* Dritte Aufl. 1897.

GIBSON, MRS. M. D. (with MRS. A. S. LEWIS), *The Palestinian Syriac Lectionary.* 1899.

Studia Sinaitica, ii, 1894 and vii, 1899.

GIFFORD, S. K., *Pauli Epistolas qua forma legerit Joannes Chrysostomus.* 1902.

GOLTZ, *Eine textkritisch Arbeit des 10 bezw. 6 Jhdts.* 1899.

GOODSPEED, E. J., *The Newberry Gospels.* 1902.

The Toronto Gospels. 1911.

The Freer Gospels. 1914.

The Bixby Gospels. 1915.

The Harvard Gospels. 1918.

The Haskell Gospels. 1918.

The Greek Gospel Texts in America (one volume combining the single volumes).

GRAMATICA, A., *Bibliorum sacrorum juxta Vulgatum Clementinam.* Nova editio. 1914.

GREGORY, C. R., *Prolegomena to Tischendorf's Novum Testamentum Graece.* 1894.

Canon and Text of the New Testament. 1907.

Die griechischen Handschriften des Neuen Testaments. 1908.

Das Freer Logion. 1908.

Textkritik des Neuen Testaments. 1909.

Einleitung in das Neue Testament. 1909.

Vorschläge für eine Kritische Ausgabe des griechischen Neuen Testaments. 1911.

A SELECTED BIBLIOGRAPHY 269

GRIESBACH, J. J., *Novum Testamentum Graece.* 1775 to 1807.
Symbolæ Criticæ. 1785-1793.
Commentarius Criticus. 1798-1811.

GWILLIAM, G. H., *The Materials for the Criticism of the Peshitto N. T.* 1891.
Tetraëvangelium sanctum iuxta simplicem syrorum versionem. 1901.

GWILLIAM (with PUSEY), *The Peshitta Revision* (Gospels only). 1901.

GWYNN, J., *The Apocalypse of St. John in a Syriac Version.* 1897.
Remnants of the Later Syriac Versions of the Bible. 1909.

HAMMOND, C. E., *Outlines of Textual Criticism.* 1872.

HANSEL, E. H., *Novum Testamentum Graece: Collatio Codicis Sinaitici.* 1864.

HARDEN, J. M., *Dictionary of the Vulgate New Testament.* 1921.

HARNACK, A. VON, *Zur Revision der Principien der neutestamentlichen Textkritik: Die Bedeutung der Vulgata für den Text d. Kath. Briefe.* 1916.

HARRIS, J. RENDEL, *The Origin of the Leicester Codex of the N. T.* 1887.
The Codex Sangellensis (Δ). 1891.
On the Origin of the Ferrar Group. 1893.
Further Researches into the History of the Ferrar Group. 1900.
Biblical Fragments from Mount Sinai. 1890.
The Diatessaron of Tatian. 1890.
Stichometry.
A Study of Codex Bezae. Texts and Studies. 1891.
Some Notes on the Verse Divisions in the N. T. (Journal of Bibl. Literature. 1900).
Four Lectures on the Western Text. 1894.
Ephraem and His Gospel. 1894.

New Testament Autographs (American Journal of Theology, No. 12, supplement).
The Annotations of Codex Bezae. 1901.
Sidelights on New Testament Research. 1908.

HASELOFF, A., *Codex Purpureus Rossanensis.* 1898.

HASTINGS, H. L., *A Historical Introduction to the Peshitto Syriac N. T.* 7th ed. 1896.

HAUTSCH, E. F., *De Quattuor Evangeliorum Codicibus Origenianis.* 1907.
Die Evangelienzitate des Origenes. 1909.

HAVET, L., *Manuel de critique verbale appliquée aux Textes Latins.* 1911.

HEMPHILL, S., *The Diatessaron of Tatian.* 1880.

HJELT, A., *Die altsyrische Evangelienübersetzung und Tatian's Diatessaron.* 1901.

HENSLOW, G., *The Vulgate the Source of False Doctrines.* 1909.

HILL, J. H., *Tatian's Diatessaron: The Earliest Life of Christ.* 1893 and 1911.

HOGG, *The Diatessaron of Tatian.* 1896.

HOLL, K., *Die handschriftliche Ueberlieferung des Epiphanius.* 1910.

HOLZEY, C., *Der neuentdeckte Codex Syrus Sinaiticus unterucht.* 1896.

HORNER, G. W., *The Coptic Version of the N. T. in the Northern Dialect, otherwise called Memphitic and Bohairic.* 4 vols. 1898-1905.
The Coptic Version of the N. T. in the Southern Dialect, otherwise called Sahidic and Thebaic. 3 vols. 1911.

HORT, F. J. A. (with WESTCOTT, B. F.), *The New Testament in the Original Greek.* Vol. I Text. 1882.
Many reprints without Schaff's Introduction; with and without lexicon.
Vol. II Introduction and Appendix. 1882.

The ablest treatise on N. T. Textual Criticism. Out of print. Written by Hort.

HOSKIER, H. C., *Codex B and Its Allies.* 2 vols. 1914.
A Full Account and Collation of the Greek Cursive Codex 604 (100). 1890.
The Golden Latin Gospels in the Library of J. Pierpont Morgan. 1910.
Concerning the Genesis of the Versions of the N. T. 1911.
Concerning the Date of the Bohairic Version. 1911.

HUTTON, E. A., *An Atlas of Textual Criticism.* 1911.

HYVERNAT, R. B., *Études sur les versions coptes de la Bible.* Revue Biblique. 1896–97.

JACQUIER, E., *Le Texte du Nouveau Testament.* 1913.
Études de Critique et Philologie du Nouveau Testament. 1920.

JORDAN, H., *Writing* (Hastings' D Ap C. 1918).

KENYON, F. G., *Facsimiles of Biblical Manuscripts in the British Museum.* 1901.
Papyri (Extra Vol., Hastings D. B. 1904).
Writing (Hastings D. B. 1902).
Palaeography of Greek Papyri. 1899.
The Evidence of the Greek Papyri with Regard to Textual Criticism. 1904.
Text of the New Testament. (Hastings One Vol. D B. (1909).
Handbook to the Textual Criticism of the New Testament. 1901 and 1912.

KNOPF, R., *Der Text des Neuen Testaments.* Neue Fragen. 1906.

LACHMANN, CAR., *Novum Testamentum Graece et Latine.* With Praefatio. 1842 and 1850. See also *Theol. Studien und Kritiken.* 1830.

LAGRANGE, M. J., *Une Nouvelle Édition du Nouveau Testament.* Revue Biblique. 1913.

LAKE, KIRSOPP, *The Text of the New Testament.* First edition. 1900. Fifth Edition, 1916.
Codex 1 and Its Allies. 1902.
Facsimiles of the Athos Fragments of the Codex H of the Pauline Epistles. 1905.
Professor H. von Soden's Treatment of the Text of the Gospels. Reprint from Review of Theology and Philosophy. 1908.

LAKE, K. (and MRS. LAKE), *Facsimile of Codex Sinaiticus.* 1908.

LECLERCQ, DOM H., *Afrique Chrétienne.* 2 vols. 1904.

LE HIR, *Étude sur une ancienne version syriacque des Evangiles.* 1859.

LEWIS, MRS. A. S., *The Four Gospels translated from the Sinaitic Palimpsest.* 1894. Studia Sinaitica.
Light on the Four Gospels from the Sinai Palimpsest. 1913.
Some Pages of the Four Gospels Retranscribed. 1896.
The Old Syriac Gospels.
(and MRS. GIBSON, M. D.), *The Palestinian Lectionary.* 1899. Studia Sinaitica. 1897.
Codex Climaci Rescriptus. 1909.

LIGHTFOOT, J. B. (with TRENCH and ELLICOTT), *The Revision of the English Version of the New Testament.* 1873.

LINDSAY, W. M., *An Introduction to Latin Textual Emendation.* 1896.

LITTMANN, *Geschichte der äthiopischen Literatur.*

LUCAS, *Brugensis* (of Bruges), *Notae ad Varias Lectiones Editionis Graecae Evangeliorum.* 1606.

MAHER, M., *Recent Evidence for the Authenticity of the Gospels.* Tatian's *Diatessaron.* 1893.

MARGOLIOUTH, G., *The Palestinian Syriac Version of the Holy Scriptures.* 1897.

MARTIN, ABBÉ J. P. P., *Introduction à la Critique Textuelle du Nouveau Testament.* 6 vols. 1883-86.

MANGENOT, E., *Texte du Nouveau Testament* (Vigoroux, *Dictionnaire de la Bible*. 1912)

MERX, A., *Die vier Kanonischen Evangelien nach ihrem ältester bekannten Texte*. 3 vols. 1897–1911.

MILL, J., *Novum Testamentum Graecum*. 1707.

MILLER, E. (with BURGON), *The Traditional Text of the Holy Gospels*. 1896.
   A Textual Commentary upon the Holy Gospels. Matt. 1–14. 1899.

MILLER, E., *The Present State of the Textual Controversy*. 1899.
   Fourth Edition of Scrivener's Plain Introduction. 1894.
   The Oxford Debate on the Textual Criticism of the New Testament. 1897.

MILLIGAN, G., *The New Testament Documents*. 1913.
   Selections from the Greek Papyri. 1910.

MITCHELL, E. C., *Critical Handbook to the N. T.* 1880.

MONCEAUX, P., *Histoire Littéraire de l'Afrique Chretienne*. 4 vols. 1901.

MURRAY, J. O. F., *Textual Criticism of the New Testament* (Hastings D B, Extra Volume. 1904).

NESTLE, E., *Novi Testamenti Graeci Supplementum*. 1896.
   Novum Testamentum Graece cum apparatu critico ex editionibus et libris manuscriptis collecto. 7th ed., 1908. Same edition in 1904, without apparatus by British and Foreign Bible Society. Also edition of the *Textus Receptus* with variants. Novum Testamentum Latine. 1906.
   Einführung in das Griechische Neue Testament. 1897. Zweite Aufl., 1899. Engl. Tr., Textual Criticism of N. T. Dritte Aufl., 1909. Vierte Aufl., by E. Dobschütz, 1923.
   Introduction to the Textual Criticism of the N. T. (Tr. of 2nd ed. 1901).
   Text of the N. T. (Hastings D. B., 1902).

NORTON, W., *A Translation of the Peshitto-Syriac Text*. 1889.

PALMER, E., *The Greek New Testament with the Readings adopted by the Revisers of the Authorized Version.* 1881.

PISTELLI, C., *Papiri Evangelici* (Papiri della Societa Italiana, Vol. I).

POTT, A., *Der abendländische Text der Apostelgeschichte und die Wir-Quelle.* 1900.

Der Text des N. T. nach seiner geschichtlichen Entwicklung. 1916.

PUSEY AND GWILLIAM, *The Peshitta Revision* (Gospels only). 1901.

RAMSEY, W. M., *The Church in the Roman Empire.* 1893.

St. Paul the Traveler. 1896.

RANKE, E., *Codex Fuldensis.* 1868.

RESCH, A., *Aussercanonische Paralleltexte zu den Evangelien.* Four vols. 1893, 1894, 1895, 1896.

Das Kindheitsevangelium. 1897.

Agrapha. 1906.

REUSS, E., *Geschichte der heiligen Schriften.* 1860.

ROBINSON, J. ARMITAGE, *Philocalia.* 1893.

Euthaliana. Texts and Studies. 1895.

ROPES, J. H., *Die Sprüche Iesu die in den Kanonischen Evangelien Nicht überliefrt sind.* 1896.

Agrapha (Extra Vol. Hastings D. B., 1904).

Three Papers on the Text of Acts. Reprint from Harvard Theological Review, April, 1923.

RÖNSCH, H., *Das Neue Testament Tertullians.* 1871.

SALMON, G., *Some Thoughts on the Textual Criticism of the New Testament,* 1897.

SANDAY, W., *The Gospels in the Second Century.* 1876.

K with photograph. Old Latin Biblical-exts. Vol. II, 1886.

SANDAY, W., AND TURNER, C. H., AND SOUTER, A., *Novum Testamentum Sancti Irenaei Episcopi Lugdunensis.* 1923.

SANDERS, H. A., *The N. T. Mss. in the Freer Collection,* Part I. The Washington Manuscript of the Four Gospels. 1912.

Photographic Copy. 1912.

Part II. The Epistles of Paul. 1918.

SAVARY, *Les papyrus grecs et la critique textuelle du Nouveau Testament.* (Revue de l'Orient Chrétien, 1911, p. 414).

SCHAFF, P., *A Companion to the Greek Testament and English Versions.* 1889.

SCHOLTZ, J. M. A., *Novum Testamentum Graece.* 2 vols. 1830–6.

SCHUBART, W., *Das Buch bei den Griechen und Römern.* 1907.

SCRIVENER, F. H. A., *Collation of about Twenty Greek Mss. Deposited in the British Museum.* 1853.

Exact Transcript of the Codex Augiensis. 1859.

A Plain Introduction to the Criticism of the New Testament. 1861. 3rd ed. 1883.

Fourth edition revised by Miller in 1894 with larger list of minuscules and fuller treatment of versions.

Codex Bezae.

Six Lectures on the History of the New Testament. 1875.

The N. T. in Greek with the Variations in the Revised Versions. 1881.

Collation of the Codex Sinaiticus with the Received Text of the N. T. 2nd ed. 1867.

Nov. Test. Textus Stephanici A.D. 1550 cum variis lectionibus. 1887.

Novum Testamentum Graece. Editio Major. 1887.

Text of Stephanus with Variations to Westcott and Hort.

SIMON, R., *Histoire Critique du Texte du N. T.* 1689. Eng. tr. 1689.

Histoire Critique des Versions du N. T. 1690 (Tr. 1692).

Nouvelles Observations sur le Texte et les Versions du N. T. 1690.

SITTERLY, C. F., *Texts and Mss. of the N. T.* (International Standard Bible Encyclopaedia).

Praxis in the Manuscripts of the Greek Testament. 1888.

SODEN, H. VON, *Das lateinische Neue Testament in Afrika zur Zeit Cyprians.* 1909.

Die Schriften des Neuen Testament in ihrer ältesten erreichbaren Textgestalt, hergestellt auf Grund ihrer Textgeschichte.

I. Teil: Untersuchungen. 1902–1910.

II. Teil: Text mit Apparat. 1913.

Griechisches Neues Testament. Text mit Kurzem Apparat. 1913.

SOUTER, A., *Study of Ambrosiaster.* 1905.

Novum Testamentum Graece, textui a retractoribus anglis adhibito brevem adnotationem criticam subjecit. 1910.

Progress in the Textual Criticism of the Gospels since Westcott and Hort (Mansfield College Essays. 1909).

The Text and Canon of the New Testament. 1912.

Pelagius's Expositions of Thirteen Epistles of St. Paul: Introduction. Texts and Studies. 1922.

The New Testament Text of Irenaeus (ch. V in Sanday and Turner's Novum Testamentum Sancti Irenaei Episcopi Lugdunensis. 1923).

STEPHENS (STEPHANUS), ROBERT ESTIENNE, Ἡ Καινὴ Διαθήκη. 1546 to 1551. Editio regio 1550.

STREIBERG, W., *Die gotische Bibel.* 1908.

SWETE, H. B., *Theodore of Mopsuestia on the Epistles of Paul.*

THOMPSON, E. M., *Handbook to Greek and Latin Palaeography.* 2nd ed. 1894. New ed. 1913.

TISCHENDORF, A. F. C., *Notitia editionis codicis Bibliorum Sinaitici.* 1860.

Bibliorum Codex Sinaiticus Petropolitanus. 4 vols. 1862.

Novum Testamentum Sinaiticum. 1863.

Novum Testamentum Graecum ex sinaitico Codice. 1865.

Die Sinaibibel. 1871.

Novum Testamentum Graece. Editio octava critica maior. 2 vols. 1869–72.

TREGELLES, S. P., *An Account of the Printed Text of the Greek N. T., with Remarks on the Revision upon Critical Principles.* 1854.
Introduction to Textual Criticism of the New Testament. 1860.
The Greek New Testament, edited from Ancient Authorities, with the Latin Version of Jerome, from the Codex Amiatinus. Seven Parts. 1857 to 1879. Parts I to VI the Text with apparatus. Part VII Prolegomena. Published after the death of Tregelles in 1879.

TURNER, C. H., *Textual Criticism of the N. T.* (Murray's Illustrated Bible Dictionary. 1908).
Historical Introduction to the Textual Criticism of the New Testament. (Journal of Theological Studies, 1908 to 1910.)
The Study of the New Testament. 1920.
(WITH SANDAY AND SOUTER), *Novum Testamentum Sancti Irenaei Episcopi Lugdunensis.* 1923.

VALENTINE-RICHARDS, A., *The History and Present State of New Testament Textual Criticism* (Cambridge Biblical Essays. 1909.)

VERCELLONE, C., *Dell' antichissimo codice Vaticano della Biblia greca.* 1860.

VERCELLONE AND COZZA, *Codex Vaticanus.* 1868. With Consent of Papal authorities. Superseded in 1889-90 by photographic facsimile of B.

VINCENT, M. R., *A History of the Textual Criticism of the New Testament.* 1889.

VOGELS, H. J., *Novum Testamentum Graece.* With various readings. 1920.
Handbuch des Neutestamentlichen Textkritik. 1923.
Die altsyrischen Evangelien in ihrem Verhältnis zu Tatian's Diatessaron. 1911.

WALTON, B., *Polyglot Bible,* 6 tom. fol. 1657. Tom. V. N. T.

WARFIELD, B. B., *An Introduction to the Textual Criticism of the N. T.* 1886.

WEISS, B., *Series in Texte und Untersuchungen:*
   VII. 1. Die Johannes Apokalypse, 1891; viii. 3. Die Katholischen Briefe, 1892; ix. 3, 4. Die Apostelgeschichte, 1893; xiv. 3. Textkritik der Paulinischen Briefe, 1896; N. F. ii. 1. Der Codex D in der Apostelgeschichte, 1897. N. F., N. F., iv. 2, Textkritik der Vier Evangelien, 1899.
   Das Neue Testament: I Teil, Apostelgeschichte, Katholische Briefe, Apokalypse. 1894. II Teil, Die Paulinischen Briefe. 1896. III Teil, Die Vier Evangelien. 1900.
WESSELY, C., *Griechische und Koptische Texte theologischen Inhalts II.* 1911.
WESTCOTT, B. F., AND HORT, F. J. A., *New Testament in the Original Greek.* 1882.
   Vol. I. Text.
   Vol. II. Introduction and Appendix.
WETSTEIN, J. J., *Novum Testamentum Graecum Editionis Receptae cum Lectionibus*, etc., 2 tom. fol. 1751–2.
WEYMOUTH, R. F., *The Resultant Greek Testament.* 1892.
WHITE, H. J., *Selections from the Vulgate.* 1919.
WHITNEY, S. W., *The Revisers' Greek Text.* 1892.
WILCKEN, U., AND MITTEIS, L., *Grundzüge und Chrestomathie der Papyruskunde.* 1912.
WILSON, J. M., *The Acts of the Apostles Translated from the Codex Bezae with Introduction.* 1923.
WORDSWORTH, SANDAY, AND WHITE, *Old Latin K.* No. II Old Latin Biblical Texts. 1886.
WORDSWORTH, J., AND WHITE, H. J., *Novum Testamentum Latine secundum Editionem Sancti Hieronymi.* 1912.
WRIGHT, A., *Fragments of the Curetonian Gospels.* 1873.
XIMENES, FRANCES DE CISNEROS, *Novum Testamentum Graece et Latine in Academia Complutensi Nouiter Impressum.* Printed in 1514, published with O. T. in 1522.
ZAHN, TH., *Introduction to the N. T.* Second Translation. 3 vols. 1910. Revised ed. 1 vol. 1917.
ZIEGLER, L., *Italafragmente der paulinischen Briefe.* 1876.

INDICES

INDEX OF NEW TESTAMENT REFERENCES

MATTHEW

i: 1–iii:10 123
i: 1–vi: 10 109
i-1-viii: 22 113
i: 1–xxv: 6 84
i: 1 47
i:1–9, 12, 13, 14–20 76
i:1–20 ....87, 229
i:16 ....110, 113
i: 18, 18 ff 110
i:19–25 110
i: 25 110
iii: 16 ....136, 201
iii: 17 ....136, 137
iv: 2–xiv: 7 123
iv: 23–24 79
v: 20 168
v: 21–48 168
v: 22 ....136, 170
v: 32 219
v: 39 201
v: 45 64
vi: 1 ....61, 168 ter
vi: 1–8 168
vi: 4, 6..130, 162, 166, 175, 178,
                196, 206
vi: 9–13 ....79, 158
vi: 10 203
vi: 13..113, 146, 149, 162, 166,
                175, 178, 206
vi: 15 226
vi: 20–ix: 2 87
vi: 25 226

MATTHEW (*Continued*)

vii: 22 235
viii: 3–xvi: 15 109
viii: 12 202
ix: 13 ....158, 207
ix: 29 154
ix: 34 226
x: 3 189
x: 32–xi: 4 78
x: 32–xxiii: 25 113
xi: 5 235
xi: 16 153
xi: 23 219
xii: 24–33 78
xii: 47 110
xii: 49–xxiv: 50 123
xiii: 1 ....56, 60 bis, 62
xiii: 15 153
xiii: 33 226
xiv: 15 204
xv: 5 152
xv: 8 ....154, 158
xv: 20–36 123
xv: 30 238
xv: 32 ....157, 204
xvi: 2–3 110
xvii: 11–xx: 24 109
xvii: 21 110
xviii: 11 ....110, 113
xviii: 17 219
xix: 9 219
xix: 16 211
xix: 17 ....111, 159

MATTHEW (*Continued*)

xix: 22	219
xix: 24	219
xx: 22–23	111
xx: 28	87, 113, 202
xxi: 20–xxviii: 7	109
xxi: 23	157
xxi: 28–31	238
xxi: 44	202, 218, 226
xxii: 14	134
xxii: 37	154
xxiii: 26	226
xxiii: 35	157
xxiv: 20	212
xxiv: 36	111, 207 ter
xxv: 1	235
xxvi: 56, 57	155
xxvii: 2–12	87
xxvii: 9	157
xxvii: 16, 17	111
xxvii: 17	152
xxvii: 28	219
xxvii: 49	176, 182 bis, 217, 226 bis, 227
xxvii: 50	176, 217
xxviii	216
xxviii: 2–20	123
xxviii: 7	238
xxviii: 19	219

MARK

i: 1	81
i: 2	200
i: 10	201
i: 12–44	109
i: 20–iv: 8	123
i: 23	98

MARK (*Continued*)

i: 27	229
i: 40	220
i: 41	236
ii: 21–iv: 17	109
ii: 22	226, 230
iii: 3	153
iii: 7	236
iii: 29	212
iii: 31	236
iv: 19–vi: 9	123
iv: 21	176, 219, 221
iv: 28	238
iv: 29	240
iv: 41–v: 26	109
v: 14	151
v: 29	152
vi–xi	179 bis, 180
vi: 5–xvi: 8	109
vi: 14	220
vi: 20	230
vi: 22	207
vi: 33	188, 211
vii: 4	212
vii: 24	236
viii: 8–11; 14–16	123
viii: 19–xvi: 9	123
viii: 26	188, 211, 240
ix: 5	92
ix: 9–13	240
ix: 15	125
ix: 24	208
ix: 26	157
ix: 29	158, 203
ix: 38	188, 211
ix: 44–46	111
ix: 44, 46	208

MARK (Continued)

ix: 48	208
ix: 49	188 bis, 208, 211
x: 2	226, 236
x: 32	240
xii: 26	47
xii: 37–40	123
xiii: 2–3; 24–27; 33–36	123
xiii: 32	207
xiv: 39	226, 230
xiv: 65	155
xv: 25	157, 206
xv: 28	111
xvi: 1	236
xvi: 7	215
xvi: 8	89, 92, 214, 215 bis, 216 ter
xvi: 9–20	22, 100, 111, 129, 187, 214, 215, 216, 231
xvi: 14	88, 214
xvi: 17–20	113 bis, 231

LUKE

i: 1–4	103
i: 1–16	109
i: 1–viii: 30	123
i: 1–xi: 33	92
i: 15–28	92
i: 38–v: 28	109
i: 63	47
i: 74–80	76
ii: 14	101, 111, 130, 146, 149, 160, 162, 169, 176, 182, 187, 195, 198, 208
ii: 48–iii: 16	113
iii: 14	47

LUKE (Continued)

iii: 22	136
iv: 1, 11	76
iv: 16	159
iv: 18	111, 154
iv: 20	75
iv: 44	208
v: 3–8	76
v: 30–vi: 4	76
v: 32	158
v: 39	202, 226, 230
vi: 1	154, 208
vi: 4	86
vi: 5	202
vi: 6	208
vi: 12–xxiv: 53	109
vi: 36–38	134
vii: 13	188
vii: 18 ff	76
vii: 33–xvi: 12	113
vii: 36–43	76
viii: 31	160
viii: 48–xi: 4	123
ix: 10	188, 211
ix: 54, 55	233
ix: 55	111, 113, 231
x: 15	219
x: 22	160
x: 38–42	76
x: 41	111, 113
x: 41 f	226
x: 42	190, 211
xi: 2	203
xi: 2–4	111, 158
xi: 24–xxiv: 53	123
xi: 35	238
xi: 54	188, 211

LUKE (*Continued*)

xii: 18 .... 188, 211
xii: 19 226
xii: 21 .... 226, 230
xii: 39 226
xiv: 8–11 .... 87, 202
xiv: 17 153
xv: 19 .... 218 bis
xv: 21 .... 168, 218
xvi: 30 189
xvii: 1–2 134
xvii: 1–xxiv: 44 113
xviii: 39 152
xx: 42 47
xxi 210
xxi: 19 b, 20 227
xxi: 38 95
xxii: 17, 18 113
xxii: 19 .... 213, 218
xxii: 19 b, 20 226
xxii: 20 218
xxii: 43–44 111
xxii: 62 227
xxiii: 34 .... 111, 113, 220
xxiii: 42 114
xxiii: 43–44 121
xxiii: 45 .... 186, 208
xxiii: 53 120
xxiv: 3 .... 227, 230
xxiv: 6 227
xxiv: 6, 12, 36 231
xxiv: 9 227
xxiv: 12 227
xxiv: 12, 20, 36, 40, 51 ... 87
xxiv: 17 208
xxiv: 36 227
xxiv: 42 111

LUKE (*Continued*)

xxiv: 52 .... 227, 230
xxiv: 53 ...... 188, 189, 211, 227

JOHN

i: 1–42 113
i: 1–xviii: 12 123
i: 13 241
i: 16–iii: 26 87
i: 18 .... 159, 209, 214
i: 23–31 76
i: 25–47 109
i: 28 .... 139, 157, 204
i: 33–41 76
ii: 16–iv: 37 109
iii: 5–viii: 19 113
iii: 13 111
iii: 31, 32 227
iv: 1 238
iv: 9 .... 112, 202, 218, 227
v: 1 205
v: 4 .. 121, 154, 182, 183, 209, 232
v: 6–25 109
v: 7 .... 183, 209
v: 37 189
v: 46–xviii: 31 109
vi: 4 238
vi: 8–12, 17–22 78
vi: 39 152
vi: 50–viii: 52 84
vi: 69 .... 112, 211
vii: 4 169
vii: 4, 10 210
vii: 8 .. 162, 169, 173, 176, 180, 182, 198, 209
vii: 10 169

INDEX OF NEW TESTAMENT REFERENCES 285

JOHN (Continued)

vii: 53–viii: 11 .. 95, 100, 112, 115, 121, 154, 210
viii: 14–22 78
viii: 59 112
ix: 4 212
xi: 39 112
xi: 45 76
xii: 7 201
xii: 8 235
xii: 12–15 76
xiii: 2 .... 170, 210
xiii: 4 210
xiii: 24 189
xiv: 10–12, 15–19, 21–24, 26–29, 113
xv: 20 98
xv: 25–31 78
xvi: 14–30 78
xviii: 24 112
xviii: 25–xxi: 25 123
xix: 14 .... 157, 206
xix: 33 213
xix: 34 .... 176, 182 bis, 217
xix: 40–xxi: 25 109
xx: 11–17 76
xx: 19–25 76
xx: 30 .... 47, 210
xxi: 25 .... 47, 210

ACTS

i: 20 47
ii: 30 211
ii: 47 210
iv: 25 238
iv: 31–37 76
v: 2–9 76

ACTS (Continued)

vi: 1–8 76
vi: 8 189
vi: 8–15 76
vii: 37 154
vii: 42 47
vii: 46 238
viii: 10 89
viii: 29–x: 14 87
viii: 37 .... 54, 64, 202
ix: 5, 6 158
ix: 31 201
x: 30 158
xi: 20 .... 166, 236
xi: 27 ff. 167
xii: 25 .. 151, 154, 167, 176, 236, 238
xiii: 14 87
xiii: 32, 42 238
xiv: 11 103
xiv: 20 87
xv: 18 213
xv: 20 202
xv: 29 233
xv: 34 203
xvi: 3 155
xvi: 12 238
xvii: 28 153
xix: 1 233
xix: 19 47
xix: 40 238
xx: 15 129
xx: 28 .... 159, 189, 193, 211, 238
xxi: 2–10, 15–18 87
xxii: 10–20 87
xxii: 29 74

ACTS (Continued)

Reference	Page
xxii: 29–xxviii: 31	87
xxv: 13	170, 210, 238
xxvi: 7, 8, 20	78
xxvi: 14, 15	158
xxvi: 28	238

JAMES

Reference	Page
i: 10–18	78
ii: 19–iii: 9	78

I PETER

Reference	Page
i: 7	238
ii: 3	153
iii: 19	240
iii: 21	238
v: 5–13	78
v: 12	51

II PETER

Reference	Page
iii: 10	238, 239
iii: 12	238

I JOHN

Reference	Page
ii: 3	201
ii: 23	152
iii: 1	201
iv: 11–13	77
iv: 15–17	77
v: 7	17, 18, 19, 27, 64
v: 7, 8	124, 158, 160, 214
v: 10	238

Reference	Page
II John 12	53, 75
III John 13	49
Jude 1, 7, 22 f	238
Jude 22–23	116

ROMANS

Reference	Page
i: 1–7	77
i: 1–16	78
i: 7–15	135
i: 32	238
iv: 12	238
v: 1	153, 201
v: 6	238
viii: 2	238
viii: 12–ix: 9	78
xii: 3–8	78
xii: 11	151
xiii: 3	238
xv: 32	238
xvi: 22	51

I CORINTHIANS

Reference	Page
i: 2	125
i: 17–20	77
i: 25–27	77
ii: 6–8	77
iii: 8–10, 20	77
vi: 13–18	77
vi: 20	68, 185, 188, 196, 201
vii: 1 ff	97
vii: 3, 4, 10–14	77
vii: 5	158, 201
vii: 12–14	97
vii: 18–viii: 4	77
xi: 24	213 bis
xv: 51	159

II CORINTHIANS

Reference	Page
ii: 9	153
iii: 3	50
iii: 3, 17	238

INDEX OF NEW TESTAMENT REFERENCES

II CORINTHIANS (*Continued*)
iv: 13–xii: 7 84
viii: 4, 5 154

GALATIANS
iv: 18 153
v: 1 238
vi: 11 .... 44, 51, 75

Eph. i: 1 .... 40, 64, 203

PHILIPPIANS
i: 30 152
iii: 9–iv: 1 77

COLOSSIANS
ii: 2 211
ii: 2, 18, 23 238
iv: 16 204

I THESSALONIANS
iii: 2 211
iv: 3–II Thess. i: 1 78

II THESSALONIANS
i: 10 238
iii: 17 51

HEBREWS
i: 1, 2 77
ii: 14–v: 5 77
iv: 2 238
vi: 14 152
ix: 12 155
ix: 12–19 77
ix: 13 .... 82, 213
ix: 14 82
x: 1 238

HEBREWS (*Continued*)
x: 8–xi: 13 77
xi: 4, 37 238
xi: 28–xii: 27 77
xii: 1–3 100
xii: 11 238
xii: 28 153
xiii: 10 89
xiii: 21 238

I TIMOTHY
iii: 16 .. 22 bis, 151, 158 bis, 160, 213, 214
iv: 3 239
vi: 7 239

II TIMOTHY
i: 13 239
iv: 13 .... 53, 75

TITUS
i: 11–15 78
ii: 3–8 78
ii: 5 135

PHILEMON
9 239
19 51

REVELATION
1: 1 152
i: 4–7 77
i: 6 170
ii: 12, 13 239
ii: 20 157
v: 1 .... 48 bis
v: 2 48
v: 5–8 78

REVELATION (*Continued*)

vi: 5–8	78
ix: 10	239
x: 2	48
x: 2, 8 ff	47
xi: 3	239

REVELATION (*Continued*)

xiii: 10, 15, 16	239
xviii: 12	239
xix: 13	239
xxii: 15	96
xxii: 16–21	96

INDEX OF SUBJECTS AND PERSONS

A

Abbot, Ezra..... 33
"Notes on Scrivener's Plain Introduction"... 94
Acta Barnabae........... 60
Alexandrian class, 67, 68, 85, 195, 197, 204–206
Alford
  Gk. Testament 35
Ambrose of Milan... 144
Ambrosiaster............ 143
Andreas................. 142
Aphraates............... 146
Apparatus Criticus........ 65
Assa in Egypt............ 42
Assyrian Monuments...... 42
Athanasius.... 141
Augustine.... 144
Augustine (Retr).. 122
Autograph..............52–54
  " of Mark in Venice. 54
Autograph of Peter in Hebrew............... 54

B

Baljon
  Novum Testamentum Graece.............. 39
Basil The Great. 141
Barnard ....
  Clement of Alexandria's Bib. Text.132, 138, 224, 228

Barton and Spoer,
  The Four Gospels in Syriac.............. 107
Bengel.................28, 29
  Gnomon.............. 26
Bengel, J. A.
  Textus Receptus, Defence of The Gk. N. T..... 25
Bentley, Richard
  (1662–1742)..25, 26, 28, 29, 30, 31
Berger
  Histoire de la Vulgate 127, 159
  Le Palimpseste de Fleury 124
Bethabara...... 139, 157, 204 f
Bethany........ 139, 157, 204 f
Beza...................23, 84
  Nine editions of The Gk. N. T................ 20
Birt
  Das Antike Buchwesen, Die Buchrolle in der kunst.............. 41
Blass.................... 87
  Evangelium sec. Lucam. 233
Book, Meaning and materials used........... 41
Bousset................. 140
Bruyne, de..........102, 124
Buchanan
  Old Latin Bib. Texts..124, 126, 223
Budge................... 119

Burgon
  The Last Twelve Verses
    of Mark............ 22
Burgon and Miller
  Attacks of, on Theory of
    Westcott, and Hort... 221
  The Traditional Text, 22, 115,
    191
  The Causes of the Cor-
    ruption of the Tradi-
    tional Text of the Holy
    Gospels............22, 115
  The Oxford Debate on
    Textual Criticism..... 191
Burkitt
  Ephraem and The Gospels 146
  S. Ephraem's Quotations
    from the Gospels..132, 146,
    224
  Evangelion da-Mephar-
    reshe,..108, 145, 146, 230
  Journal of Theo. Studies..117
  The Old Latin and The
    Itala..121, 124, 135, 144,
    231

C

Calamus................ 49
Canons of Criticism....160–162
Cassiodorus............. 145
Catullus................ 30
Changes demanded by the
  new knowledge of the
  Western Text.....235–237
Chase
  The Old Syriac Elements
    in the Text of Codex
    Bezae............... 86
  The Syro-Latin text of
    the Gospels.......... 86
Chapman
  Barnabas and the West-
    ern text of Acts...... 132
  Notes on the Early His-
    tory of the Vulgate
    Gospels.............. 128
  The Diatessaron and the
    Western text of the
    Gospels.............. 108
Chapter headings and con-
  tents................. 98
Chrysostom............. 141
Citations from the Fathers, 58, 66
Clement of Alexandria..97, 137
Codex Alexandrinus (A)..84, 85
"   Argenteus......... 130
"   Augiensis (F_2)...... 88
"   Basiliensis (E)....73, 88
"   Beratinus (Φ)...... 92
"   Bezae (D)..20, 73, 82,
          86, 125
"   Bibliothecae Angeli-
        cae (L_2)............. 89
"   Bobiensis (k)....... 123
"   Bobiensis (edited by
        Wordsworth, Sanday
        and White).......... 223
"   Boernerianus (G_3)... 89
"   Boreeli (F)......... 88
"   Borgianus (T)...... 90
"   Campianus (M).... 89
"   Claramontanus (D_2), 73,
          88
"   Coislinianus (H_3)... 89
"   Cyprius (K)....... 89

INDEX OF SUBJECTS AND PERSONS

Codex Dublinensis (Z).... 91
" Ephraemi Rescriptus
   (C)................ 85
" Freer (I).......... 89
" Guelpherbytanus A
   (P)................ 90
" Guelpherbytanus B
   (Q)................ 90
" Latinus Monacensis. 125
" Laudianus (E₂)....73, 88
" Macedonianus (Y).. 91
" Mosquensis (V)... 91
" Mosquensis (K₂).... 89
" Munacensis (X).... 91
" Mutinensis (H₂).... 89
" Nanianus (U)...... 91
" Nitrensis (R)...... 90
" Palatinus......... 123
" Petropolitanus (Π). 92
" Porphyrianus (P₂).. 90
" Purpureus Petropoli-
   tanus (N)........... 90
" Regius (L)........ 89
" Rossanensis (Σ)... 92
" Sangallensis (Δ).... 91
" Sangermanensis (E₃) 73
" Seidelianus (G).... 88
" Seidelianus II (H). 89
" Sinaiticus (ℵ) 30, 83
" Sinaiticus, its discov-
   ery...., ... 34
" Sinopensis (O).... 90
" Tischendorfianus III
   (Λ).................. 91
" Tischendorfianus IV
   (Γ).................. 91
" Vaticanus (B)73, 77, 81, 82

Codex Vaticanus 354 (S).. 90
" Vaticanus 2066 (B₂). 92
" Vaticanus (Vercel-
   lone's edition). 32
" Vercellensis........ 125
" Veronensis.. 125
" Washington (W).... 87
" Zacynthius (Ξ) 92
" Θ (Gregory's 038)... 91
" Ψ (Gregory's 044)... 92
" Ω (Gregory's 045)... 92
Colon writing............ 100
Comparative Criticism of
   Tregelles............ 32
Complutensian Polyglot
   Edition of Ximenes..17, 18,
                         19, 24
Confirmation of theory of
   West. and Hort...221–225
Conflate readings......187–192
Conjectural emendation,237–241
Constantine, Emperor.. .. 52
Cosmas Indicopleustes.... 142
Crum.. 120
Coptic Ostraca......... 46
Cureton
   Remains of a Very An-
   cient Recension of the
   Four Gospels in Syriac 112
Cyprian.........17, 31, 37, 143
Cyril of Alexandria....... 142
Cyril of Jerusalem........ 141

D

Deissmann
   Light from The Ancient
   East............42, 46, 53

Licht Vom Osten 46
Diatessaron of Tatian
  Commentary, on by Ephraem of Syria 107
Dobschütz, E. Von
  Einführung zur Textkritik, ... 69, 79, 93, 94, 97, 128, 211, 241
Documents copied from Manuscripts 177

E

Edmunds and Hatch. 224
Ellicott 35
Elzevir
  Editions of the N. T. 20
  Text 24, 26, 30, 57, 62
Ephraem Syrus 146
Epiphanius 141
Epistle of Barnabas 80
Erasmus ... 19, 20, 23, 24, 29, 54
  Corrections from Complutensian text 18
  Edition of the Gk. N. T. 1516 18
  Editio Princeps 96
Errors of the Copyist
  Accidental 150–155
  Errors of the eye 151
  "   of the ear 152
  "   of memory 153
  "   of judgment 154
  "   of the pen 155
  "   of speech 155
Errors of the Copyist
  Intentional 156–160
  Clearing up historical difficulties 157
  Doctrinal corrections 158
  Harmonistic corruptions. 157
  Liturgical corruptions ... 160
  Rhetorical changes 156
Estienne, Robert (Stephanus)
  Editio Regia 1550 20
Eumenes II of Pergamum .. 43
Eusebian Canons 83, 98
Eusebius 52, 80, 97, 140
Euthalian Chapters 99
Evidence of Classes
  Actual number of classes. 185
  Alexandrian class (See Alexandrian)
  Examples of three readings 211–216
  Neutral class (See Neutral)
  Possible Western in B in the Gospels 218–220
  Proper procedure 197–199
  Readings Supported by one class 200–206
  Readings supported by two classes 206–211
  Recognizing the classes 194–196
  Relation of classes 185
  Syrian class. (See Syrian)
  Weighing evidence of classes 196–197
  Western class (See Western)
Evidence of Groups
  Confining a group to one section 181
  Confounding groups 181

Evidence of Groups
  Group represents an old
    document.........179–180
  Group not the addition of
    single documents...180–181
  No perfect group....... 182
  Where a group falls short 183
External evidence........37, 38
  Steps in use of it....... 171

F

Families.................. 37
Fathers, Chief Syriac..145–147
Fathers
  List of names and abbre-
    viations............60–62
Fayûm.................. 45
Ferrar Group............ 95
Fleury Palimpsest........ 123
Flinders-Petrie, W. M..... 46
Freer, C. L.............. 87
Frey.................... 29
Fritzsche................ 30
Froben, printer at Basel... 18

G

Gaius................... 30
Gebhardt
  Edition of Tischendorf... 34
Gebhardt and Harnack
  Texte und Untersuchun-
    gen................. 224
Genesis in Codex Vaticanus
    (B)................. 82
Gibson, Mrs............. 60
Gifford.................. 132
Goltz................... 139

Goodspeed, E. J.
  The Freer Gospels....87, 224
Gramatica, A............ 128
Greek N. T. first printed... 36
Greek Anthology......... 70
Gregory
  Canon and Text of the
    N. T..25, 49, 52, 53, 74,
    93, 94, 97, 106, 121, 124, 127,
    131, 138
  Die Griech. Hands. des
    N. T........26, 92, 94, 95
  of Nazianzus........... 141
  of Nyssa............... 141
  Prolegomena..56, 60, 61, 64,
      71, 92, 94, 97, 130, 146
  Textkritik des N. T..69, 71,
      92, 94, 114, 115
  Theol. Liter............ 69
  Vor. für eine Krit....... 94
Grenfell and Hunt.......46, 79
Griesbach..27, 28, 29, 30, 31, 57,
      58, 62
  Gk. N. T. (1774–77).... 26
Gutenberg Bible.......... 41
Gwilliam
  The Materials for the
    Criticism of the Pesh-
    itto N. T............ 115
  The Pal. Version of the
    H. Scriptures......... 118
Gwynn
  The Apoc. of St. John in
    a Syr. Version........ 116

H

Hammurabi.............. 52

Harnack
  Zur Rev. der Prin. der
    N. T. Text............ 128
  Die Bed. der Vulg. für den 128
Harris, J. Rendel
  A Study of Codex Bezae. 86
  The Expositor Feb. 1924 225
  On the Origin of the Fer.
    Group............... 95
  Further Research into the
    Hist. of the Ferrar
    Group............... 95
  Sidelights on N. T. Res..130,
                          159, 240
  Stichometry............ 100
Hastings, H. L........... 116
Hautsch
  Die Evang. des Origenes 132
Helbing
  Gram. der Sept......... 237
Henslow.................. 128
Herculaneum
  Library of papyrus rolls, 45, 52
Herodotus................ 42
Hilary................... 31
Hill..................... 107
Hippolytus............... 140
Hogg..................... 107
Horner
  The Coptic Version of the
    N. T. in So. Dialect.. 120
  Edition of the Bohairic
    Version.............. 224
Hort
  Introduction..115, 117, 136,
    148, 161, 162, 163, 164, 171,
    181, 185, 187, 188, 189, 200,
    217, 223, 237, 239

  Intr. Notes on Selected
    readings..........167, 239
  Intr. Vol. II of the N. T.
    in the original Gk..... 28
Hoskier
  Codex B and its Allies, 224–225
  The Golden Latin Gospels 124
Hug...................... 27

I

Internal evidence........ 38
  Kinds of.............. 149
  of each document....... 174
  Principles applied..... 174
Intrinsic evidence
  Canon of.............. 165
  Danger in............. 164
  Nature of............. 163
Irenaeus............31, 37, 136
Isho'dad of Merv......... 146
Itacism.................. 51

J

Jacquier
  Le Nouveau Testament.. 39
  Le Text du N. T...72, 93, 102
                    128, 130, 222
James
  The Languages of Pales-
    tine................ 106
Jerome.31, 48, 61, 63, 80, 81, 144
  Contra Pelag........... 88
  De Doctrina Christina... 122
Jordan
  Hastings Dict. of the Ap.
    Church............43, 49
Justin Martyr............ 135

INDEX OF SUBJECTS AND PERSONS 295

K
Kenyon
Article in Hastings D. B., 42, 43
Paleography of Gk. Papyri..............46, 82
Textual Criticism of the N. T..54, 67, 69, 71, 72, 73, 74, 76, 79, 84, 94, 118, 128, 139, 160, 222, 241

L
Lachmann..25, 29, 30, 31, 32, 35, 37, 38, 39, 61, 62, 172
Lake, Kirsopp............ 83
  Text of the N. T...25, 26, 40, 56, 67, 94, 96, 163, 191, 222, 228, 231, 234
  Text and Studies....... 95
Langton, Stephen......... 100
Leclercq................. 124
Lectionaries.............. 96
Lewis (Mrs.) and Gibson (Mrs.)
  Palestinian Syr. Lectionary of the Gospels.... 118
Lewis (Mrs.)
  Studia Sinaitica No. I... 118
  Codex Climaci Rescriptus 118
  Light on the Four Gospels from the Sinaitic Palimpsest............. 241
Libraries of
  Rameses I, Pergamum, Alexandria........... 52
Lightfoot...............35, 39
Littmann................ 129
Lucas of Bruges......... 23
Lucifer.................. 31
Lucretius................ 30

M
Manuscript books........ 42
Manuscript
  Alexandrian, by Woide... 65
    "   by Thompson................ 65
  Gk. Minuscule 61–16th Cent...............18, 19
  Latin, Gigas........... 126
  Syriac Sinaitic.......... 39
  Washington, Photograph by H. A. Sanders..... 224
Manuscripts, Greek....... 58
  Notations.........70, 71, 73
  Designations........... 73
  Kinds................. 68
  Number............... 68
Martial.................. 44
Matthaei................ 29
Marcion................. 135
Martin.................15, 22
Mayser
  Gram. der Gk. Papyri, 46, 237
Membrana............... 48
Method of Criticism...148–149
Middleton, Conyers....... 25
Migne's Patrologia.....140, 141
Milligan
  Gk. Papyri..........46, 153
  N. T. Documents....... 54
Mill, John............... 24
  Edition of Stephens..... 19
Miller
  Present State of the Textual Controversy..... 22

Oxford Debate on the
Text. Crit. of the N. T. 22
Minuscule Codices........ 93
  List according to Kenyon
    and Gregory......... 72
Mixture in documents, 192–194
Moffatt
  New Trans. of the N.T., 110, 222
Monceaux............... 122
Moulton
  Prolegomena........... 237
  Accidence.............. 237

N

Nestle
  Einf. in das Gk. N. T., 69, 94, 130
  Intro. to the Gk. N. T., 94, 222
  Novum Test........... 39
  Text of the N. T., Hastings D.B.............. 240
Neubauer
  Dialects of Pal. in the
    Time of Christ....... 106
Neutral Class..67, 68, 76, 77, 79, 85, 195, 197, 203–204
Neutral Interpolation..216–218
New Testament in Ap. Fathers.............. 134

O

Opus Imperfectum........ 62
Origen..31, 37, 56, 60, 61, 63, 67, 138
  Quotations............. 27
Orthography and Quotations
  Notes on, Westcott and Hort................. 36
Ostraca.................. 41
Ostraca and Wax tablets.. 46
Owen.................... 29

P

Palimpsest...........44, 50, 85
Palimpsest, Sinaitic Syriac. 62
Palmer
  Gk. Text behind the Revised Eng. Vers...... 39
Pamphilus............... 140
Paper before printing..... 41
Papyri
  Discovered in the Fayûm 45
  Oxyrhynchus.....46, 77, 229
  Growth and use.......44, 45
  Fragments............. 74
  List of fragments....... 76
Paragraph............... 51
Parchment..............42, 43
Patristic Quotations....... 24
Pelagius................. 144
Pen and ink.............49, 50
Philology, Classical....... 30
Philoxenian and Harklean Syriac............116–117
Pistelli.................. 79
Polyglot
  London................ 23
  Persian text............ 62
Pope Leo................ 18
Primasius..............31, 145
Priscillian..............17, 143
Prolegomena to Tischendorf (Gregory).............. 33

INDEX OF SUBJECTS AND PERSONS 297

Propertius.............. 30
Psalms in Codex Vaticanus 82
Pusey and Gwilliam....... 224

Q
Quintilian (Inst. Orat).... 44

R
Rameses I in Egypt....... 52
Reuss
  Gesch. der heiligen Schriften................. 43
Revision Committee (1881) 39
Robinson, J. A.
  Euthaliana in "Texts and Studies"............. 99
Roll, the................ 47
Romance of Erasmus's Gk. N. T. in
  Froude's "Life and Letters of Erasmus"..... 18
  Robertson's "The Minister and His Gk. N.T." 18
Rönsch.............132, 143
Robertson, A. T.
  Aorist Part. for Purpose, in Journal of Theol. Studies.............. 170
  Gram. of the Gk. N.T. in the Light............ 237
  The Minister and His Gk. N.T............ 102
  Trans. of Luke's Gos. with Gram. Notes.... 102

S
Samarcand.............. 42

Sanday
  Gospels in the Sec. Century................ 143
  Old Latin Bib. Texts... 143
Sanday, Turner and Souter 224
Sanders, H. A............ 87
Savary.................. 79
Schaff........28, 29, 34, 35, 59
Scholz.............27, 57, 62
Schubart
  Das Buch bei den Griechen und Romern..... 41
Scribes.................. 51
Scrivener
  Edition of 1881......... 23
  Gk. N.T. (1887)........ 22
  Plain Intro. to the Criticism of the N. T....22, 71, 84, 94
Septuagint..............34, 46
Shepherd of Hermas...... 80
Simon, Richard........... 23
Simonides............... 30
Smith, Payne
  Thesaurus Syriacus..... 113
Soden, H. von. 30, 40, 55, 67, 71, 72
  Das Lateinische.....124, 143
  Die Schriften des N.T..94, 241
  Griechisches N.T....... 243
  New Notation.......241-243
  Text................... 222
Souter
  Pelagius's Exp. of the Ep. of St. Paul..127, 132, 135, 144, 224
  Progress in the Text. Crit.

of the Gospels since
Westcott..223, 232, 235, 243
Revisers' Gk. N.T....... 74
Study of Ambrosiaster,
132, 143
Text and Canon..39, 42, 49,
86, 108, 116, 117, 122, 124,
135, 136, 139, 140, 142, 143,
144, 145, 146, 151, 158, 197,
222, 226, 230
Text of the N.T........ 242
Stephanus, Robert........ 100
Third edition........... 23
Text.............24, 57, 62
Stichometry.............. 99
Streiberg................ 130
Study of the author....... 164
Stunica.................17, 19
Styles of writing.........50, 75
Syrian Class..67, 68, 76, 85,
194, 196, 200-201

T

Tacitus, Annals of........ 70
Tatian's Diatessaron..95, 106-
109, 145
Tertullian..........37, 97, 142
Testing documents.....178-179
Text
Asiatic (Bengel)........ 31
Beza................... 22
Blass's Roman......... 39
Byzantine............. 31
Elzevir............... 22
Lachmann............. 23
Nestle, ed. 1901........ 23
Oriental............... 31
Occidental............ 31

Revisers, Gk. Text of... 23
Stephanus............22, 23
Stephanus, Beza, Elzevir. 21
Tregelles.......23, 34, 35, 39
Types of.............. 67
Westcott and Hort...... 23
Textus Receptus
of Britain.............. 20
Origin of phrase........ 20
Unlimited reign........ 23
Period of Struggle...... 23
Thackeray
Gram. of the O. T. in Gk. 237
Thecla, the Martyr....... 85
Theodore Mopsuestia..... 142
Thomas of Harkel........ 116
Thomas, Judas
Acts of................ 145
Thompson.............82, 84
Intro. to Latin and Gk.
Paleography......... 46
Tibullus................. 30
Tischendorf
Die Sinaibibel.......... 84
Discovery of Aleph..... 34
Eighth edition, 55, 56, 59, 71, 84
Novum Test. Graece...27, 87
Seventh edition.......57, 84
Transcriptional evidence,
examples............ 162
Tregelles
An Account of the printed
text of the Gk. N. T.. 30
Trench.................. 35
Turner
Study of the N. T..225, 229,
235, 240, 242, 243

U

Uncial codices............ 79
Date of.............. 82
Distinguished from cursives............... 26
Primary.............. 82
Unfinished tasks.......... 243

V

Valentine-Richards....... 235
N. T. Text. Criticism... 19
Valla, Laurentius......... 18
Varro
(apud Pliny H. N.)..... 43
Vatican library........... 18
Vellum.................. 43
Venerable Bede.......... 145
Versions
Aethiopic............23, 129
African Latin.......122–124
Arabic................ 23
Armenian............. 129
Authorized, Eng. (1611) 20
Bashmuric or Mid. Egyptian 120
Bohairic (Coptic or Memphitic)............. 120
Egyptian..26–27, 37, 118–121
European Latin.....124–126
Gothic................ 129
Latin...............121–128
Latin, Old............24, 67
Latin Vulgate..18, 31, 66, 70, 126–128
List of, with abbreviations................ 59
Primary.............. 105

Revised, Eng........... 35
Sahidic, or Thebaic..... 119
Secondary......105, 129–130
Syriac................ 106
Syriac, Curetonian...112–114
Syriac, Jerusalem, or Pal.
117–118
Syriac, Old..........67, 109
Syriac, Peshitta..23, 24, 114–116
Syriac, Sinaitic......... 109
Syriac, Sinaitic, list of
books on........112, 114
Vienna
Corpus Scriptorum Ecc.
Lat................ 143
Vogels
Die Alts. Ev. in ihrem
Ver................ 108
Die Harm. im Ev. des
Cod. Cant.......... 107

W

Walker, John........... 25
Walton's Polygot........23, 84
Warfield..32, 37, 68, 97, 133, 150, 153, 154, 155, 158, 160, 161, 163, 164, 165, 172, 173, 175, 179, 180, 196, 222, 239
Weiss, B................ 39
Texte und Unter........ 221
Westcott and Hort..26, 32, 34, 35, 36, 37, 38, 39, 40, 55, 87
Wesseley............... 79
Western Class..67, 68, 76, 86, 194, 196, 201–203
Origin of..........233–235

Western Readings, new interest............225–237
Western text
　Date...............227–230
　Different strata......230–233
Wettstein, J. J.
　Gk. N. T.............. 26
Weymouth
　Resultant Gk. N.T..... 39
White, H. J...........102, 128
Whitlock................ 62
Whitney................ 29
Wilcken
　Grund. und Chrest. der
　　Pap................. 46

Wordsworth and White
　Novum Test. Dom. Nos.
　　Jesu Christi Latine, 128, 224
Wordsworth, Sanday and
　White............124, 223
Wright, A.............. 113
Writers, Chief Gk.....134–142
Writers, Chief Latin...142–145

X

Ximenes............17, 19, 20

Z

Ziegler................. 124

www.ingramcontent.com/pod-product-compliance
Lightning Source LLC
Chambersburg PA
CBHW052339230426
43664CB00041B/2304